HOW
THE BRAIN
LOST ITS MIND

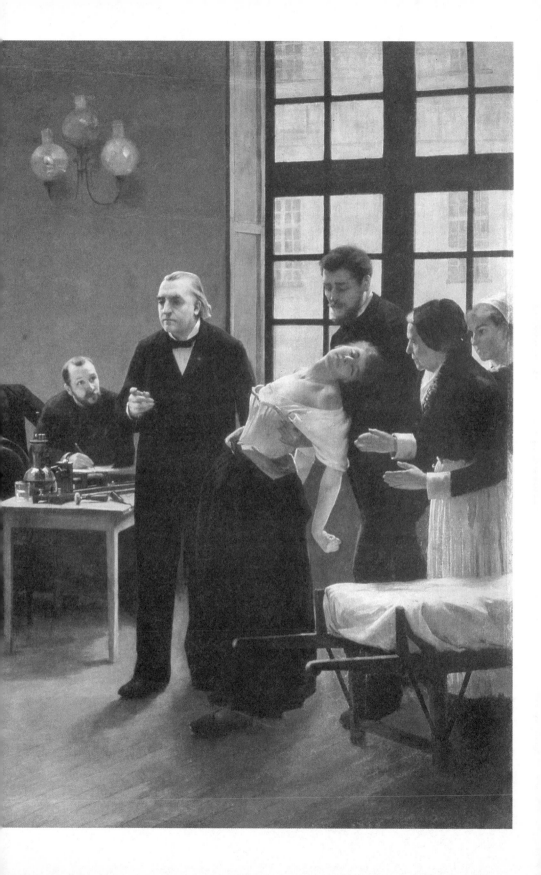

By the same authors

Reaching Down the Rabbit Hole

HOW
THE BRAIN
LOST ITS MIND

SEX, HYSTERIA,

AND THE

RIDDLE OF

MENTAL ILLNESS

Dr. ALLAN H. ROPPER

AND

B. D. BURRELL

Atlantic Books
London

Published by arrangement with Avery, an imprint of Penguin Random House LLC.

First published in hardback in Great Britain in 2020 by Atlantic Books, an imprint of Atlantic Books Ltd.

1 2 3 4 5 6 7 8 9

A CIP catalogue record for this book is available from the British Library.

Hardback ISBN: 978-1-786-49180-0
Trade paperback ISBN: 978-1-786-49181-7
Paperback ISBN: 978-1-786-49183-1
E-book ISBN: 978-1-786-49182-4

Printed in Great Britain by Bell and Bain Ltd, Glasgow

Designed by Nancy Resnick

Frontispiece: *Une Leçon Clinique à la Salpêtrière* by André Brouillet 1887, FNAC 1133, Centre National des Arts Plastique. Copyright © Public domain/ Centre National des Arts Plastique. Photo courtesy Musée d'Histoire de la Médecine, Paris.

Atlantic Books
An imprint of Atlantic Books Ltd
Ormond House
26–27 Boswell Street
London
WC1N 3JZ

www.atlantic-books.co.uk

For Dr. Raymond D. Adams, master clinician and author of the definitive book on neurosyphilis, who taught that there was only one brain and it belonged to both neurology and psychiatry.

—AHR

For Jennie Bujnievicz, who taught us for a while, allowed us to see particular things, and then sent us on.

—BDB (via TRP Jr.)

CONTENTS

AUTHORS' NOTE

This book tells the story of a disease known for its uncanny ability to mimic the symptoms of almost any illness, mental or physical. Its root cause—syphilis—was the driving force behind five centuries of fear and loathing, and though now viewed with little cause for concern in the developed world, it is epidemic elsewhere. *Neuro*syphilis, or syphilis of the brain, first appeared in Europe in the late 1700s, and produced a rapidly expanding wave of debilitating insanity that filled asylums and cut lives short in a grotesque and frightening way. As traumatizing and destructive as AIDS proved to be two hundred years later, neurosyphilis cast a pall over the sexual lives of people from all walks of life for the better part of a century, while its cause and nature remained a mystery. Its shadow may no longer haunt us, but it is still with us today, although shunted into the neglected corners of medicine.

When a cure for syphilis was found and the threat of neurosyphilis receded, so did popular awareness of brain-based mental disorders. Into this conceptual vacuum a seductive new theory of the unconscious emerged emphasizing mind over brain. Sigmund Freud's psychoanalytic system would dominate the treatment of mental disease for most of the twentieth century, and it still colors our conversations about the mind while largely ignoring the brain. We have written this book to redress this derailing of a coordinated neurological and psychiatric approach to mental illness.

How does a germ-borne venereal disease produce insanity? Do we really understand the difference between a sick brain and a sick mind? In setting out to write a book about neurosyphilis, we ended up with a book about sex, hysteria, psychosis, hypnotism, psychoanalysis, mind cures, synthetic dyes, sensation fiction, psychotropic drugs, genius, and madness. Which is to say, we ended up with a book about neurosyphilis—a far more expansive subject than we first imagined.

We have relied on the resources of many libraries and their staffs, notably the Countway Library of Medicine at Harvard Medical School and the Robert Frost Library of Amherst College. We greatly appreciate the invaluable assistance of Sandy Ropper, MLS, in providing extensive library research. Several of our colleagues provided essential assistance with our investigations, including Drs. Emily Stern, David Silbersweig, and Daniel Talmasov of Brigham and Women's Hospital, Drs. Michael Fox and William Greenberg of Beth Israel Deaconess Medical Center, Dr. Paul McHugh of Johns Hopkins University School of Medicine, Dr. Thomas D. Sabin of Tufts Medical Center, and Dr. Joseph B. Martin of Harvard Medical School. Professor Hans Vaget of Smith College provided valuable insights into the life and works of Thomas Mann. Our sincere thanks go out to our editors at Avery Books, Megan Newman and Nina Shield, for their astute input and hard work; to our agent, John Thornton of the Spieler Agency, for kick-starting the project; and to Fran Shifman for reading early versions of the manuscript. We would also like to thank colleagues who led us to the stories of their patients, some of which appear here with identifying features altered to protect their privacy.

INTRODUCTION

I took special notice of Mr. M the moment he entered my field of vision. Anyone would have. A study in contrasts—tall, thin, and handsome, wearing crisply cuffed Brooks Brothers slacks, polished wing-tip shoes, and a shabby white T-shirt—he was pacing, as people tend to do in hospital corridors, deep in conversation, sometimes excitedly. Sans Bluetooth, oblivious to anyone around him, he was immersed in a heated argument with himself.

I had been called down to the psych ward to check on Mr. M, to see if he might be having seizures. He was not, but in our initial interview he insisted that the sugar in his coffee was the source of the voices he was hearing; it was poisoning not just him but everyone. His argument was articulate and intense, and as I later decided while contemplating a Danish pastry in the hospital café, unconvincing. I wondered why patients like him are admitted to a psych ward in the first place. They don't belong there.

Twenty-seven years old, Mr. M has a degree from the Wharton School, a wide vocabulary, and a brain problem. He impressed me as being an intelligent, exceedingly perceptive, engaging man, yet completely psychotic. I noted many hints, some of them highly suggestive: involuntary grasping responses when I put my fingers in his palm, darting eyes, head tossing, lip smacking—what we call soft neurological

1

signs. Yet every test we ran, every scan, no matter how sophisticated, ruled out many things, and ruled in nothing. He seemed to have a normal brain. I was sure he did not; I just couldn't prove it.

To my dismay, I found his patient file dense with psychiatric jargon, as if he did not have a brain disease at all, as if the roots of his psychosis were wrapped up in the tangled filaments of his life experiences. By general agreement, he was insane. But the word itself means different things to different people. The identifiable mental illnesses, the big-ticket items including bipolar illness and schizophrenia, are diseases of brain structure and function. Most neurologists believe this, as do most academic psychiatrists. Yet we do not have the irrefutable evidence to prove it. As a result, these conditions are treated clinically as mental illnesses rather than as brain diseases. Neurologists by and large have tacitly condoned this practice, and even abetted it, partly because we cannot nail down the structural or functional brain problems that produce most abnormal behaviors. This is a serious problem and a long-standing one.

In 1801, the pioneering French psychiatrist Philippe Pinel invented the term *aliénation mentale* as a catchall for all forms of insanity. Pinel meant alienation in the sense of loss, a state in which the patient has become estranged from reason. Pinel attributed it, as medicine had only recently begun to do, to the brain, but he also saw alienation as a disorder of sensibility (perception), of intelligence, and of the will, without associating those things with specific brain structures. In other words, insanity was also a problem of the mind.

Pinel's classification efforts mark the very beginning of the practice of psychiatry and the first stirrings of my own profession, neurology. It was the dawn of a new era. Minds and brains took precedence over manners and morals. Specialists known as alienists were now charged with deciding whether persons detained for "reasons of madness" belonged in a hospital, in a prison, or back out on the street. Prior to Pinel, anyone exhibiting erratic behavior would have been dumped, somewhat indiscriminately, into an asylum or *maison d'aliénés*, chained to the wall and left to wallow in their own filth. Pinel would soon reform the asylums out of his sense of humanity, but also because he perceived differences of type, severity, and cause of insanity, and he believed many of his patients could be reclaimed through what he called "moral treatment." He also hoped to put psychiatry on a par with biological science by establishing a classification scheme for all mental illnesses.

In Pinel's time, my patient Mr. M would have been committed to an asylum and declared *aliéné*. The English word *insane* is not equivalent and would not be appropriate in his case. Unlike *aliéné*, insane defines a state of mind by what it is not, and glosses over our inability to distinguish the many categories and causes of bizarre thoughts and erratic behaviors. It is a declaration rather than a placeholder. As though in compensation, we now possess a wealth of subclassifications of insanity, including schizophrenia, bipolarity, psychosis, conversion disorder, and so on through the 947 pages and 297 descriptors catalogued in the *Diagnostic and Statistical Manual of Mental Disorders*. The sheer scope is impressive, but what the *DSM* fails to do is identify which disorders arise in specific brain pathology. This is because in most cases we still do not know.

In the early 1800s, no one had mustered a serious argument for the brain as a source of mental instability. Phrenology, the only viable theory of mind at the time, treated the brain as a muscle in need of toning, its faculties capable of being strengthened through exercise or repressed through restraint. The expert would feel the bumps on the skull, consult an atlas of the underlying brain, map the patient's character and proclivities, and write out a detailed diagnosis and a prescription. As a logical and medically approved system for understanding the mind, it was very appealing, and most customers walked away contented. If insanity was the result of unfortunate deformations of the skull, the phrenologist could tailor his examinations to flatter his clients. If a cranium did not measure up to the ideal, he would provide the owner with helpful suggestions. Nothing was at stake because the theory could not be disproven. At least at first.

The seed of phrenology's undoing was sown in 1822 when a medical student working in a French asylum published a thesis with an intriguing premise: Could a mental breakdown be caused by a disease of the brain?

He found the evidence in a small cohort of patients in their thirties and forties who had died at the asylum after a period of florid insanity. Although he could not say how the affliction had come about, he accurately described its dramatic effects. In the months before their deaths, all of the patients had exhibited similar patterns of delusion, depression, mania, and later, paralysis. At autopsy, they displayed a consistent pattern of damage in their frontal lobes, seemingly caused by an inflammation of the brain's outer lining. The idea that a physical disorder of the brain could produce insanity was unprecedented—and decidedly non-phrenological. An outside agent appeared to be invading these patients' bodies and crippling their mental faculties. The medical establishment instantly rejected the notion.

The brain had long been conjectured to be the organ of the mind, but even the phrenologists could not provide a coherent explanation of how it worked. Clearly it controlled the muscles. Epileptic convulsions, for example, were assumed to indicate an underlying brain disorder, one affecting motor control, while unconnected to the thought process. Epilepsy did not alter personal identity. This new syndrome, on the other hand, vastly distorted the victim's sense of self. How did it do that?

At first no one took the young student seriously, but as soon as the asylum superintendents recognized the advantages of a *medical* diagnosis for insanity, the idea caught on. Such a disease would establish their bona fides as real doctors, not merely as custodians relegated to the grimy back wards of medicine. The superintendents were also astute enough to recognize that the clinical details provided by the medical student matched a large proportion of the patients under their care. Within a few years, thousands of cases had been catalogued, all with the same pathology. Whatever it was, it seemed to have become epidemic, and it spurred the building of newer and larger asylums.

The disease soon acquired a name: general paralysis of the insane (today known as GPI). Its symptoms included colorful delusions of grandeur, psychosis, slurred speech, periods of deep melancholy, a gradual spread of paralysis, and death usually within a few years of onset. Although the diagnosis could be made with some precision, no one was entirely sure what caused it or what could be done about it. It was impossible to say whether it was a brain state or a mind state, germ-based or hereditary, due to lifestyle or due to bad luck.

Today we know all about it. It is caused by syphilis, and it manifests itself as a mental illness. For that reason, it provides the ideal lens through which to view all forms of mental alienation. For a time it even bridged the gap between neurology and psychiatry. Perhaps it can bring them together once again.

Mrs. B sits in a wheelchair, clutching a leather-bound, jewel-encrusted Bible while a young man in a white lab coat excuses himself and steps into a conference room. He will be only a minute, he says. The room is full of young doctors and medical students, two dozen or so. This is the neurology group at Boston's Brigham and Women's Hospital. We have gathered for Chief's Rounds, a weekly teaching exercise. Mrs. B has graciously agreed to participate.

The young man, who happens to be our senior neurological resident, sets the stage. Today's patient is seventy-five years old, of Jamaican descent, and has been living in the Dorchester section of Boston for fifty years. She lives alone, but in the last few months has been unable to manage her affairs. Her walking has deteriorated. She falls frequently, especially in the dark. Her behavior has become increasingly bizarre and disorganized. She has stopped cooking. Family members describe her as "not who she is," and her religious fervor has crescendoed to a euphoric pitch. She carries her Bible at all times, and speaks constantly of the end of the world and of her important role in it.

Once Mrs. B is wheeled into the room, the chief begins the classic neurological examination. She responds slowly and deliberately to his questions, and admits only to some vision problems. Wielding a penlight and moving his face to within inches of hers, the chief notices how her pupils fail to narrow in response to the light, yet they constrict when he asks her to focus on his thumb as he moves it closer. "Pupils accommodate," he says, "but they don't react to light."

After she is wheeled out, the guessing game begins, starting with the medical students, then the residents in reverse order of seniority, and finally the academic faculty. Only the senior resident knows the results of her tests. The round table conjectures touch on every cause of premature dementia, as well as brain tumors, strokes, and ophthalmic problems, but nothing seems to fit her signs and symptoms, especially her recent mental decline, one too abrupt to qualify as an ordinary dementia. No one gets it right. In fact, no one in the room under the age of sixty-five has ever seen a case like hers. A century ago, almost everyone would have recognized it instantly. Even a country doctor would have seen it. Finally the chief weighs in: "What about syphilis?"

Most people do not realize that syphilis, a venereal disease, can invade a brain and quickly destroy the mind within, reducing the patient to a hopeless wreck. It can take two years or thirty, but in any case, if left untreated, it is unrelenting. Neurosyphilis is now uncommon, at least in the developed world, which explains why a roomful of doctors in a major teaching hospital failed to spot it. It is not on the list of usual suspects in cases of dementia. A blood test can identify it quickly, but before the first such test was developed, syphilis was extremely difficult to pin down. It could manifest itself as almost anything. It still does.

The senior resident put Mrs. B on a series of penicillin injections— our first line of defense. They would rid her body of the infection and rid her mind of its overblown religiosity, but fall short of producing a complete recovery. The neurological damage had been done.

Meanwhile, up on the neurology ward, Sara J, a nursing student— nineteen years old, the first in her family to go to college—lies on her side, salivating onto her pillow, clenching her teeth in obvious distress. Her family, all five of them, huddle at the foot of her bed. A week earlier, she had been preparing for final exams, acting "completely normal," according to the roommate who brought her to the ER.

In cases involving neurological symptoms—convulsions, tremor, paralysis, numbness, coma, seizures, palsy, migraine, hallucinations, disorientation, catatonia, even blindness—I begin by ruling out the biggest threats. One of these is epilepsy. As my residents and I enter, Sara rolls over and it begins. Her muscles tense, her teeth gnash so violently she almost breaks her incisors. Arching her back in a half circle, supporting herself by only her heels and the back of her head, she goes into grand mal convulsions. Her mother, frantic, yells at us, "Can't you stop this? Do something!"

The wires attached to the electrodes stuck to the young woman's scalp lead to an electroencephalograph behind the bed, carrying signals from her brain activity during her frenzied behavior. There is nothing unusual in the waveforms of the electroencephalogram. She is not having a seizure; her spasms and convulsions do not look genuinely epileptic. Even so, she has no control over them, and for the first time in her life, it seems, her parents have no control over her. I ask the family to step out, but her brothers are emphatic that she can't be left alone in a room with men, even with a doctor. "She is a virgin," they say.

We have our theories. The overprotective family and their odd insistence that she is a virgin raise a few red flags. A social worker pays a visit, but neither the young woman nor her parents will give anyone a peek into their lives. The blood tests, along with a battery of other tests costing an astronomical sum, all come back negative. She does not have a disease we can identify, but Sara would have been quickly diagnosed by any nineteenth-century physician. He would have called it hysteria.

Three patients in the same week: one a case of general paralysis, also known as neurosyphilis, a disease of the brain; one a case of pseudo-epileptic seizures, an affliction of the mind; and the third, Mr. M, fell somewhere in between. He seemed normal in many ways. He spoke in full sentences; he had no paralysis, blindness, or incoordination; yet his mind was a mess. The attending psychiatrist gave him Seroquel, an antipsychotic, and he became almost catatonic. When switched over to Valium, he began talking again—about good and evil, about righteousness. "If you had a choice between being on the right or the wrong side of evil," he asked me, "and you could do it forever, which would you choose, Doc?" I had no answer. He was not confused, just crazy.

As a resident in the 1970s, I treated "crazy" patients with penicillin. We still had a lues clinic for the treatment of neurosyphilis (*lues* is a euphemism for syphilis). Every few months we took spinal taps to test whether the drug was working. We could see the white blood cells in the cerebrospinal fluid go from a count of about fifty down to one or two over the course of a year, a measure of the disappearance of the syphilis bacterium within the nervous system. The clinic is long gone, but the memory of it has stayed with me. We were curing mental illness by treating the body. Mr. M reminded me of the extent to which we have drifted away from that. Instead of curing his disease, we were merely moderating his symptoms.

A friend recently asked me, "You're a neurologist, right? Why am I anxious and can't focus? I can't figure out what is making me feel this way. Nothing special has happened to me." I could only shake my head. He's wrong that being a neurologist would allow me to deduce the cause of his nervousness. My friend is anxious, he believes, because something in his brain is not functioning properly—perhaps a chemical imbalance. He is angling for a societally legitimized pseudo-medical diagnosis. Thanks to drug company advertising, every uncomfortable state of mind has morphed into a medical problem with a brain-based explanation. Freud took the opposite tack: he assumed that anxiety and neurosis are *psycho*pathologies, not organic but experiential in origin. This assumption was still dominant when I started practicing medicine. Patients suffering from mental distress wanted to know what events in their lives had led to their feeling like this, and the medical profession was happy to oblige them. Now they want to know what events in their brain have brought them down.

Today we know a lot more about the brain than Freud and his contemporaries did. As for the mind, history has taken us on a circuitous journey, and what we *think* we know has outpaced what we really do know. Only in the last few decades have we doubled back, somewhat chagrined, to our original route, weighed down by the baggage we acquired along the way. The baggage goes by many names—Freudian, neo-Kraepelinian, Jungian, Pavlovian, Skinnerian, and so on—and it continues to divide neurology and psychiatry into opposing camps.

The causes of bipolar disorder, schizophrenia, depression, autism, alcoholism, attention deficit disorder, criminality, sociopathy, and neurosis, despite the optimistic pronouncements of popular scientists, remain out of reach. The question of what makes one person act ethically and reasonably while another becomes a thief and a liar has been relegated to the social sciences, where it remains highly speculative. Why someone becomes agitated and confused in the absence of a recognizable pathology is equally baffling. For a clinical neurologist like me, the situation is frustrating and somewhat absurd, much like the case of the blind men describing an elephant: their descriptions vary wildly depending on which part of the animal they latch onto. Mental illness is just such a beast. Neurologists and psychiatrists, each enamored of the part that makes the most sense to them, describe the pathology from their own vantage point, uncertain what the whole animal looks like. Instead of sharing our perspectives, we continually return to our comfort zones: mind versus brain. In order to begin the conversation anew, we could use some common ground: a disease of both mind *and* brain. Syphilis, for example.

When Sir William Osler, widely acknowledged as the greatest diagnostician ever to wield a stethoscope, declared that "he who knows syphilis knows medicine," he elevated what had been considered a lowly disease, one treated mostly by dermatologists, into something all encompassing. Almost always sexually transmitted, it can attack any organ, usually starting with the genitals in the form of ugly lesions and dry ulcers known as chancres. From there it moves inward. The heart, liver, lungs, and spinal cord are at its mercy, as is the brain. Only careful examination can distinguish the true nature of syphilis from the many things it merely appears to be. For this reason, it was called the Great Imitator—not just an imitator of biological disease, but of almost any mental illness. This made it a crucial nexus of neurology and psychiatry.

Osler had it mostly right. Understand syphilis, and you will indeed understand all of medicine. He might have added that if you understand how a mental disturbance due to a brain disease differs from a purely psychological problem, you will gain a deeper understanding of disease in general. This book sets out to do just that.

CHAPTER 1

A CLINICAL LESSON

On a warm Paris afternoon in late spring, throngs of weary tourists swarm the narrow streets off the Boulevard Saint-Michel in search of a place to unwind after a day spent in the grueling pursuit of checklist tourism. Led around by docents and modern-day Baedekers, most of these vacationers have dashed through a handful of the city's five-star attractions, waved selfie sticks while plugged into audio tours, and can now be seen flowing into the Place Saint-Michel in a movable feast fanning out across the sidewalks and down the clogged alleyways feeding into the Rue de la Huchette.

Just around the corner from this bustling warren of conviviality, one of the most historically significant artworks in the city goes unnoticed, unvisited, and unappreciated. Sheltered in a vestibule of a stately neoclassical building, it presides over an oasis of solitude and calm. Because none of the guidebooks mention it, very few people are even aware it exists. It is a large painting, and over the century and a quarter since it was painted, it has lost its notoriety but not its significance. To understand this one painting is to understand everything that went wrong in the modern concept of mind and brain. It portrays nothing less than the original sin of neurology and psychiatry, one from which we are still trying to recover.

The colonnaded building housing the painting is perched on the Rue de l'École-de-Médecine, a two-minute walk from the bustle of the Place

Saint-Michel. It is the home of Paris Descartes University, a satellite of the Sorbonne. Among other things it contains a museum of medical history: a cabinet of gruesome curiosities including an amputation kit used at the Battle of Waterloo, crude-looking instruments once used to remove bladder stones, and boxes of glass eyes. Admission costs three euros, but the painting can be viewed for free. At nine and a half by fourteen feet, it is too big for the museum's limited wall space and has been accommodated just outside of the main gallery, as if in an afterthought, in a skylighted foyer where, on a sunny day, the glare makes it difficult to take in as a whole. As a further indignity, it is unframed and almost casually hung, a sad fate for a work once hailed as "the success of the Salon of 1887."

The painting is by André Brouillet, a journeyman artist who studied with the great Jean-Léon Gérôme, had a moment of passing fame, and then slid back into obscurity. He titled the work *Une Leçon Clinique à la Salpêtrière* (*A Clinical Lesson at the Salpêtrière Hospital*), and at the Salon des Beaux Arts of 1887, an annual showcase of established and aspiring academically trained artists, it stood out by virtue of its striking subject. Rather than drawing upon the distant past, Brouillet chose to depict a contemporary event, one very much of the moment. The setting is a window-lit room in a hospital. A medical demonstration is in progress before a male audience. At first glance, it appears to be a group portrait of thirty finely rendered individuals. The center of attention is a young woman in a state of semiconsciousness and semi-undress. The scene is highly sexualized and frankly voyeuristic, hardly unusual in the world of academic painting. Two of its more obvious points of reference include a scandalous canvas by Gérôme entitled *The Slave Market in Rome*, featuring a nude young woman standing on an auction block as buyers frantically make their bids. The other, a more subdued work, depicts Philippe Pinel, the aforementioned pioneer in the humane treatment of the insane, as he orders the unshackling of the madwomen at an asylum. Stripped of all context, the subjects of these works are young, vulnerable, exposed, unseeing or semiconscious women under the complete control and watchful eyes of men. In each case the historical moment trumps the sensational content, allowing the paintings to be peddled as art rather than as pornography.

A salon-goer of 1887, unlike the viewer of today, would have known exactly what was going on in Brouillet's canvas. A young woman under hypnosis will be induced to act out a series of seemingly unexplainable physical and mental tasks, during which needles will be passed through her hand with no sensation of pain, paralyses will appear on one side of her body, only to switch sides after the application of a magnet, and her perception, having become sensitized, will allow her to read thoughts and exhibit astounding feats of clairvoyance. Finally, as the pièce de résistance, she will respond to a series of random suggestions from her handlers, ranging from the banal—"You are smelling a flower," "You see a snake"—to the fantastic—"You have survived a violent train crash," "You are Kutuzov at the Battle of Borodino." In response to each suggestion she will act out a series of tableaux vivants, all in service of advancing knowledge of one of the most baffling forms of neurosis known to medical science: hysteria.

The swooning woman at the center of the painting has a name: Blanche Wittman, also known as the Queen of the Hysterics. The man presiding over the scene is Jean-Martin Charcot, known as the father of clinical neurology, more reservedly as the father of French neurology (as if neurology were as regional as cuisine), and sometimes derisively as the Napoléon of the Salpêtrière. Everyone in the painting can be identified by name and by profession, and a legend posted on the wall does just that. The group includes not just medical men but literary figures, artists, and statesmen, and they are there to lend gravitas to what was an elaborately crafted ritual and a highly controversial practice that might otherwise have appeared somewhat shady, if not scandalous.

Une Leçon Clinique is a bright and crisp painting, both real and unreal: real in its vivid attempt to capture the likenesses of living men and women, unreal in its frozen formality. The more you look at it, the more impossible the scene appears. It was not commissioned, a rarity in a historical painting. Brouillet took a chance that the public and the press would want to see the most-talked-about phenomenon in Paris, especially if it featured the city's most famous physician and his most celebrated patient. He was right. Hailed by the critics of the time as "one of the most important artworks of the Salon," and possibly "the most sensational painting" out of the more than five thousand other works on display, it drew large crowds from the opening day. The Salon itself, an annual event put on by the French Academy of Beaux-Arts, drew up to a half million people to the Palais de l'Industrie during its two months' duration. Most of them would have made a beeline for Brouillet's large canvas because of its subject, its overt sexuality, its composition, and its sheer size. According to contemporary accounts, the crowds also came for the same reason Beatles fans were drawn to the cover of the *Sgt. Pepper* album. They wanted to see how many faces they could identify. Perhaps this explains the critic Louis de Meurville's dismissive remark, in the *Gazette de France*, that "it takes only a minute to admire the truthfulness of the characters and the light. Beyond that, there is nothing more to discover."

Meurville can be forgiven for focusing only on the surface quality of the work. He was not in a position to understand how Brouillet, in this one canvas, had inadvertently captured a seminal moment in the history of medicine. The scene he so carefully composed would foretell not only the birth of psychoanalysis but also a regrettable split between neurology and psychiatry, and the failure of medical science to take ownership of the study and treatment of mental illness. In short, Brouillet attempted to portray the culmination of a century's worth of bad science on the threshold of giving way to good science. In the end, he showed the very opposite.

Jean-Martin Charcot deserved better. In the 1860s, at the outset of his career, he laid the groundwork for the medical specialty of neurology through a remarkable sequence of discoveries. He differentiated multiple sclerosis and Parkinson's disease from a multitude of similar-looking ailments, naming the latter for the English physician who first described it. He identified the symptoms of poliomyelitis and of tabes dorsalis, or syphilis of the spinal cord. He detected the role of uric acid buildup in cases of gout. More famously, he differentiated the pathology of amyotrophic lateral sclerosis, or Lou Gehrig's disease (known in France as Charcot's disease), from other forms of paralysis. In short,

Charcot deciphered the workings of the human nervous system through a careful and perceptive examination of the many ways in which it can go wrong. He correlated fanatically precise observations during his patients' lives with careful examination of their brains after their deaths. In doing so, he left behind centuries-old preconceptions and prejudices in favor of an objective empiricism. He then built a research enterprise that served as the model for the modern teaching hospital and for the entire enterprise of medical investigation. According to a contemporary, the writer Léon Daudet, "No one anywhere in the civilized world would publish a book on diseases of the nervous system without seeking his approval, his *imprimatur*, in advance."

But just when everything seemed to be going his way, Charcot stunned his colleagues by redirecting his efforts toward a paradoxical phenomenon regarded by mainstream physicians more as a nuisance than as a real disease. Charcot plucked hysteria, long thought to be an affliction unique to women, from its marginalized place in medicine, and set it alongside epilepsy, ALS, MS, and Parkinson's as a very real disease of the body. But that wasn't all. He ventured into even more treacherous territory when he introduced hypnotism into his arsenal of diagnostic tools, and he achieved an initial breakthrough with a group of patients consisting mostly of attractive young women. Charcot's reputation alone brought this unlikely enterprise some legitimacy within the French Academy of Sciences, but outside of the academy not everyone was on board.

Hysteria is an umbrella term denoting afflictions of body and behavior displayed vividly by a patient while remaining awkwardly unverifiable even with an autopsy. Today we resort to less controversial terms, including conversion disorder, functional illness, somatization disorder, dissociative states, pseudoepileptic seizure, and psychogenic pain disorder to describe the same phenomenon. It is hard to say what distinguishes hysteria from a genuine illness, or a pseudoseizure from a real one, but one hint is the sheer outrageousness of its manifestations. Charcot left behind a trove of photographs showing a woman suspended between two chairs, supported only at the neck and ankles, stiff as a board; a patient with arms outstretched, as if crucified; a scantily dressed woman with her right arm rigidly extended and her right leg provocatively stretched out of her gown. None of these images accords with the way the human brain is wired. They look more like stunts than symptoms.

By any name, hysteria was and still is the bane of every neurologist's existence. It produces a constant white noise of symptoms and signs, some real and some feigned. Hysterical patients—meaning those whose condition is ultimately classified as "functional," or structurally normal—parade through every major hospital on a daily basis. The manifestations are only a bit less flagrant than in Charcot's time, but they are no less peculiar. There is no objective way to verify what the patient is feeling or of telling whether his or her actions, no matter how extreme, are beyond conscious control. You have to take the person's word for it. Estimates place the proportion of such cases in neurology departments at up to 30 percent. It is a serious and nagging problem for the profession, not to mention for the patients themselves.

The word is unfortunate. *Hysteria,* from the Greek for uterus, shows up as early as the Hippocratic texts of the fifth century BC, reflecting an ancient belief in a wandering womb as the source of many women's health issues. According to the Greeks, the uterus traveled around the body, creating sensations of pressure and unease, especially in the throat, including a feeling of choking and the loss of the ability to speak. Such was the theory, and it established hysteria exclusively as a disease of women. It was a neat explanation, it fit the known facts of the time, it let men off the hook, and it exonerated the brain completely. Its fabulistic limitation and its eventual downfall is its anatomical impossibility.

In her book *Hystories*, the feminist literary critic Elaine Showalter calls hysteria "a mimetic disorder." It mimics what she calls "culturally permissible expressions of distress." These expressions change over time and between cultures. In Charcot's Paris, permissible expressions included convulsions, fainting, numbness, paralysis, and blindness. According to Showalter, most of these have gone out of fashion, and in their place have arisen chronic fatigue, repetitive stress, and eating disorders. This is not entirely correct. If Showalter had spent any time in my neurology clinic, she would have seen what Charcot saw. There are always new twists, but old-fashioned hysteria has not disappeared.

The pleasant walk from the medical school housing Brouillet's painting to the Salpêtrière Hospital where Charcot worked takes about twenty minutes. Charcot would still recognize the route today. At the halfway point, the buildings turn modern, but once at the hospital gate, he would be reassured: the place looks much the same as he left it. It does, however, look very different than when he first arrived, and the changes had everything to do with Charcot himself.

The Pitié-Salpêtrière Hospital constitutes a walled city within a city. It lies between the Place d'Italie and the Gare d'Austerlitz in Paris's 13th arrondissement. The hospital within this vast complex is the house that Charcot built. When he first came on the scene, it was little more than a hospice on the lowest rung of Paris's social welfare system, a dumping ground built on the outskirts of the city as a place to dispose of unwanted women. In their collective misery, Charcot saw vast potential. Within the span of a decade, drawing upon the reservoir of neurological disease at his disposal, he made his landmark discoveries, laying the groundwork for modern neurology. He lectured in pathological anatomy, trained a generation of pioneering physicians, and made his lectures and demonstrations an obligatory stop for any aspiring researcher, including a young Sigmund Freud. He built laboratories, invented new physiological measuring devices, introduced the use of photography, and was instrumental in excising religion from the institutional practice of medicine. But in one sense the sprawling abundance of the Salpêtrière posed a great danger. The self-sufficient isolation of the place set Charcot up for the biggest mistake of his career.

The building got its name from a gunpowder factory and storage annex (a saltpetery) erected on the site in the early 1600s. Within a few decades, King Louis XIV repurposed the buildings. The saltpetery gave way to a hospice for the indigent, but the original name stuck. At the time, Paris was increasingly overrun by society's castoffs, and the Salpêtrière became a destination for women and wayward girls deemed unsuitable for the streets of Paris—thieves, vagrants, prostitutes, alcoholics, blasphemers, epileptics, syphilitics, foundlings, the elderly, and the criminally insane. Rounded up on nightly patrols, many were housed in a prison on the site prior to being deported to America, as happened to Manon Lescaut in the famous novel of that name by Abbé Prévost. Those left behind added to a burgeoning population. In due course, a hospital was added.

The Salpêtrière gave Charcot access to what he called a "grand asylum of human misery" and a "museum of living pathology." He put it to good use. In the 1870s he raised funds, ordered the construction of specialized laboratories, staffed them with bright young interns, developed a curriculum and a research agenda based on detailed observation, and attracted students from around the world. Breakthrough discoveries followed in quick succession and revolutionized the study and understanding of the nervous system. It is easy to see why. He opened the hospital to the surrounding community by establishing a free outpatient clinic. He built a dormitory for men in order to diversify his patient pool. He outfitted a four-hundred-seat amphitheater in order to give demonstrations to the public, and these began to attract large audiences. Not just aspiring researchers, but the literati, the entertainment world, politicians, and a host of hangers-on descended upon the hospital each week to witness Charcot's lectures. A lot of this had to do with his star patient.

Blanche Wittman's life story reads like a horrific fairy tale. A young girl living in squalor finds a golden ticket to a magical place presided over by a real-life Willy Wonka. Once there, she is installed as the queen. During her reign she receives visitors from the cream of society, from the stars of the theater and the literary world. She becomes the toast of Paris. When she finally steps down from her throne, she is slowly poisoned, chopped into pieces, and dies. As fantastical as this might sound, it is a fairly accurate account of Blanche's life and fate.

Marie Wittman, her real name, was born in Paris in 1859 to an abusive out-of-work carpenter father and a laundress mother who toiled sixteen-hour days. Before she was in her teens, Marie saw her father sent off to an insane asylum, where he died; she saw five of her eight siblings die in childhood; and then she had the misfortune of being apprenticed to a furrier who made constant sexual advances to the point where she often collapsed in convulsions. She ran away at age fourteen to rejoin her family, but her mother died a year later. With her remaining siblings packed off to foster homes and orphanages, and being too old to be placed herself, Marie had no choice but to return to the furrier, at whose hands she endured sexual abuse for eight months before fleeing again, this time to a friend's house. She managed to secure a job at the second-lowest rung of the career ladder available to young women by becoming a ward girl at a local hospital. Hours were long, the work filthy and backbreaking, and she contended with dizziness, convulsions, and fainting spells. Frequently belligerent and combative, she did not last long in school, could not read or write very well, had a string of brief romances, and continued to suffer from the trauma of her abuse. Eventually the convulsive attacks landed her at the Salpêtrière, where she was admitted to the epilepsy ward. For whatever deep-seated reason, once there she continually barked out the name Blanche. It might have been the name of one of her dead siblings, or simply a reaction to having to wash sheets, but the name stuck, and she thenceforth became Blanche Wittman. She was just eighteen years old, and she would remain at the Salpêtrière for the rest of her life.

Why Charcot took an interest in her is not clear. She was one of dozens of women who, although not epileptic themselves, mimicked the convulsive attacks of the patients whose quarters they shared. Pseudoseizures were contagious; scores of women at the Salpêtrière came down with them. But contagion is not synonymous with disease. Charcot called it "hystero-epilepsy" at first, in order to distinguish it from the real thing. He then decided to delve deeper. As he knew very well, some patients feigned seizures to get attention, and his staff became adept at distinguishing simulated from real convulsions. But Blanche Wittman and a few others defied categorization—they were neither epileptic nor simply acting. Their fits and altered minds seemed more neurological than psychiatric. Skeptics—and there were many—assumed the entire phenomenon had been manufactured by Charcot himself, that it was nothing more than a carefully choreographed act.

Hysterical, madame, here is the great word of the day." Guy de Maupassant had had enough of hysteria. In 1882, the emerging literary star and cultural commentator penned an editorial for the Parisian literary journal *Gil Blas*, in which he let loose:

> Are you amorous? You are a hysteric . . . You are a gourmande? Hysteric! You are nervous? Hysteric! You are this, you are that, you are just like any woman since the beginning of time? Hysteric! Hysteric! I tell you. We are all hysterics, since Charcot, that grand priest of hysterics, that breeder of chamber hysterics, maintains at great cost in his model establishment a number of nervous women among whom he inoculates with madness and of whom he makes demoniacs in no time.

In his wanderings through various Parisian social circles and haunts, both high and low, Maupassant had visited the Salpêtrière. He may even have sat alongside a young Sigmund Freud while witnessing a phenomenon seen almost exclusively within its walls. He was not impressed. "[Charcot] produces on me the effect of those storytellers of the school of Edgar Allan Poe who go mad through constantly reflecting on queer cases of insanity," one of his fictional characters says. "He has set forth some nervous phenomena that are unexplained and inexplicable; he makes his way into that unknown region that men explore every day and, not being able to comprehend what he sees, he remembers perhaps too well the explanations of certain mysteries given by priests."

Maupassant had a difficult relationship with doctors in general. Outwardly, he was the picture of robustness. An avid outdoorsman, he spent hours rowing his boat down the Seine or sailing off the coast of

Étretat. He was also a notorious ladies' man. In his early years in Paris, just after getting out of the navy, he lived on the ground floor of an apartment house populated by prostitutes. They got along very well. Maupassant even used his neighbors' experiences in some of his early short stories. It should have come as no surprise to him when, at the age of twenty-seven, he made an astounding discovery. "I've the pox!" he wrote to a friend. "At last! It's true! . . . and I'm proud, by God, and despise above all the bourgeoisie. Hallelujah! I have the pox, and so have no need to fear catching it." By the pox, he meant syphilis.

It seemed to worry him hardly at all. He blamed it on a fisherwoman he had encountered by the banks of the Seine, although the pool of suspects was vast. Maupassant was almost pathologically drawn to women. From the river to the streets to the cafés to the salons, he had scores of casual encounters. In a letter to his mother, of all people, he wrote: "I am obsessed by women. I cannot pass up their caresses. And when a woman stops me in the street, by chance, despite her fetid breath and her repugnant filth, I cannot resist for long that silent and powerful call of the flesh that wells up like the waves from below, from the depths of my entrails, and places a blindfold on my eyes, a gag on my conscience, and reduces you in an instant to the mercy of these bitches."

Maupassant claimed not to have noticed the first stage of his disease, although in looking back, he remarked, "Many symptoms to which I attached no importance served to make that discovery extraordinary." Two years later, in 1877, his hair began to fall out, but not in a typical balding pattern. A physician immediately recognized it as syphilis, but his symptoms receded quickly enough to allow the writer to ignore this diagnosis, and he easily found other doctors who assured him his condition was merely degenerative and hereditary, not syphilitic. Meanwhile, he enjoyed a streak of success as a popular novelist and editorial journalist. Under the mentorship of Gustave Flaubert, another syphilitic, his reputation soared. But behind the scenes, the harsh reality of Maupassant's declining physical state became increasingly difficult to ignore. While his womanizing continued almost unabated, Maupassant took the precaution of using condoms when sleeping with his mistresses. Prostitutes did not receive the same consideration. Though publicly arrogant and boastful, he understood the impossibility of marriage. His eye problems, well documented in his letters, were the most telling sign of his worsening condition. To Flaubert he wrote, "I can hardly see out of my right eye. My doctor is a bit worried and thinks there's a congestion of some part of the organ." The doctor, Jean Marie Charles Abadie, told him, "Syphilis is often the cause of such paralyses." Grudgingly, Maupassant sought out Charcot. He was desperate.

The consultation occurred in 1886, the same year André Brouillet was immortalizing Charcot in oils. Maupassant explained his symptoms in detail. For years he had struggled with migraine, hair loss, toothache, intestinal bleeding, nervousness, insomnia, and vision problems. "I live with an abominable hypochondria," he admitted, "and suffer still from a neuralgia of the neck from the nape extending up to the interior of the skull to the base of my eyes and ears. . . . I'm half-broken with fatigue, with headache and nervous illness. Everything pains me and I've no relief except for those hours when I write. . . . I only have a sense of well-being when near the sea or in the mountains."

His drinking and womanizing were by then the talk of Paris. So was the fact that his brother had been sent off to an asylum, and that his mother was perpetually ill with one thing or another. Nervous complaints seemed to run in the family. Charcot examined him carefully. He concluded it was nothing serious, and he recommended rest and a water cure. Though the subject of syphilis may have come up, it did not stand out as the primary problem. It was a commonplace condition of the time, a background annoyance much like shingles or eczema. It usually cleared up after treatment with simple remedies. Maupassant left, bitter and disappointed. The great Charcot could do nothing for him. He dutifully sojourned at a spa and took the waters as advised, but to no avail. His condition worsened.

"I assure you I'm losing my mind," he wrote to another doctor. "I'm going mad. I spent yesterday evening at Princess Mathilde's, searching for words, unable to speak, losing my memory altogether. I came home to sleep, and the sensation of my distressed state of mind kept me up. I took sulfonal; nothing happened. I walked and walked. Please come see me. We must find the cause." The wellspring of his inventiveness began to dry up. He could no longer write. His output dwindled to a few letters, most of them chronicling his list of complaints. A few years later, a friend recalled,

> On the last occasion on which I saw him, at a garden party in Sèvres . . . it had struck me that there was something strange in his conversation. He kept talking of money and of fashionable folk whom he had met or whom he had hoped to meet, as though by birth and by talents he was not very far superior, even from a social point of view, to all of the silly people whose names he mentioned. I suppose that if I had been a pathologist I should then and there have recognized in this talk the prodromes of megalomania and general paralysis.

Prodrome is a word heard very little these days. It describes an early sign of the onset of a disease or condition, and Maupassant's condition was now recognizable even to the man on the street.

The following January, while in Cannes, his faithful valet François found Maupassant holding a knife, his mouth open, saying, "Look, François, at what I've done. I've cut my throat, an absolute case of folly." He was placed in a straitjacket, bundled into a railway carriage, and taken to an asylum in Paris. Delusions soon set in. According to his biographer, "He accused François of embezzling his money and plagiarizing his work, he insulted God and said he was God's son by his mother, referred to his urine as diamonds, was obsessed with the idea of piles of eggs, and constantly mentioned his train journey to Purgatory and his dialogue with Lucifer about taking over the world." By April he could no longer stand. In late June he slipped into a coma, and on coming out of it a week later was racked by convulsions. Mercifully, on July 6, 1893, his heart stopped. He was forty-two years old.

Hindsight is a luxury. We now know what was wrong with Guy de Maupassant. Charcot should not be faulted for missing it. Facing an uncharted landscape of so-called *névroses*—generalized diseases of the nervous system—few of which could be verified by examination of tissues or even cells, Charcot believed that most patients like Maupassant were not suffering in body, but in mind. In the parlance of the day, he had a case of the nerves combined with a weakened constitution. Such a condition could not be verified; it could only be intuited. Someday, Charcot assumed, technology would provide the means of confirming the underlying condition, but at the time of his examination, Maupassant's illness had not progressed far enough to be conclusive. The multitude of physical symptoms struck Charcot as being neurasthenic, a euphemism for hysteria in men. He did not connect them to syphilis because neurosyphilis did not yet exist as a disease; it would not be revealed as a neurological condition for another two decades. And even if he had correctly diagnosed the problem, Charcot could have done nothing about it. Maupassant was doomed.

A month after the writer's death, Jean-Martin Charcot also dropped dead. His heart gave out. From that day forward his most famous patient, Blanche Wittman, never again had an attack of hysteria. Maupassant had proven Charcot wrong on two counts. Blanche's convulsions had originated entirely in her mind, while Maupassant himself, diagnosed with the nineteenth-century catchall of hysteria, had instead died from a disease of the twentieth century, a disease of the brain.

The medical profession no longer recognizes Blanche Wittman's diagnosis, at least not officially, yet we continue to acknowledge it. After Pluto was demoted in 2006 to the status of a dwarf planet, many people, scientists included, resisted that reclassification, just as many doctors continue to speak of hysteria as if it is a valid label. This is what André Brouillet's *A Clinical Lesson* is about. It depicts an early attempt to pin down the meaning of mental illness: whether it is a state of mind or an altered state of the brain. Charcot attributed it to the brain, but failed to prove it. Instead, he inadvertently linked sex and neurosis, as Brouillet was happy to show us, and set neurology and psychiatry on an impossible quest to resolve the question of hysteria. All the while, in the person of Guy de Maupassant, the neuropsychiatric disease par excellence escaped his notice entirely.

CHAPTER 2

WHAT IS A DISEASE?

In the mid-1950s, when a developer announced plans to demolish a service station in Fairmount, New York, Michael Chomentowski knew he had to do something about it. His family had been leasing the property for years, he worked there, and he was not about to let a shopping center snuff out his livelihood. After rebuffing all appeals to vacate the premises, Chomentowski took to patrolling the gas station with a rifle slung over his shoulder. As he later described it, he was simply "walking his post in a military manner." When two men approached and tried to put up a sign advertising the new construction, Chomentowski fired two warning shots into the air. The men fled, and when the police arrived and arrested Chomentowski, they discovered a French-manufactured machine gun in the trunk of his car. It was nonfunctional, but illegal nonetheless. Chomentowski kept saying, "I'm a soldier for the people," which didn't help matters. At the local lockup, under questioning, he claimed there was gold buried under his gas station, that Jesus Christ had been born somewhere on the premises, and that he felt as though nailed to a cross during the whole ordeal. To a reporter, he added, "The people now have the original Davy Crockett. This will be the biggest story in history and I'm glad it happened."

In the state of New York at the time, judges did not have the authority to declare someone unfit to stand trial by reason of insanity, the privilege having been ceded to the psychiatrists, two of whom declared Chomentowski "oriented in all spheres," though suffering from a schizophrenic reaction. They deemed him incapable of standing trial, and he was shipped off to the Matteawan State Hospital, where he remained for seven years. No charges were ever filed.

At a habeas corpus hearing in 1962, Chomentowski's family brought their own expert witness, hoping to rebut the judgment of the original psychiatrists. His name was Thomas Szasz, and he had just written a book on mental illness. It had earned him a sudden notoriety because of its startling central premise, declared rather forthrightly in its provocative title, *The Myth of Mental Illness*. On the first page of his book, Szasz declares, "Psychiatry is conventionally defined as a medical specialty concerned with the diagnosis and treatment of mental diseases. I submit that this definition . . . places psychiatry in the company of alchemy and astrology and commits it to the category of pseudoscience. The reason for this is that there is no such thing as 'mental illness.'"

As a newly minted professor of psychiatry at the State University of New York's Upstate Medical University in Syracuse, Szasz had begun to question the legal principle behind the insanity defense. By this time, neither the state of New York, in the person of Dr. Abraham Halpern, one of Szasz's colleagues at the university, nor the county of Onondaga, represented by its commissioner of mental health, had an interest in detaining Chomentowski any longer. But both men had a highly vested interest in putting Szasz and his controversial book on trial. Szasz, for his part, hoped to put the psychiatric profession on trial. The Chomentowskis had no idea of this subplot, mistakenly believing the hearing was all about their son.

Throughout the hearing, Dr. Halpern coached the prosecutor and whispered questions for the witness. Some of them, relevant to bias but not much else, drifted far from Chomentowski's appeal and into the expansive domain of Szasz's ideas on religion, politics, and Sigmund Freud. When it finally got down to the claims he had made in his book, the prosecutor had to ask, "How does mental illness constitute a myth?"

"People say these are illnesses that doctors can cure," Szasz replied. "I say they are wrong. These are not illnesses people can cure. They are using the term *mental illness* mistakenly." The phenomenon of so-called mental illness, Szasz insisted, is not illness or disease as medicine defines those terms. To a casual observer, this would seem to be a matter of semantics, but to Szasz it made all the difference in the world. If there is no discernible problem with the body, or specifically with someone's brain, he argued, how can that person be diagnosed with an illness? If a psychiatrist has the power to deem someone insane based solely on the subject's words and actions, where is the gold standard of that diagnosis? Would every psychiatrist, after interviewing Michael Chomentowski, call him insane?

There is a simple answer to these questions. Each organ of the body expresses dysfunction in a specific way. The liver produces jaundice, the heart produces chest pain, the lungs shortness of breath. Not only does the brain produce movement and register sensory experience, but to its self-referential misfortune, it also creates thoughts, ideas, and words. When these products of the brain become "deranged," the brain is diseased. The derangement *is* the disease. Szasz countered with a strictly biological interpretation. Derangement of the mind without any evidence of a defect in the body is a problem, but not a disease. Treating it as one opens up Pandora's box. "We have thus come to regard addiction, delinquency, divorce, homosexuality, homicide, suicide, and so on almost without limit, as psychiatric illnesses," he wrote. "This is a colossal and costly mistake." If the standards of diagnosis are not medical standards, they are subject to interpretation, he continued. Clearly the simple answer does not suffice. It is not enough to say of a disease, "I know it when I see it." In Szasz's view, "this distinction—between fact and facsimile, object and sign, physics and psychology, medicine and morals—remains the core problem of contemporary psychiatric epistemology."

His testimony lasted two days and ate up almost the entire hearing. It took that long for the prosecutor to finally get Szasz to expose himself by saying: "Being called a psychiatric patient when one does not want to be called a psychiatric patient, being given drugs, psychiatric drugs, when one doesn't want psychiatric drugs—I would consider all of these things together as brutality." In that era, this was apostasy, and precisely the sound bite Halpern wanted.

In the end, Szasz's testimony did not help his client; Chomentowski's appeal was denied. Later that year, the Supreme Court overturned the constitutionality of Chomentowski's arrest, and he was released. Szasz himself did not get off so easily. He became a public whipping boy for academic psychiatry and for orthodox psychoanalysis. Half a century later, although the profession claims to have moved on, leaving Szasz a distant speck in the rearview mirror, his book still haunts psychiatry if not neurology, and remains historically if not epistemologically relevant. The proof of this lies in continual attacks launched on Szasz himself rather than on the main argument put forth in his book.

What is a disease? To anyone suffering from one, it may seem obvious, but from a scientific standpoint, it is anything but clear. Historically, the method of diagnosis emerged through a process of observing patients with similar symptoms, and if these occurred frequently as an ensemble, calling it a syndrome. The great Thomas Sydenham, a medical pioneer of the seventeenth century, saw such a collection of symptoms in the rapid flinging and twisting movements of some pregnant women, as well as in children in the wake of infections. He recognized that the symptoms, known as chorea, abated after a few days. At the time, the wild flinging phenomenon was popularly ascribed to demonic possession, and was called St. Vitus's dance. Sydenham decided that if a suite of symptoms, a syndrome, had a predictable course over time, it would qualify as a disease. The medical establishment eventually endorsed this idea, as well as the ailment that inspired it, and called it Sydenham's chorea. It was later found to be due to antibodies from streptococcal infection. This established the classic method of medical classification in the evidentiary progression from symptom to syndrome to disease. Many famous examples would soon follow.

From the age of thirty onward, the folk singer Woody Guthrie suffered a series of health setbacks, and they affected his behavior in dramatic ways. He was described as being "erratic." When he began to also make erratic flinging arm movements, like a windmill, twisting his torso, and twitching his head, those close to him suspected a mental illness. It was easy, perhaps too easy, to attribute his troubles to alcohol. He was indeed an alcoholic, but was that his disease, or was it merely a symptom of something else? In 1952, his doctors diagnosed him with Huntington's chorea, something characterized by the same involuntary movements seen in Sydenham's chorea, but in Woody's case they were due to degeneration of nerve cells rather than to an infection. It would ultimately lead to dementia. Guthrie was not mentally ill. He had a brain disease.

Cases of Huntington's chorea were first described on New York's Long Island in 1872. It occurred frequently within families, suggesting a strong genetic element. George Huntington, a twenty-two-year-old general practitioner, assumed it was a true disease because the syndrome worsened gradually in a consistent fashion, and it did so only to members of specific local families. As with St. Vitus's dance, the symptom profile did not qualify as a disease until Huntington described its symptoms, its heritable nature, and its time course. This transition from nonexistence to legitimization occurs for almost every major medical disorder. Still, Huntington could only chronicle what he saw. He did not understand the underlying mechanics of the phenomenon that now bears his name. Fifty years after Huntington described the syndrome, scientists found pathologic changes in the brain corresponding to the disease: the caudate nuclei, part of the basal ganglia deep within the brain, were shrunken. By backward reasoning, the shrunken caudates had to be the cause of the chorea. The next logical question was: What caused the damage to the caudate nuclei?

In 1983, James Gusella at Massachusetts General Hospital, along with a consortium of researchers, found an abnormal gene on chromosome 4 in successive generations of Huntington's patients. The mutation was an excessively long series of repeated segments of three nucleotides, the backbone chemicals of DNA. Some patients with 36 to 39 consecutive triplets got the disease. For those with higher numbers, the symptoms of chorea and dementia were almost inevitable, although we still do not know how this particular genetic variant leads to the death of nerve cells in the caudate. This raises the question of whether the fundamental cause of Huntington's disease is the genetic mutation, the lost nerve cells, or a yet-to-be-discovered mechanism that links them. And what of people who have an intermediate number of repeat segments? If they have no clinical manifestations even late into life, can they be said to have the disease? In medicine, we say yes, because the mutation is dominant, meaning one copy is enough to cause Huntington's disease, and because it has high penetrance, meaning it will always eventually express itself. A comparable situation exists in forms of inherited Alzheimer's disease, in which virtually everyone with the genetic marker will eventually get demented. Those who have the marker can be said to have the disease even without the symptoms. All they can do is wait.

The philosopher Catherine Dekeuwer has defined such genetic states as "hereditary diseases whose fundamental (molecular) defect has been identified at the level of DNA. This defect explains the disease's characteristics on higher levels (cellular, tissue, physiological)." The disease is the genetic code, and the availability of genetic analysis by commercial testing companies such as 23andMe will create a dilemma for those who discover they have a high susceptibility to Huntington's, diabetes, or Alzheimer's. Even if their condition takes fifty years to manifest, Dekeuwer would say these people have had the disease all along, even though many of them (most, actually) will never experience symptoms.

The historical process of identifying *mental* illnesses sidestepped these questions. The model established by Thomas Sydenham was faithfully followed, except that the symptoms consisted of behaviors and experiences rather than physical alterations in the brain. If a series of symptoms and signs cohered to a pattern and followed the same trajectory in every afflicted patient, they were assigned a disease name. According to the historian Edward Shorter, the German psychiatrist Emil Kraepelin "provided the single most significant insight that the late nineteenth and early twentieth centuries had to offer into major psychiatric illness: that there are several principal types, that they have very different courses, and that their nature may be appreciated through the systematic study of large numbers of cases." The two types of psychosis he distinguished were dementia praecox, now known as schizophrenia, and manic-depressive insanity, now known as bipolar disorder.

Born in northern Germany in 1856, Kraepelin studied medicine in Leipzig, specialized in neuropathology, and used this as a springboard into the study of psychiatry. In 1886 he began to collect clinical histories of disturbed patients in order to come up with a scheme for the classification of mental illness. He recorded his thumbnail patient histories on notecards, so-called Zählkarten, or counting cards. "I ensured that a Zählkarte was made . . . for every patient and that all the important features of the clinical picture were noted on those cards," he wrote. His team collected around a thousand such cards, fewer than half of them done by Kraepelin himself, and they represent an incomplete and somewhat vague data set, although Kraepelin regarded them as scientific gold. It has been suggested that rather than using the cards to formulate criteria and theories of mental illness, he used them selectively to reinforce what he had already decided. Even so, his classification of mental disease, and in particular of the psychoses, profoundly influenced the writing of psychiatric diagnostic manuals in the twentieth century.

In 1893, the year of Charcot's death, Kraepelin introduced his iconic dichotomy into the psychiatric literature. He chose the term *dementia praecox* because he viewed it as a degenerative form of dementia with a precocious nature, thus rarely if ever emerging in late adulthood. He cared little about the content of psychotic speech: the bizarre nature of the thoughts traversing the patient's mind and distorting his perception of the world. The underlying problem had to reside in the brain. If a patient exhibited behaviors or responses at odds with objective reality, then he fit the description, especially if his mental state deteriorated over time into a premature form of dementia. Kraepelin's other category—manic-depressive insanity—applied to those afflicted with wild mood changes. Rather than being unable to recognize reality, these patients seemed unwilling to accept it.

Unlike Kraepelin, Eugen Bleuler, a Swiss psychiatrist who had trained under Charcot, developed a deep interest in the content of his patients' speech. He too amassed a database of diagnoses, but in contrast to Kraepelin, Bleuler based these on intense face-to-face sessions, usually employing word associations. He recognized that what Kraepelin called dementia praecox did not always involve true dementia, but rather a "splitting off" of personality. He gave the condition a new name: "I call dementia praecox 'schizophrenia' because (as I hope to demonstrate) the 'splitting' of the different psychic functions is one of its most important characteristics." The first psychiatric diagnostic manuals of the twentieth century grew out of both men's classifications, acknowledging how problems with the brain could produce even more serious problems with the mind. But as Szasz would later note, these categories broadened and became less focused over the decades, especially with the incursions of psychoanalysis into mainstream psychiatry. Like *hysterical*, the word *schizophrenic* became a universal adjective for out-of-control behavior. Moreover, there was considerable lack of agreement within the psychiatric community about the diagnostic criteria. Psychiatrists, Szasz complained, had been abetting this kind of imprecision and abuse of classification since the days of Philippe Pinel. Where would it end?

Szasz saw himself as a counterbalance to assumptions and received ideas within his chosen profession. He placed the blame for these ideas on Charcot, Freud, Kraepelin, and Freud's writing partner, Josef Breuer. They and many others "lent their authority to the propagation of this socially-enhancing image of what was then 'hysteria,' and what in our day has become the problem of 'mental illness.'" The turning point in the history of psychiatry, he believed, was the discovery of neurosyphilis. "Paresis [syphilis of the brain] was *proved* to be a disease," he notes, "hysteria was *declared* to be one." Unfortunately, as Szasz saw it, the discovery of the tangible, physical basis of neurosyphilis fueled an expectation that all forms of mental illness eventually would be shown to have an organic basis. Charcot believed this about hysteria, and Kraepelin believed it about dementia praecox. This belief in the underlying if undiscovered biological basis of mental illness enhanced the prestige of psychiatry while casting a wide net over all forms of mental distress, what Szasz dismissed as "problems with living." With an insanity-causing brain disease in hand, psychiatry could attribute all abnormal behavior to unspecified, unlocalized bodily diseases with undetected pathology in the brain. Charcot and Freud, among others, anticipated this trend. By defining hysteria as an illness, wrote Szasz, "Charcot made it easier for the sufferer, then commonly called a malingerer, to be sick."

Midcentury was a good time to be a psychotherapist in America. The G.I. Bill was financing the building of Levittowns, finished basements, and backyard bomb shelters, while writers like John Cheever, William H. Whyte, and David Reisman were chronicling the alienation and paranoia of life in burgeoning bedroom communities. In the 1950s, the population of American psychiatrists was growing at twice the rate of the U.S. population. Psychiatry promised to reshape society by relieving it of the burden not just of neurosis but also of serious mental illness. But in this boom industry, Szasz grew increasingly uneasy about the way in which psychiatrists had come to serve as accomplices of civil authority. If a husband tired of his wife, he could, with a cooperating psychiatrist's declaration of insanity or hysteria, have her committed to an asylum. If a government tired of a dissident, it could have him declared mentally incompetent, jailed, and drugged into a stupor. Szasz was aware that the Soviet regime had perverted the use of psychiatric practice to deal harshly with political opposition. Coercive psychiatric measures could graduate from involuntary incarceration to forced sterilization, insulin coma therapy, electroshock therapy, and even lobotomy—and they did. "The enterprise of inventing mental diseases," Szasz wrote, "unconstrained by fixed criteria or the requirements of empirical evidence, must eventuate in the conclusion that any phenomenon studied by the observer may be defined as a disease."

Szasz's "myth" of mental illness may sound like a stunt, but it grew out of a legitimate frustration with science overstepping its bounds. Instead of solving the problem of psychosis, academic medicine had indeed multiplied the number of disease classifications, in some cases simply by inventing diseases to serve a particular agenda. Back in 1843, American slaves who tried to escape had been given the medical diagnosis of drapetomania. A century later, Soviet psychiatrists created a similar category for dissidents: sluggish schizophrenia. Homosexuality was treated with hormone injections because of its presumed endocrine origin; later, as a presumed mental disorder, it was treated with electroshock. The lines separating the boundaries of normal human behavior from pathology became increasingly blurred. For any Szaszian, the problem is now pervasive. Today Szasz (he died in 2012) would probably include chronic fatigue, gluten sensitivity, chronic Lyme, hypoglycemia, sick building syndrome, chronic candida infection, even grief or sadness diagnosed as depression in his list of "problems with living." But of course it is not that simple.

Thomas Szasz was a provocateur, and his uncompromising argument for the myth of mental illness undercut his more important point about the danger of trying to psychopathologize everyday life. This habit of assigning a classification to almost every troubled thought or pattern of behavior did not come about by accident. Nor was it entirely Charcot's fault. In fact it predated Charcot by a century and can be traced back to one man, to his therapeutic innovation, and to the supporting theory he invented. Like phrenology, it should long ago have been consigned to the junk heap of history, yet it is still alive in many guises, even within mainstream medicine. Its inventor's name lives on as well: Franz Mesmer.

CHAPTER 3

PYGMALION AND GALATEA

In 1894, the Franco-British writer George du Maurier, the grandfather of novelist Daphne du Maurier (*Rebecca, Jamaica Inn*), wrote a bestselling novel entitled *Trilby*. It became an even more successful play and made two lasting contributions to the English language. The first is the name of the short-brimmed fedora known as a trilby, so called after the hat worn by the British actress who created the title role on the stage. The other is the term *Svengali*, from the name of a memorable rogue and hypnotist who guides Trilby's career. The word now describes any domineering man who manipulates a young woman into doing his creative bidding. In the novel, Trilby O'Ferrall, an orphan with a squalid past, makes a living as an artist's model. She has no discernible talent or skill, and is plagued with traumatic memories. According to the narrator, she has "a singularly impressionable nature, as was shown by her quick and ready susceptibility to Svengali's hypnotic influence." A musician of no great talent, Svengali insinuates himself into Trilby's life, and he projects his artistic ambitions onto her. Under his spell, she becomes an astonishingly successful singer and soon achieves international fame as a diva. Yet without Svengali behind her, pulling the strings, she cannot sing at all. When her lack of talent is finally revealed, Trilby succumbs to a nervous disorder and dies.

There are several precedents for Svengali and Trilby going back to the myth of Pygmalion and Galatea. What is remarkable is the extent to which du Maurier, without knowing it, reproduced in the character of Trilby O'Ferrall the mutually opportunistic relationship not just between Charcot and Blanche Wittman, but even before them, between the original mesmerist and his reluctant muse.

At the age of four, Maria Theresia von Paradis informed her loving parents that she had gone blind. The von Paradis family lived in a bourgeois neighborhood of the Vienna of Mozart and Haydn, and Herr von Paradis himself served as imperial secretary to the empress Maria Theresa, for whom his daughter was named. In a panic, Herr von Paradis sought out the top specialists in the city, and though they attempted various primitive remedies, they could not help the girl. There was nothing wrong with her eyes. She appeared to be in the bloom of health, and yet she could not see.

With the remarkable adaptability of youth, the girl compensated in extraordinary ways. She mastered her surroundings so well she could navigate the house with ease. She took up music and became a prodigy on the piano. She even enjoyed playing cards. It was as though her other senses stepped up to cover for her loss of sight, allowing her to carry on as a normal if somewhat precocious child. On the piano, her precocity soon graduated into a prodigious talent. She performed at the court of the empress (who was Marie Antoinette's mother), and so impressed Her Highness that a royal allowance of two hundred gold ducats was bestowed upon and gratefully accepted by the girl's parents. With access to the funds, they consulted more doctors, whereupon Maria Theresia endured yet more barbaric treatments, including bloodletting and purging. Still, nothing availed. None of the specialists could find a single defect in her optic nerve, retina, or corneas. Meanwhile her education continued and she refined her musical skills. At the age of thirteen, she prepared to perform on a public stage for the first time on a tour that would take her first to Vienna, then Paris, and finally to London. Little Maria Theresia, the blind girl for whom Mozart himself had allegedly composed a sonata, had risen from obscurity to celebrity in less than a decade to become the darling of Viennese society.

In her sixteenth year, after her debut as a performer at the salons of the city, a physician by the name of Franz Anton Mesmer approached Maria Theresia's parents, offering to cure her with a novel method. Wouldn't it be wonderful, he said, if the young lady could at last regain her sight? After a decade of failures by the cream of the Viennese medical community, what chance did this upstart have? The parents nonetheless agreed, perhaps out of desperation, but more probably because they had heard something of this Mesmer. Apparently he could work miracles.

If Mesmer's name sounds familiar, it is because of the eponyms *mesmerism* and *mesmerized*. Two years prior to approaching Maria Theresia's parents, Mesmer hit upon one of the most influential and counterproductive ideas of the Age of Enlightenment. In the dustbin of history, the ashes of mesmerism would mingle with those of phrenology and astrology. But like the phoenix, Mesmer's idea would be reborn several times over. It would inspire the founding of Mary Baker Eddy's Church of Christ, Scientist; it would also serve as a model for the Church of Scientology and for dozens of self-help movements of the nineteenth and twentieth centuries, including the autosuggestive self-healing of Émile Coué ("Every day in every way I'm getting better"), Erhard Seminars Training (aka EST), Norman Vincent Peale's "power of positive thinking," and all of its variants. Most significantly, within the world of academic medicine, it would also bring Jean-Martin Charcot and Blanche Wittman together, as shown in André Brouillet's painting, and shortly thereafter, it would provide Sigmund Freud with the therapeutic springboard for psychoanalysis. Thomas Szasz put it more bluntly: "Mesmer stands in the same sort of relation to Freud and Jung as Columbus stands in relation to Thomas Jefferson and John Adams."

As with Freud a century later, Mesmer cloaked spiritualism in the guise of natural science while championing "mind over matter" as the key to overcoming disease. What he found, rather than discovered, was the very human susceptibility to the idea of all forms of illness as a state of mind, coupled with the power of one's own mind, providentially assisted by an unseen force, to effect its own cure. Mesmer believed he had found a way to harness something analogous to gravity and electricity, and pass along its healing qualities. He called it animal magnetism.

Mesmer never set out to become a con artist. He truly believed he had discovered a universal fluid and its healing properties by pursuing a simple and legitimately scientific question: What if he were to give a hysterical woman a tonic containing iron, then applied magnets to various parts of her body? The test patient, a certain Fräulein Oesterline, had suffered for years from, as Mesmer described it, "a convulsive malady, the most troubling symptoms of which were that the blood rushed to her head and there set up a most cruel toothache and earache, followed by delirium, rage, vomiting, and swooning." His treatment worked. The woman felt a wave of energy, and with it her tension dissipated. This is not quite as outlandish as it sounds. The chi of Chinese acupuncture and the pranas of Hindu medicine are similar in concept.

Mesmer was also no fool. He carefully assessed the symptom profile of prospective clients before offering his services. He was a physician, after all, with a medical degree from the University of Vienna. He knew the medical history of Maria Theresia and was aware of the absence of any pathological signs associated with her blindness or visual impairment. It had to be hysterical.

Whatever Maria Theresia may have thought of Mesmer's plan, she dutifully moved into his home clinic, joining a few other patients, and the good doctor set to work. Within a few weeks, he had partially restored the young woman's sight. Her parents were delighted, but she herself seemed dubious, then disappointed, then depressed. "Why is it that I am now less happy than I was when I was still afflicted?" she asked. "Everything I see gives me an unpleasant sensation."

There is a difference between looking and seeing, and for a dozen years Maria Theresia had not been held to account for looking at anything. She could most definitely see, but at some point had simply decided she would not see, all the while still processing some visual data. In this way she convincingly imitated true blindness. But once she acceded to Mesmer's cure, everything struck her as being unbearably ugly, especially Mesmer's face, one of the first things she cast her gaze upon.

Like any successful man, Mesmer had enemies and competitors on the alert for ways to bring him down. Now his detractors found their opportunity. Mesmer had staked his reputation on Maria Theresia's cure, and over the course of a few weeks had induced her to recognize the broad outlines of images. She was able to detect varieties of brightness. She could distinguish simple geometric shapes in black and white. Mesmer felt he was on the verge of a miracle worthy of the New Testament. Now was the time for his adversaries to strike. If Mesmer had talked her out of her blindness, they reasoned, she could be talked back into it. They began a whispering campaign aimed at Herr von Paradis, suggesting that if his daughter could see, he would forfeit her annual pension. Maria Theresia herself seemed to realize, somewhat late in the game, what she stood to lose. Her audience knew her as the astonishingly talented blind girl. If she could see, there would no longer be anything special about her. Within days she regressed to a worse state than the one in which Mesmer had found her. In addition to a return to total blindness, she now became racked by convulsions. Her father demanded her return, but Mesmer refused, citing the importance of completing her treatment. His enemies charged him with fraud and sexual impropriety, and a scandal ensued. At the order of the empress, Mesmer was forced to return the young woman to her parents. The treatment over, his reputation in Vienna now in tatters, Mesmer decamped for Paris, hoping the story wouldn't follow him there.

It didn't. Franz Anton Mesmer was a man with a plan to conquer the world, and to a large extent he succeeded. Like his contemporary, Napoléon, he came, saw, conquered, then was exiled, returned to Paris in a last hurrah, and in the end was permanently banished. His first downfall was brought about by a clever and talented young blind woman; his second one by none other than Benjamin Franklin.

In Paris, Mesmer's practice flourished, and he adopted the accoutrements of a mystical healer. He entered his sessions wearing a flowing purple robe. He even carried a wand. Although he spawned many imitators, he kept a tight rein on his own operation, limiting himself to few students, making sure he alone was the center of attention. He wrote a book, *Memoir on the Discovery of Animal Magnetism*, and conducted therapeutic séances around an oaken tub filled with jars of water, each with a conductive rod sticking out. Clients came in droves, and he took to treating them in groups, up to twenty at a time. But within a decade the man in the purple robe went from A-list celebrity to social pariah yet again. A scientific panel convened by King Louis XVI in 1784, numbering Benjamin Franklin, Antoine Lavoisier, and Joseph-Ignace Guillotin (yes, *that* Guillotin) among its members, did not question the results of the therapy—people did feel better after the sessions—but demurred on the question of whether animal magnetism had anything to do with it. They could find no evidence it even existed. Without royal backing, Mesmer was effectively run out of town.

A second royal commission, convened in 1826, voiced a more hopeful opinion, but by that time Mesmer was long gone. A generation of practitioners had carried on his craft in his stead with spectacular results and equally spectacular profits. Mesmerism was capable of putting subjects into trances, of jolting stultified clients to the core. It even served as an effective form of anesthesia for surgical and dental patients. Through the power of suggestion, hysterics could be relieved of pain or cured of their malaise or depression. However it worked, and the second commission's members had no idea how or if it did work, they conceded it a place within the firmament of medicinal science. Its scientific basis, they said, should at least be investigated.

While mesmerism enacted on the stage provided entertainment, in other settings it offered cures where medicine could offer nothing. The limits of medical science have always opened the door to various forms of faith healing, and Mesmer played up the shamanistic aspect of his technique. So did his imitators. And like Svengali with his Trilby, they occasionally produced remarkable outcomes.

In the 1860s, Phineas Quimby, a spiritual and magnetic healer from Belfast, Maine, treated Mary Morse Baker, a fragile New Hampshire woman, for a variety of nervous ailments of long standing. As a child, Mary would routinely collapse in response to her father's overbearingly strict treatment. A stern and religious man, her father had refused to allow her to attend school, claiming that her brain was too large for her body. Instead she was educated by a series of tutors. In the 1840s, she suffered through the losses of her husband, brother, and mother. Her own health, never good to begin with, kept her bedridden for extended periods. She sought out Quimby in 1865. Her account of his treatment verges on the ecstatic.

> With this physical and mental depression I first visited P. P. Quimby, and in less than one week from that time I ascended by a stairway of one hundred and eighty-two steps to the dome of the City Hall, and am improving ad infinitum. To the most subtle reasoning, such a proof, coupled too as it is with numberless similar ones, demonstrates his power to heal.

A decade later, drawing upon her revelatory experience with animal magnetism, Mary Baker, better known now by her married name of Eddy, went on to write a book called *Science and Health with Key to the Scriptures*, and the First Church of Christ, Scientist was born.

Phineas Quimby was a healer in the tradition of New Thought, which itself had grown out of what William James referred to as the mind-cure movement. In turn, mind-cure had evolved from music hall entertainments that had sprung up in the wake of Mesmer's departure from Paris. The direct inspiration for the character of Svengali is said to have been an itinerant Swiss magnetist named Charles Lafontaine, who toured Europe with a pseudomedical act in the 1840s. Lafontaine, a failed actor, brought people up onstage, put them into trances, and to the delight of his audiences, made them do his bidding. The trance states were real enough. They still are. Given the right setting and a talented hypnotist, many people will yield to the power of suggestion. But did animal magnetism have anything to do with it?

At a performance in Manchester, England, in 1841, Lafontaine caught the attention of Dr. James Braid, a Scottish surgeon and inquisitive experimentalist, who enjoyed the show immensely even though animal magnetism struck him as a clumsy dodge. But he also saw something very real in Lafontaine's technique and in the possibility of utilizing trance states for some greater purpose. Braid decided to experiment. Some mesmerists would magnetize objects and pass healing powers through them. In one instance, a healer magnetized a tree, and people came from all around to touch it. Braid wanted to reproduce the sensation of being mesmerized, but without the hocus-pocus. If he could mesmerize himself, he reasoned, it would disprove the existence of animal magnetism. The idea sounds preposterous. If he succeeded, who would bring him out of his trance? How would he know he was in one? With his tub, Mesmer had personally imparted animal magnetism to his clients through its protruding metal rods, much like a tour guide, and he had then brought them back out again. But Braid was aiming for the kind of unconscious consciousness he had witnessed on the stage, a fugue state in which his five senses would be suspended. He had never been magnetized, had never touched a magnetized tree or wand, so he was the perfect control subject. As he suspected, through concentration alone he could place himself in a kind of artificial sleep and then wake up from it. Once he got the hang of it, he could also do it to others, even though he had no access to animal magnetism. In order to distinguish his own form of mesmerism without magnetism, he initially called it neurypnology, then neurohypnotism, and eventually just hypnotism, although he did not coin the term. He published a book on the subject in 1843.

There is something to be said for attaching an exotic if unverifiable frisson to a tentative scientific theory. A hint of mystery often can lend a sense of legitimacy. (Think of cold fusion.) Unfortunately for Braid, his neurohypnotism lacked any performance drama or mystery, and it failed to gain a foothold outside of its limited use as a surgical anesthetic. Even there, it gradually gave way to chloroform, whose properties were sufficiently understood by 1850 to make it reliable. Hypnosis remained a sideshow attraction until a series of serendipitous events brought it back into the medical mainstream two decades later.

When a dormitory on the grounds of the Salpêtrière complex was condemned in the 1870s, the hospital administrators decided to house epileptic and hysterical patients in a single building. Inevitably the patients intermingled, and the hysterics began to imitate the epileptics. According to one of Charcot's assistants, Pierre Marie, "Living in this way among the epileptic, checking them in their falls, and taking care of them during their seizures after they had fallen, the young hysterics were susceptible to powerful impressions, and because of their tendencies to mimic, which is so characteristic of their neuroses, they duplicated in their hysteric fits every phase of a genuine epileptic seizure." Charcot instantly recognized the artificiality of the phenomenon, but also its potential utility.

A few years later, Charcot was asked to sit on a committee charged with evaluating the efficacy of James Braid's hypnosis as a psychotherapeutic technique. He was impressed. Egged on by a colleague, Charles Richet, Charcot decided to incorporate hypnosis into his study of hysteria. Specifically, he wanted to distinguish real seizures from pseudoseizures, a difficult task even today. With an entire ward of subjects at his disposal, mostly women, he set his assistants to work on the project, tasking them with reproducing the symptoms of an epileptic fit through the use of hypnotic suggestion. What they discovered convinced Charcot of a key difference between hysteria and epilepsy: hysterical women had "attacks," whereas epileptic women had "seizures," a more serious phenomenon and a measurably different one. He could not find a brain lesion corresponding to either, but assumed there had to be one. He called it a dynamic lesion, describing it as "ephemeral, changeable, always prone to disappear."

At about the same time, a competing school at the University of Nancy, under the direction of the French neurologist Hippolyte Bernheim, also took up hypnotism, not as an investigative tool but rather as a therapeutic one. If people could be made to act out suggestions on a stage for the purpose of entertainment, Bernheim reasoned, they could also be induced to confront and overcome the fears and habits making them miserable. Charcot and Bernheim eventually feuded over the nature of hypnotism and its effectiveness as therapy. It was a time when mainstream medicine ventured into psychic research, when discoveries in electromagnetism launched theories about invisible forces, when almost anything, from magnetism to ESP to conversing with the dead, seemed possible. Out of this scrum of competing ideas and feuding factions, Sigmund Freud borrowed a little from almost everyone and emerged with his own mind-cure.

As told in Ovid's *Metamorphoses*, Pygmalion created a sculpture of his ideal woman, and the goddess Athena granted his wish to wed such a woman when she made the statue come to life with the artist's kiss. Real life may imitate art, but it cannot always pull off the happy endings. Mesmer's failure to bring back Maria Theresia's sight led to his disgrace and banishment. Charcot should have known he was tempting the same fate when he decided to hypnotize Blanche Wittman.

CHAPTER 4

THE INVENTION OF HYSTERIA

Jᴇᴀɴ-ᴍᴀʀᴛɪɴ Charcot, a man ruled by habit, passed through the gates of the Salpêtrière in a coach at exactly the same time every morning. At the end of the day, he departed, also as if by clockwork. The days and weeks and months unfolded according to an unwavering schedule— lectures on Tuesdays, demonstrations on Fridays, outpatient clinics, inpatient visits, meetings, conferences, private time for writing— everything hinged on the comings and goings of the Master. His schedule was rounded out by soirees on Tuesdays held at his impressive art-filled home on the Boulevard Saint-Germain. Writers, artists, politicians, and physicians attended the salon-style evenings. Eventually even young Sigmund Freud, a perpetually miserable and down-at-the-heels student, would be invited.

Despite his charismatic reputation, J. M. Charcot was taciturn, slow of movement and gesture, and almost silent during clinical exams. His students would wait patiently for his pronouncements, usually to be disappointed. Freud idolized Charcot, but found him to be difficult, somewhat remote and inscrutable, his methods opaque. He either could not or would not say how he reached his conclusions, merely that after observing something long enough the nature of it would become clear. According to Pierre Marie (sitting third to Charcot's right in Brouillet's painting): "More than once his closest pupils heard him answer to their

'Why?' or to their 'How?' sometimes impatiently, because of his inability to better satisfy them: 'Oh, why? I cannot tell you, but I know it is this disease, I can sense it.'"

He was not a natural orator. Each week Charcot gave carefully prepared lectures, memorized in full and delivered with faultless diction but almost no theatricality or bravado. He was deliberate, highly organized, and obsessed with classification and description. This obsession extended to his uncanny ability to mimic almost any disorder of speech, posture, tremor, or gait. His entire research enterprise came to revolve around the idea of re-creation. As another assistant, Pierre Janet, recalled, "Everything in his lectures was designed to attract attention and to capture the audience by means of visual and auditory impressions." Charcot hired the artist-physician Paul Richer (first on his right in the painting, with a pencil and paper) to reproduce the poses of afflicted patients. Charcot also built a photography studio on the premises and hired the medical photographer Albert Londe (seated on the far left of the painting, wearing an apron and cap) to document exemplary cases. The resulting publication, in three volumes, the *Iconographie Photographique de la Salpêtrière*, may have greater claims to art than to science, but it was a major breakthrough in the classification and understanding of mental illness.

It is not entirely clear whether the man who inspired the loyalty of students and gratitude of patients was in fact cold and aloof. But the man portrayed in Brouillet's *A Clinical Lesson* appears to be more concerned with symptoms than with people, as his reputation would suggest. Charcot is the only man in the painting who is facing away from the patient, the only one who seems more interested in what he is saying than in what is happening behind him. His assistant Joseph Babinski, with his matinee-idol looks, stands center stage, ready to catch the swooning Blanche. Georges Gilles de la Tourette, an odd-looking duck by his own admission, is mercifully rendered in profile. Gilles's lookalike, Charles Féré, who had just completed an exhaustive study of animal magnetism, sits in rapt attention by the window. Charcot's son Jean-Baptiste, then a medical student, stands at the rear. Then there is Charcot himself. He stands with his right hand extended in an odd gesture, probably drawn from life, of thumb and forefinger held out as if indicating a measurement of a few centimeters. According to a contemporary, Félix Platel, "There is something mystical in his gaze, astonishing in a materialist. His gaze is oblique—which is surprising in a mask of Bonaparte. . . . The Roman nose is solid and well defined. It is like the tip of the prow of a Roman galley, destined to cleave the waves, despite wind and tide." It could also be the gaze of a man beginning to doubt what he is saying.

In the decade of his astounding series of discoveries in neurology, Charcot had become well known in scientific circles, but not beyond. This would change. His decision to tackle hysteria, to lend his considerable reputation to it, brought his fame to another level. He was taking on not just one of the biggest unanswered questions in medicine, but perhaps one of the most intriguing and unsettling aspects of human existence: What makes us who we are, and what can cause us to forget who we are?

Today, epilepsy has a set of diagnostic criteria backed by the technology of electroencephalograms, yet hysteria has only a generic and vague profile. In 1870, hysteria drove diagnosticians to distraction. One physician called it a "mockingbird of nosology" because of its tendency to run the gamut from migraine to paralysis, numbness, fainting, sweats, difficulty in breathing, insomnia, and even nymphomania. No one could say whether it was real or imagined, structural or functional, all in the head or lurking in damaged tissue. Charcot decided to find out.

At the end of a decade-long investigation involving scores of patients, he was ready to publish. In a report of 1878, he rejected the idea of a purely psychological basis for all forms of hysteria. Even though he could not find any anatomical basis for his conclusions, he isolated an extreme form of hysteria as a "physiological disturbance," or a *névrose*: a general affliction of the nervous system. Not only was it a true disease, he said, but hysterical attacks had a classic identifying profile consisting of four distinct phases. In phase one, the so-called tonic phase, the subject exhibits all the signs of a grand mal epileptic seizure: muscle spasms and jerks, then muscle contractures, eyes rolled upward, rapid breathing, and possibly the loss of consciousness. Phase two, the clonic phase, brought on contortions and postures, culminating in a backward arcing of the entire body, with only the feet and head touching the ground. This is the *arc-en-circle* depicted by Paul Richer in the diagram mounted on the easel behind the last row of viewers in *A Clinical Lesson*. The third phase consisted of a series of "*attitudes passionnelles*," essentially a range of highly charged emotional states, including ecstasy and even religious rapture, bracketed by sexually suggestive poses. In the final phase, the subject drifted into a languid, sleepy delirium. The phases occurred spontaneously. They were not induced. They could be observed on the ward. The contractures of the tonic-clonic phases were difficult to distinguish from real epileptic seizures, but Charcot accomplished this by measuring subtle differences in heart rate, body temperature, and other clinical features. Once he had isolated it, he called it *la grande hystérie*, or grand hysteria. Where others saw feigning, malingering, or attention getting, Charcot insisted he discovered a true disease, one with distinct and recognizable stages. He then set out to see whether he could produce them on command.

Charcot introduced hypnosis in 1878, a year after Blanche's arrival at the Salpêtrière. His peers were mystified. Charcot seemed to be reviving mesmerism. Bad enough that he had elevated a low-priority condition to the status of a disease. Now he wanted to resurrect a discredited technique invented by a crackpot and adopt it as a clinical tool. Only Charcot could have gotten away with it, and he did, with the instrumental help of Blanche Wittman.

Up to that point, Blanche's behavior had been intolerable and uncontrollable. Charcot's assistants diagnosed her with epilepsy, then with hystero-epilepsy, then with grand hysteria. To relieve her convulsions, they tried ovarian compression in the belief that the ovaries were hysterogenic zones. That didn't work. They tried occupational therapy. She improved. Then they tried hypnotism. Whether it was a survival skill, or due to some sly coaching behind Charcot's back, Blanche emerged as the ideal hypnotic subject. She became cooperative and responsive, and while under hypnosis could reliably recapitulate the stages of what Charcot decided to call "artificial hysteria."

At the Salpêtrière, *artificial* hysteria—hysteria induced by hypnosis, as opposed to *natural* hysteria—unfolded in three distinct acts. Brouillet's painting depicts the opening of Act One, the onset of catalepsy, or the maintenance of unnatural postures. Charcot's assistant Joseph Babinski, the man supporting Blanche, has just put her into a hypnotic trance, possibly with a gong. Her left fist is clenched and bent into an awkward state of contracture, indicating that she is not merely swooning. In this stage, Babinski will arrange her limbs in various poses, and Blanche will hold those postures indefinitely. She will also become impervious to pain, to the extent that a needle can and will be passed through her arm or hand, eliciting no reaction. In the second stage, lethargy, her body will become limp and fall as though lifeless until Babinski induces muscle contractures, rendering her rigid, as though in a state of rigor mortis. When posed, Blanche could maintain awkward positions well beyond the ability of a skilled acrobat. The demonstration will reach a climax in the final stage, called somnambulism. This is what the audience had come to see. In a state of extreme suggestibility, Blanche will be induced to act out scenes requiring a full gamut of emotions. She might be told she is being threatened by a dog or a snake, and she will cower, or that she is a general marshaling her troops on the front line of a battle, and she will bark commands. In one demonstration, she was asked to kiss the plaster bust of Franz Joseph Gall, the inventor of phrenology. Upon awakening, she will have no memory of these playacted scenarios and will deny having done them. Yet she will retain some unconscious memories. In one instance, under hypnosis, she was shown a picture of a donkey and told it was a nude photo of her. It shocked her so much that she later smashed the picture when she came across it, even though she professed to have no memory of the hypnotic suggestion.

The crowd appeal of these demonstrations is obvious—they played heavily upon sexual innuendo. Similar demonstrations took place all over Paris in music halls, advertised as hypnotism "à la Charcot." Some former patients of the Salpêtrière starred in these shows, borrowing heavily from Blanche's performances. Medical men decried the lay practitioners as irresponsible and dangerous, but it was a case of the pot and the kettle. Charcot wanted to show the extent of a subject's malleability under hypnosis, but more than that, he claimed to be demonstrating genuine medical pathology. Not only was hysteria a disease of the body, but so was the susceptibility to hypnotic suggestion. In other words, according to Charcot, only true hysterics could attain the postures and maintain the poses of artificial hysteria. These could not be faked, so they had to be a pathological sign connected to real hysteria, even diagnostic of it. He called it *le grand hypnotisme*.

In 1882, Charcot presented this theory to the French Academy of Sciences as part of his bid for membership. The academy had already accepted his claim for the status of hysteria as a true disease on the strength of his reputation, although without much enthusiasm. They also signed off on his description of grand hypnotism, despite widespread skepticism. The idea had almost no support outside of Paris. According to Charcot's critics, his four stages of hysteria and three-act demonstrations of hypnosis could be observed only at the Salpêtrière, or in patients who had lived there and had learned the choreography. Moreover, as Hippolyte Bernheim of the Nancy School argued, there was nothing special about susceptibility to hypnosis. Almost anyone could be hypnotized. Yet Charcot pressed on, buoyed by the success of his weekly performances.

Why did Charcot medicalize hysteria and hypnosis? There is good evidence that he wanted to demystify all phenomena touted by the church as miracles. He hoped to substitute neurological explanations for religious ones. Auras, visions, imperviousness to pain, miracle cures (especially curing the blind): he wrote all of these off as hysterical symptoms. Epiphanies, the ecstasies of the saints, if not the resurrection itself, could be explained neurologically. Accounts of such religious phenomena, catalogued extensively by Charcot and reenacted onstage by Blanche and other hysterics as *attitudes passionnelles*, peddled a not-so-subtle form of anticlerical materialism to a hungry audience. None of this fell too far beyond the pale until Charcot began to lay on a theoretical framework. He had proposed two ideas for which he had no real evidence—grand hysteria and grand hypnotism. Absent an anatomical lesion in the brain to explain them, he fell back on something he called a "dynamic lesion" of the nervous system, a transient and undetectable disruption of brain function. The whole enterprise was poised to fall under the weight of its own improbability. Brouillet's painting depicts the moment when the public demonstrations became untethered from the clinical practice of medicine.

The first sign of trouble appeared when Alfred Binet, an unpaid intern, quit his post in 1890 and publicly denounced Charcot's theory. Binet and Charles Féré had recently published an exhaustive history of hypnotism, going back to Mesmer, in which they had summarized and defended both *la grande hystérie* and *le grand hypnotisme*. Binet then had a crisis of conscience. The public demonstrations were not genuine, he confessed. The theory of a pathological basis of hysteria could not stand up to facts in evidence. Since the birth of his daughters in 1887, Binet had become increasingly disenchanted with the hijinks perpetrated by the hypnotizers at the Salpêtrière. In one instance, they tried to induce a somnambulizing Blanche to take off her clothes and imitate taking a bath. According to Georges Gilles de la Tourette, the chief of Charcot's lab, "When it came time to take off her corset, her entire body stiffened, and we barely had time to intervene in order to avoid an attack of hysteria, which in her case always begins in this fashion." Binet abandoned neurology in favor of developmental psychology. He would go on to develop the first intelligence test, the direct progenitor of the Stanford-Binet Intelligence Scale still in use today.

The end came three years later, in 1893, when Charcot died suddenly on a trip to Nièvre, France, at the age of sixty-seven. It was a shock to his colleagues, but not to Charcot himself. A lifelong smoker who did no exercise of any kind, he had already diagnosed his own heart problem, and when stricken he knew exactly what was happening. But he did not know what would happen next. At the announcement of his death, the Paris School he had founded ceased to exist. The theory of *la grande hystérie* was shelved, the Tuesday and Friday clinics came to an end, and most tellingly, Blanche Wittman never again had a hysterical attack.

This last point, noted by Babinski, settled the matter. At first diagnosed as epileptic, then as hysterical, then treated with hypnosis, electrotherapy, and massage by a team of physicians over a fifteen-year period, Blanche was finally cured by the departure of the only audience she cared about. She had lost her Svengali.

Jane Avril, the most famous dancer at the Moulin Rouge and a favorite model for Henri Toulouse-Lautrec, wrote a memoir of her eighteen-month stay in the hysteria ward at the Salpêtrière, among the "stars of hysteria," as she called them.

> There were those deranged girls whose ailments named Hysteria consisted, above all, in simulation of it. . . . How much trouble they used to go to in order to capture attention and gain stardom. . . . In my tiny brain, I was astonished every time to see how such eminent savants could be duped in that way, when I, as insignificant as I was, saw through the farces. I have said to myself since that the great Charcot was aware of what was happening.

He was, but he had his reasons to keep the show going. Gilles de la Tourette and Babinski did not. With Charcot gone and with the hospital now trying to disassociate itself from his theories, his two senior assistants had an extremely difficult time. Both lost all academic support and were denied chairs in medicine at the Salpêtrière. Gilles de la Tourette continued to defend Charcot's legacy, but Babinski backed down and conceded the purely psychological basis for all hysterical phenomena. He renamed the condition *pithiatisme*, from the Greek, meaning curable through persuasion (the name never caught on). Babinski later discovered a curious hardwiring of the human nervous system: the stroking of the sole of the foot in someone with even subtle brain damage causes the big toe to extend upward while the other toes fan out. This is called the Babinski sign and it is performed thousands of times every day as an obligatory part of any neurological examination. No other neurological sign has had its durability or provided such a degree of certainty concerning damage to the nervous system. It made Babinski one of the most famous eponyms in medicine.

Toward the end, even Charcot had privately begun to acknowledge his mistake. *Le grand hypnotisme*, he conceded, was not a true disorder or even a syndrome. Hypnosis, it was becoming increasingly clear, was a universal susceptibility. Under pressure from almost every corner of the research community, he also backed down from his claims about hysteria as a disease of the body, at least in private. In 1891, he admitted that it was, "for the most part, a mental illness." But Charcot never openly conceded defeat. The painting shows why. His skepticism did not extend to the handful of star hysterics who packed audiences into his amphitheater each week. The standout was Blanche.

Throughout the 1880s, dancers, magicians' assistants, models, opera divas, and stage actresses traipsed over to the Salpêtrière to see the one person who embodied the fullest range of emotive performance on the Continent. When Sarah Bernhardt, the on-again, off-again darling of the European theater scene, wished to recapture her popularity upon her return to the Paris stage in 1881, she too headed to the Salpêtrière to see Blanche perform. Jules Claretie, the director of the Théâtre Français, writing for *Le Temps* in 1884, put it bluntly: "Never has an actor or painter, never a Rachel or a Sarah Bernhardt, Rubens or Raphael, arrived at such a powerful expression. This young girl enacted a series of tableaux that surpassed in its brilliance and power the most sublime efforts by art. One could not dream of a more astonishing model."

Nonetheless, Blanche Wittman lived at the Salpêtrière as an institutionalized mental patient. She was given menial tasks to perform, including laundry and other cleaning, and she was of course called upon to participate in Charcot's weekly demonstrations. By all accounts, she was one of the greatest improvisational actors of all time. In her final years, Blanche's insistence on the legitimacy of her role-playing never waned. After Charcot's death, she went to work in the Salpêtrière's photo lab, and soon was transferred to the new radiation lab. Like Marie Curie, completely unaware of the dangers, she was exposed to repeated X-rays. Within a few years she began to undergo a series of necessary amputations, first of digits, then of limbs. As she succumbed to radiation poisoning, she refused to repudiate any aspect of grand hysteria. In her mind, it had been as real as epilepsy.

She died in 1913 at the age of fifty-four, and to the end she defended Charcot. In her final year, Blanche agreed to speak to a reporter about her stint as the Queen of the Hysterics. She claimed to have feigned nothing, arguing that no one could have fooled the great Charcot. "If we were put to sleep, if we had fits, it was because it was impossible for us to do otherwise. Besides, it's not as though it was pleasant!" When asked if there had been any simulation, she replied sharply, "Simulation! Do you think that it would have been easy to fool Monsieur Charcot? Oh yes, there were certainly some jokers who tried! He would look them straight in the eye and say, 'Be still!'"

The Salon of 1887 ended after two months. The French government bought *Un Leçon Clinique* and shipped it off to Nice, where it went on display for a number of years before being consigned to storage. It was later cleaned and hung in a neurological hospital in Lyon, out of sight, but not out of mind. In 1887, Eugène Pirodon made an engraving of the painting, and this small reproduction sold very well. It brought the image to the attention of millions. Sigmund Freud purchased a copy and hung it in his examination room in Vienna, and later, after relocating to London, he did the same. Either the painting or the engraving has become the stock image of a quaint form of medical credulity, on par with phrenological heads and orgone boxes. Unfortunately for medical science and for the man himself, it is how Charcot is remembered. He didn't live long enough to ward off that impression.

The meaning of any work of art changes over time. Standing in front of Brouillet's painting today, one finds it difficult to appreciate what it meant to viewers when it debuted. Charcot saw psychiatry and neurology as cooperative specialties. They should, he wrote, "philosophically speaking remain associated with each other by insoluble ties." The painting marks the moment when that hope was dashed, and the two fell apart in the most confounding way, partly because of Charcot himself—his role in creating the very scene Brouillet depicted—and in a small yet significant way, partly because Brouillet chose to depict it at all. He unwittingly immortalized a catastrophic failure.

Charcot believed he could separate mind and brain by treating the human subject as an automaton, as a sensorimotor machine. Instead of visiting his patients on the wards, he had them brought to his office. Instead of interviewing them, he examined their bodies in silence. Instead of interacting with them, he let his assistants do it. Onstage, he treated them like servants, speaking freely as if they were not present and could not hear. Charcot thought he was removing any potential bias this way, and in doing so, he seems to have overlooked the mind entirely. Blanche Wittman and his other subjects heard everything, unconsciously processed it, and fed it back in a finely tuned performance.

Hypnosis does work as a short-term intervention. Hardly anyone uses it anymore in a hospital setting because it is paternalistic and exposes a subject's vulnerability, although it remains popular in alternative medicine. People undergo hypnosis today for the same reasons therapists used it a century ago. It can help people break habits they may or may not be aware of. It makes use of the subject's suggestibility, which exists along a spectrum of personality types. Had Charcot used it strictly for the purpose of artificially producing symptoms of hysteria and epilepsy, had he not invested himself in what most of his contemporaries viewed as sideshow antics, he would command greater respect today. But Brouillet's painting, perhaps more than anything Charcot himself ever did, exposed him in flagrante, duping himself in front of a double audience—the one portrayed in the painting and the one viewing it. Had it been an isolated incident of a great scientist exceeding the bounds of the scientific method, the painting might not merit all that much attention. But there is more to be found in it, facts unknown to the viewers of 1887, and a crowning irony even Charcot overlooked. A real neurological disease did indeed lurk behind many of the hysterical symptoms he so painstakingly observed, and he missed it, even though all along it was right there under his Napoleonic nose.

CHAPTER 5

THE PAPUAN IDOL

Aɴʏoɴᴇ old enough to have seen Al Capp's comic strip *Li'l Abner* will recall the iconic image of Joe Btfsplk, the woebegone and cursed schlemiel who walks around under a perpetual dark cloud and brings disaster wherever he goes. His last name, Capp explained, was pronounced by sticking out your tongue and blowing a raspberry, also known as a Bronx cheer. Not only was poor Joe jinxed, but anyone who got near him fared even worse. If Capp needed to get rid of a character, he would often bring Joe into the same cartoon panel. What Joe Btfsplk was to Dogpatch, U.S.A., Georges Albert Édouard Brutus Gilles de la Tourette was to Paris, France.

His mouthful of a last name has led historians to routinely and incorrectly refer to him as Tourette, rather than the full Gilles de la Tourette. In Brouillet's painting, GdT, as he signed his letters, can be seen in profile, front and slightly off-center, wearing a white apron and leaning forward to see Blanche Wittman more clearly. As his bad luck would have it, in the schematic posted on the wall across from the painting and reproduced everywhere, Gilles de la Tourette is misidentified as Charles Féré, and vice versa. Superficially, the two men look alike. Both sported widow's peaks and neatly trimmed beards. But unlike GdT, Féré was a commanding presence (he was nicknamed Grand Féré), whereas Gilles was decidedly not.

Born in a small village in central France, Gilles (as his friends called him) was an intelligent but peculiar youth. According to his mother, he had marked mood swings. After medical school, he went to study with Charcot as an intern, and by the time of Brouillet's painting he had become Charcot's right-hand man, his *chef de clinique*. Because of his awkward looks, he was not always taken seriously. Charcot and Gilles collaborated on many studies, and following his generous usual practice, the Master allowed his assistant to publish their joint results under his sole authorship, contributing only a preface himself. Such was the case with Gilles de la Tourette's most famous paper, written in 1885, entitled "A Study of a Nervous Disorder Characterized by Motor Incoordination with Echolalia and Coprolalia." In the paper he investigates a rare phenomenon involving the involuntary repetition of phrases (echolalia), highly impulsive and colorful bursts of cursing (coprolalia), often accompanied by compulsive and repetitive mannerisms and gestures, sometimes crude and often imitative in origin. As a loyal channeler of Charcot's theories of hypnosis and hysteria, Gilles was repaid by the boss by having the condition named after him: *la maladie des tics de Gilles de la Tourette*. The British neurologist Macdonald Critchley, a literary forerunner of Oliver Sacks, referred to this as "a fragment of poetry with its iambus following a dactyl." Today, less grandiloquently, we call it Tourette syndrome.

Gilles de la Tourette habitually waded into trouble and controversy. As an expert on hypnosis and a leading representative of Charcot's Paris School, he offered his opinion on high-profile criminal cases whenever the defense invoked mental incapacity due to the influence of hypnosis. In part because of Charcot's reputation, this legal tactic had become quite common. In 1887, Gilles de la Tourette published a study on the medical-legal aspects of hypnotism in which he emphasized the primacy of the moral sense even among hysterics. Hypnosis, he insisted, could not overcome someone's sense of right and wrong. Despite testimony from Charcot's rivals at the Nancy School, the courts usually upheld the dictum that hypnosis could not induce murder. Nevertheless, the scandalous nature of these trials did inestimable damage to Charcot's work, setting hypnosis back ten years, as he put it. In 1892, the French government banned all public displays of hypnotism outside of a medical setting.

In the archives of the Salpêtrière, the collaboration of Charcot and Gilles de la Tourette centers around two mysterious ailments. One is the ticcing disorder. The other was commonly known as locomotor ataxia, a term describing the loss of perception and control of the extremities. Charcot preferred a more elegant term, tabes dorsalis, emphasizing the immediate cause—the wasting of the neural tracts in the dorsal, or posterior, columns, of the spinal cord. Before Gilles de la Tourette arrived on the scene, Charcot had studied it closely. Rather ingeniously, he had used his clinical-anatomical method to correlate the spinal cord lesions characteristic of tabes with the symptoms of a stumbling gait, inability to stand with the eyes closed, excruciating lightning pains in the extremities, and the sensation of compression of the chest. Throughout the nineteenth century, tabes had emerged as an increasingly common neurological disorder, and its victims showed up frequently in Charcot's wards. They displayed not only the classic ataxic gait, but a highly distinctive affliction of the eyes known as the Argyll Robertson pupil. The pupils would accommodate—they would reduce in size when viewing an object up close, as normally expected, but they would not do the same when reacting to light. They were often referred to as "prostitute's pupils" due to their high prevalence in the brothels, but also because, in common parlance, they were said to "accommodate but not react." The phenomenon was first described in the 1860s by the Scottish ophthalmologist Douglas Argyll Robertson.

In Charcot's era, the sight of a middle-aged man stamping his way uncertainly over the cobblestones with a thumping assist from a walking cane would have elicited an instant and correct diagnosis from even a casual and untrained observer. Perhaps the worst part about tabes dorsalis was that it was not fatal. The sufferer could expect to live for decades in a state of perpetual agony and disability.

In his book *The Divine Banquet of the Brain and Other Essays*, Macdonald Critchley provided detailed accounts of the disease as it affected its most famous sufferers. The poet Heinrich Heine, for example, while only in his early forties, developed a violent pain in his eyes. "The sight failed in the left eye, and he . . . had to prop up his eyelids with his fingers in order to scrutinize an object. His heart felt 'bound as by an iron frost.' Everything he ate tasted like dirt. Later his lips became insensitive, so that kissing was devoid of feeling. . . . His finger-tips became numb and he took to a walking cane because of lameness." By the age of fifty he was virtually incapacitated. Critchley quotes Heine's biographer, William Sharp, to the effect that "the sufferings of the poet became terrible: the fire of an undying fever scorched his veins, the frosts of a living death cramped his muscles, 'unborn agonies' took possession of his racked nerves. With bent body, half-blind, lame, without senses of smell or taste, with hands unable to guide the pen save for a few roughly-scrawled lines . . . his was indeed a pitiable case." Even allowing for poetic license, the biographer has nailed the desperation and hopelessness of a wasting disease. Critchley notes how a friend asked Heine if he had made his peace with God. "Don't bother yourself," Heine replied. "God will forgive me—that's what he's there for." Maybe so, but could Heine ever forgive God?

Charcot's good friend, the novelist and playwright Alphonse Daudet, documented his own struggle with tabes in a journal published posthumously as *La Doulou*, later edited and translated by Julian Barnes as *In the Land of Pain*. A few of Daudet's entries convey his sense of ironic despair.

> Armour is exactly what it feels like, a hoop of steel cruelly crushing my lower back. Hot coals, stabs of pain as sharp as needles. . . .
>
> Long conversation with Charcot. It's just as I thought. I've got it for life. The news didn't deal me the blow I would have expected. . . .
>
> Not once, neither at the doctor's, the baths, nor the spas where the disease is treated, has it ever been given its name, its real name. I have a 'disease of the bone marrow'! Even scientific books refer euphemistically to 'the nervous system'!

Even though the cause of tabes had not been proven, Daudet could feel it in his bones. It had to be syphilis. But Charcot and Gilles de la

Tourette reserved judgment. They conceded the high degree of correlation between the two diseases, but remained unconvinced of a direct connection. In an ill-fated attempt to help, Charcot told Daudet to try a grotesque method of traction recently invented by a Russian physician. It involved the suspension of the helpless patient by the arms and even by the jaw for several extended sessions. Daudet emerged from the treatment worse than ever, and he never forgave Charcot.

The German physician Moritz Heinrich Romberg first fully described tabes dorsalis in 1845, and he invented a time-honored test for it, later named for him: Can the patient remain upright with feet together and eyes closed? One of the first things to go in tabes is proprioception—the ability to sense where one's legs and body are without looking. Failing the test is a sign of sensory impairment; the police routinely use it on suspected drunk drivers. For the tabes sufferer, unlike the drunk, the loss of proprioception is permanent.

Romberg failed to make the connection between tabes and syphilis, but Charcot's mentor, Guillaume-Benjamin-Armand Duchenne de Boulogne, did. For a time, tabes was known as Duchenne's disease. Statistics revealed the startlingly high rate of coincidence: as many as 90 percent of all tabetics had a history of syphilis. But Charcot, taking the conservative line, asked, "What about the other 10 percent?" He also pointed out how the symptoms of tabes failed to respond to the antisyphilitic treatments of the day, notably mercury injections and potassium sulfate. Quite rightly, he cautioned against conflating high correlation with causation. There could very well be another hidden explanation for the high coincidence. Quite wrongly, he thought he knew what it was. Degeneration theory explained everything—perhaps too well.

For many natural scientists in the post-Darwin era, degeneration offered a convenient foothold for racialists struggling to accommodate the theory of the common descent of mankind. Everyone may have descended from the same primitive stock, but certain family and kinship lines had been corrupted either by environment or culture, and had passed on their frailties and vulnerabilities to their descendants. Degeneration was a get-out-of-jail-free card, a Lamarckian catchall to account not only for tabes, but for hysteria, neurasthenia, and neurosis. Weak nerves, a frail constitution, alcoholism, addictive behavior: all of these could be accounted for by Lamarck's mistaken belief in the heritability of personal failings, in effect by transgenerational susceptibility. In particular, a penchant for debauchery—a family trait—could easily lead to tabes—a medical one. Used to dealing with constitutional ailments such as ALS and Parkinson's disease, Charcot lumped tabes into the broad category of bad lots and bad decisions in the game of life.

Daudet, of course, was syphilitic *and* tabetic, as was Heine, as was the painter Édouard Manet. There were countless others. Even if Charcot would not attribute their stumbling gait to syphilis, what of the many other small agonies they suffered? Still, he held out against a growing chorus of voices arguing for the syphilis connection right up until he died. Gilles de la Tourette, ever the loyal assistant, kept the faith as long as he could, until the bottom dropped out.

Late in the summer of 1893, Charcot took a trip with two friends to the Morvan region of Burgundy. He brought with him the proofs of Gilles de la Tourette's forthcoming book on the history of hysteria and hypnotism. The work represented the culmination of Charcot's efforts to understand both of these baffling phenomena. Before he could finish going over it, his heart gave out. After his sudden death, the void Charcot left swallowed up his entire enterprise, and the fortunes of Gilles de la Tourette spiraled downward. It was just the beginning of a run of horrible luck.

In the year of Charcot's death, Gilles de la Tourette's son Jean died of meningitis. Then in December, Gilles was shot in the head by a deranged patient. The story is almost always reported this way, as though Joe Btfsplk had entered the frame, though there is more to it. Her name was Rose Kamper-Lecoq; she was twenty-nine years old and a former patient at the Salpêtrière, though not Gilles de la Tourette's patient. She sought restitution of some kind, claiming she had been hypnotized at a distance and could no longer work. Gilles probably came onto her radar through his opinion pieces in the newspapers, where he occasionally weighed in on the malpractice aspects of hypnotism. Rose showed up at Gilles's office, demanded money, and when he refused, she fired three shots. One of them caught him in the neck or near the back of his head. That evening, the bullet having been removed, he wrote a note to a friend describing the incident, concluding: "What a bizarre story!" The damage to his reputation was immediate. He became the butt of jokes, a laughingstock. On top of it all, he was passed over for an academic chair at the Salpêtrière. His career was put on hold.

Four years later, Alphonse Daudet dropped dead at the head of the family dinner table. Though relations between the Daudet family and Gilles de la Tourette had been strained ever since Charcot made his disastrous recommendation for suspension traction, they summoned him. He arrived immediately with another physician and made a furious and rather alarming attempt to revive Daudet by pulling on his tongue repeatedly for over an hour (the artificial respiration method of the time). The family was horrified, the attempt failed, the immediate cause of death was apoplexy, and the root cause was indeed syphilis. Gilles de la Tourette could no longer hold out against that fact. The evidence was overwhelming, and he conceded the connection and finally admitted his mentor had been wrong. Two years later, he published a book on spinal paralysis and syphilis of the brain, describing only its sensory-motor symptoms, while ignoring any associated cognitive impairments. He never mentioned, on a personal note, a concern that must have been rattling around inside his mind for a while. He too had contracted syphilis many years earlier as a student. It seemed to have passed without producing any of the harbingers of tabes. He had seen what it had done to Daudet. The possibility remained that it might do the same to him.

It did not. Instead, it did something quite different. In 1901, Gilles's behavior began to deteriorate in a disturbing way. Léon Daudet, Alphonse's son, noticed it upon seeing him on the street one day. Gilles clapped him on the back and became so effusive as to make Daudet uncomfortable. "I was unable to shake off his panting declarations of tenderness and devotion," he later wrote. What was going on? They were no longer friends. In fact, Daudet had publicly ridiculed the man.

"Gilles de la Tourette was ugly," he once wrote, "like a Papuan idol covered with patches of hair. . . . He had a raspy and scorched voice, abrupt gestures and a grotesque demeanor. He was seen as unusual." But his behavior had now become even more unusual. One day his wife discovered Gilles naked in his office, hiding under his desk, while a patient cowered in the corner. His speech became notably affected, his ideas grandiose. Léon Daudet knew something was wrong and had a fairly good idea what it was, but he had no idea it was related in any way to the cause of his own father's death.

As Gilles's public speeches became more and more bizarre, his colleagues stepped in. He was placed on leave from the hospital in late 1901. Charcot's son Jean-Baptiste came up with a plan. He told Gilles of a celebrity patient in Lausanne, Switzerland, who needed his help. They would travel together. Once there, instead of seeing the patient, Gilles became one. He was involuntarily committed to the institution. He protested bitterly, but nothing could be done. He descended into madness and died two years later.

Most present-day accounts of the landscape of disease in the nineteenth century overlook its most important aspect, not simply its connection with sex, in the case of syphilis, and sexual abuse, in cases of hysteria, but the very real fear associated with sexual contact of any kind. The same fear and foreboding looms over Édouard Manet's café paintings (for example, *A Bar at the Folies-Bergère*). It lurks behind Freud's invention of psychoanalysis, and it probably accounted for the convulsions that landed Blanche Wittman in the Salpêtrière. It is the X factor in André Brouillet's painting. Brouillet rendered Blanche in the way insane women have always been portrayed in art: partially clothed, swooning, out of her right mind. Many of those madwomen were likely infected with syphilis; in fact, it would have been the *cause* of their madness. The same goes for many of Charcot's epileptic and hysterical patients, and for some of his colleagues as well. Syphilis was rightly known as a great imitator, its profile indistinguishable from epilepsy, hysteria, neurasthenia, and insanity. In their attempts to understand hysteria, both Charcot and Gilles de la Tourette were initially in denial about the link between sex and mental illness, between syphilis and hysteria. Neither man could fully appreciate the extent to which they really had two great imitators on their hands. By the time Gilles de la Tourette finally made the connection in his own case, it was too late. The deterioration of his mind left him unable to write about what he now knew, what he had been so reluctant to accept. Syphilis had forced him into an insane asylum. After deranging his mind, it sent him to his grave.

CHAPTER 6

HEARTS OF DARKNESS

Joseph Conrad's *Heart of Darkness*, once a staple of high school and college reading lists, chronicles the atrocities committed by colonial trading companies in the Belgian Congo of the 1890s as they went about raping the African continent. The story may be more familiar today in Francis Ford Coppola's retelling in *Apocalypse Now*. The narrator of the original version, a stand-in for Conrad, relates a tale told by a man who is hired to travel up the Congo River in search of the legendary Mr. Kurtz, a station agent who has apparently gone native. "The wilderness . . . had taken him," the narrator says, "loved him, embraced him, got into his veins, consumed his flesh, and sealed his soul to its own by the inconceivable ceremonies of some devilish initiation."

The route up the river is one Conrad himself took on behalf of the Belgian government years earlier. In the book, the journey is largely allegorical, the slant is blatantly racist, and the tale has not aged well. Mr. Kurtz, reportedly having divested himself of the mores of civilized society, needs to be brought back home, but he is located too late and dies on the return journey in the grip of a distinctive form of madness.

> You should have heard him say, "My ivory." Oh, yes, I heard him. "My Intended, my ivory, my station, my river, my—" everything belonged to him. . . . Sometimes he was

contemptibly childish. He desired to have kings meet him at the railway stations on his return from some ghastly No-where, where he intended to accomplish great things.

The narrator never divulges it, but with these fevered words, the author left a damning clue as to what was really ailing Mr. Kurtz.

A "heart of darkness" serves as an apt metaphor for the depravity lurking beneath all civilized societies. But just as the contemporary audience for André Brouillet's painting would have been intimately familiar with hypnotism and hysteria, the contemporary audience for Conrad's novella would have been equally familiar with Kurtz's incipient madness and delusions of grandeur. At the time, there were plenty of real-life models. The insane asylums were full of Kurtzes. Lord Randolph Churchill, the father of Winston Churchill, was one prototype. He died in 1895 at the age of forty-five after a rapid physical and mental decline, during which his speaking ability deteriorated and paralysis set in. Guy de Maupassant died insane in an asylum at the age of forty-two, raving about the diamonds flowing out of his urine; the poet Charles Baudelaire, similarly at age forty-six; the composers Hugo Wolf and Gaetano Donizetti at forty-two and fifty—early and ugly deaths preceded by manias and extravagantly wild delusions. Georges Gilles de la Tourette was only forty-six when he suffered the same fate. For Mr. Kurtz's madness, Conrad simply latched onto a convenient stereotype, almost a cliché.

People no longer go mad in the haunted, ill-fated, somewhat random, and ultimately spectacular way glorified in the novels of Charlotte Brönte or the stories of Poe and Maupassant. Madness is a very nineteenth-century idea. The life stories of famous cases—Nietzsche, Wilde, Schubert, Schumann, Van Gogh, Smetana, Randolph Churchill—add to the sense of a mind operating apart from the brain, of excess passion tilting creative artists over the edge, of the intimate, even necessary, link between profound genius and lurking insanity. What was the nature of this madness? Looking back, we find it impossible to say, leaving the door open to the kind of postmortem if not postmodern speculations that routinely show up in medical journals as historical filler. Did syphilis cause Beethoven's deafness? Did Robert Schumann exhibit signs of mercury poisoning from his treatment for syphilis? Was *Dracula* conceived out of the fever of Bram Stoker's venereal disease? No one knows, and no one will ever know for sure. Such questions produce a lot of sound and fury, adding nothing to our understanding of art or of disease. Postmortem evidence of syphilitic infection is hard if not impossible to find, and we are left with rare cases where we have the contemporaneous reports of capable clinicians, as well as an indisputable disease profile. Guy de Maupassant was such a case. He did indeed have syphilis, and he died from it. But no one could prove it at the time.

Prior to the year 1913, syphilis of the genitals and skin was well known, but there was no such thing as *neuro*syphilis. The word was invented, it is not clear by whom, to describe two diseases—tabes dorsalis and general paresis of the insane—after direct evidence of their common origin came to light under a microscope. Until that point, the term *para*syphilis, connoting coincidence without proof of causation, had to suffice. But then syphilitic diseases had gone through many name changes throughout the course of history. The word *syphilis* itself is an insult meaning "pig lover," even though the origin of the term has nothing to do with pigs. It has to do with oxen and sheep.

According to legend, at the time of the summer solstice in the reign of King Alcithous, a young shepherd boy named Syphilus tended to the king's flock, consisting of some one thousand oxen and one thousand sheep swarming the banks of a parched river. Sirius, the sun god, had cast a torrid and unending heat over the land, scorching the groves and the fields, and neither wood nor wind could offer any relief. Syphilus, full of indignation, railed at the god. "We make our offerings in good and humble faith, and this is how you reward us? Better we should make our offerings to the king. At least he would try to help us." Hearing of this outburst, the king, besotted with himself and flattered by the boy's rebuke, decreed an end to the worshiping of gods in favor of his own earthly self. Sirius, in his anger, then visited a scourge upon the earth. For the sin of being the first to offer sacrifices to the king, Syphilus was the first to suffer horrific sores over his entire body. He was the first to endure horrid pains in his limbs and the banishment of sleep. From him, the first victim, the scourge derived its name—syphilis—and it soon spread across the land, not sparing even the king himself.

This vignette, liberally paraphrased, comes from a lengthy Latin poem written by the Italian physician Girolamo Fracastoro in 1530. The shepherd's name was plucked from it a few decades later and adopted in medical textbooks. Fracastoro knew the disease very well, having treated many cases at a time when its severity rivaled that of the bubonic plague. His poem is less an epic than it is a treatise on syphilis, its history, its description, and the various treatments for it. Fracastoro specialized in infectious diseases. He believed they were spread by tiny particles, either through direct contact, by contact with objects such as dirty clothing, or through the air. His writings present the first expositions of the germ theory of infectious disease, another example of a brilliant theoretical leap based on close observation. The world would have to wait three hundred years for Robert Koch and Louis Pasteur to found modern bacteriology and validate Fracastoro's conjectures.

Contagion itself was well enough understood. Fracastoro's early germ theory competed with the miasma theory, in which diseases were borne by fetid, polluted air called miasma. Wherever it originated, syphilis was known to be sexually transmitted. Every nationality blamed it on their worst enemy. Because the retreating French army under Charles V first brought the miasma of syphilis northward, the disease became known, especially in Italy, as *morbus gallicus*, or the French disease. As Voltaire acerbically noted, "On their flippant way through Italy, the French carelessly picked up Genoa, Naples, and syphilis. Then they were thrown out and deprived of Naples and Genoa. But they did not lose everything—syphilis went with them." Because they did indeed pick it up in Italy, the French referred to it as the Italian disease. The Russians called it the Polish disease and the Muslims called it the Christian disease. No one wanted to own it. Other euphemisms included lues venerea (*lues* means plague), Cupid's disease, grandgore (in Scotland), and the Great Pox.

After a few centuries, the severity of syphilis seems to have modulated somewhat. Victims still bore its scars, often on their faces, but it became less lethal. The Phantom of the Opera, in the original tale, wears a mask to hide the loss of a nose and half of his face due to syphilis. The disease could and did gnaw holes in bone and eat chunks out of cartilage. Or not. Some of those infected got off easy, and the initial phase of the disease passed with nothing more than some ulcerous sores and a rash, and it never came back. A lucky few escaped with no symptoms at all. Then again, it is hard to say. Given the protean nature of syphilis, it could be a very difficult diagnosis to make.

Until the early 1800s, syphilis and gonorrhea were thought to be the same disease, or at least closely related. The same was true of syphilis and leprosy. The situation was complicated by the Scottish surgeon John Hunter, a giant in medical history, who in 1767 botched an experiment in which he inoculated either himself or an assistant (it is still not clear) with gonorrhea, unaware that the needle he used was also infected with syphilis. When he came down with the symptoms of syphilis as well as those of gonorrhea, he assumed a common pathogen must lie behind both diseases. His mistake would not be corrected for another half a century.

In 1879, the English venereologist Jonathan Hutchinson delivered a speech to the British Medical Association in which he called syphilis "the great imitator" because of its varied presentation, and the difficulty of distinguishing it from smallpox, psoriasis, lupus, leprosy, and epilepsy. William Osler, the Canadian physician sometimes known as the father of modern medicine, advised all young physicians to "know syphilis, and the whole of medicine is opened to you." For the purposes of diagnosis, it may be useful to treat it as a kind of versatile thespian, capable of acting out roles in any part of the human body. How it traverses the body and how the body responds do not follow a script. It can literally be all over the place. In the 1830s, Philippe Ricord, a French physician, corrected Hunter's mistake, and managed to distinguish syphilis from gonorrhea. He also described how it tended to progress through three basic stages. In the first stage, round, hard-edged chancre sores appear on the genitals or the mouth. These ulcerous sores usually clear up after three to six weeks. This is followed in weeks or months by a second-stage rash over the entire body, including the palms and soles. Fever is common, hair loss less so, and headaches, flu-like symptoms, and aches and pains are typical. These too will disappear after another few weeks, and the disease will settle into an asymptomatic latency, a kind of truce with the body. In about a third of all untreated cases, the patient will enter the third stage. At that point any organ may come under siege, although the heart and the brain present the biggest targets. Gummatous tumors, essentially balls of inflamed tissue, may appear almost anywhere and can be extremely disfiguring. So can the wasting of bone and cartilage, a collapsed "saddle nose" being one of the characteristic features.

Where did syphilis really come from? Fracastoro's fanciful poem places the blame squarely on the gods, but its true origin lies somewhere between a compelling folkloric narrative and an inconclusive archaeological record. The spotty archaeological record says syphilis has always been with us, hidden behind many guises—leprosy, smallpox, pellagra, and various other plagues. Folklore points the finger at Christopher Columbus and his crew, in a cautionary tale of anticolonial comeuppance. According to the Columbian theory, syphilis already existed on Hispaniola (Haiti) in a mild form, more an annoyance than a pestilence, and it had little effect on the locals because of their evolved immune response. While confined to the islands, it did minimal harm. For the European explorers, who had no such built-up resistance, it was catastrophic. Eyewitness reports describe the condition of Columbus's crewmen upon their return to Spain in 1493. "The entire body is so repulsive to look at," wrote one Venetian doctor, "and the suffering is so great, especially at night, that this sickness is even more horrifying than incurable leprosy or elephantiasis, and it can be fatal." Historians have gone back and forth over the Columbian theory, with the most recent evidence indicting the explorer and his men. It seems they did indeed come back to Naples with the Great Pox.

Diseases ride on the backs of armies. When King Charles VIII of France invaded and conquered Naples in 1495, he took with him an army of mercenaries who laid waste to the countryside. Among these were the Landsknechte, German pikemen who fought in almost every European war of the period. Emperor Ferdinand of Spain eventually sent his own army to Naples to expel the French, and his soldiers carried syphilis and passed it along to Charles's troops through the brothels. When the French army retreated to all corners of Northern Europe, the Neapolitan disease, as they called it, went with them.

Albrecht Dürer's famous woodcut of a pikeman covered with bulbous sores combines both folklore and fact. Above the pikeman, Dürer has sketched astrological symbols indicating the supposed cause of the disease in the conjoining of two planets under the sign of Scorpio. The accompanying text lays out this origin story and the forlorn hope for a cure. The pikeman himself, in the classic garb of a Landsknecht, embodies the vector of the disease's transmission from Spain to Northern Europe.

The French pox was unusually protean. Most doctors' accounts noted how varied its symptoms could be. All cases began more or less the same way. After a sexual encounter, pustules or chancres appeared on the genitals within days, sometimes accompanied by fever and pain. A variety of secondary symptoms waxed and waned. Its immediate effects could range from mild to severe and disfiguring. This was the syphilis of Shakespeare's time, the pox Mercutio wishes on the houses of Montague and Capulet, the "hoar leprosy" from *Timon of Athens*. The barber-surgeon William Clowes, a contemporary of Shakespeare's, noted that "the disease itself was never in my opinion more rife with the Indians, Neapolitans, or in France or Spain, than it is in the present day in England." He complained that the population of London's hospitals consisted mostly of syphilitics, and he blamed the alehouses for spreading it, calling the disease "the just punishment of God upon our sins." It deserved the name of the Great Pox because of its severity and ubiquity compared with smallpox, and it frequently drew comparisons to the Black Death.

By the nineteenth century, syphilis had become less virulent and less deadly. Philippe Ricord's description of the disease's three stages circa 1830 pales in comparison to the horrors described during the Elizabethan era. As many as half of all cases advanced no further than the first stage, and the symptoms then disappeared. Ricord assumed, incorrectly, that the person became immune. "You cannot catch a double dose of syphilis," he noted. "It is now a question of determining the specific cause, the fatal poison which produced syphilis." But he was underestimating the resilience of the infection while overestimating the medicines used to treat it. The first was guaiac, a resin obtained from the guaiacum tree, native to subtropical America. It was applied topically and was thought to cure the ulcers and sores. Maybe it did, but it did not cure the underlying infection. Mercury became even more popular. When it was rubbed on, swallowed in pill form, or breathed in with steam vapors, its side effects rivaled those of the syphilis infection itself, and could produce many of the same symptoms, notably blackened or loose teeth, hair loss, aches, pains, and bleeding of the bowel. Looking back over firsthand accounts, it is difficult to distinguish the disease from the supposed cure. In the wrong form or in the wrong hands, mercury can be as lethal as lead and arsenic.

In 1810, during the hostilities of the Napoleonic Wars, the 74-gun British warship HMS *Triumph*, operating with a crew of 650 off the Spanish Bay of Cádiz, came upon two wrecked Spanish vessels carrying a cargo of elemental mercury. The liquid metal, also known as quicksilver, had been stored in kidskin bladders, stuffed two to a keg, with the kegs then packed into crates and stowed in the holds. In all, the crew of the *Triumph* unloaded 130 tons of the stuff.

At the time, Spain was one of the world's largest exporters of mercury, a metal used in gold mining, gilding, hat making, and a host of other industrial applications. Although not rare, it was in high demand and worth salvaging. The captain of the *Triumph* split the booty into two lots. He ordered one of the lots to be loaded onto his orlop (lowest) deck and the other onto a smaller vessel, the armed schooner HMS *Phipps*. The nature of the cargo was not revealed to either crew, and according to eyewitness testimony given years later, the sailors may have thought the prize was *silver* rather than quicksilver. This inspired some of them to pierce the bladders and withdraw a small share for themselves. Or perhaps more than a small share. On both ships, liquid mercury leaked out of the bags and began to fill up niches in the lower decks. Within days, headaches, ulcers, excessive salivation, and breathing difficulties had stricken over half of each crew. As the weeks passed, the symptoms expanded to include tremor, tooth loss, loss of coordination, partial paralysis, and skin eruptions. The ship's doctor ordered the *Triumph* to be ventilated. Gunports were opened, affected sailors had to sleep on the main deck, and the orlop was abandoned. The crew of the *Phipps* succumbed in much the same way, and it was no mystery to the officers or the ships' doctors what was happening. Mercury vapors emanating from the spilled cargo had filled the unventilated lower decks. Everyone was breathing a toxic poison. Immediate ventilation stemmed the problem somewhat, but the ships were forced to return to England to be cleaned. Holes were drilled in the hulls to allow the mercury to flow out. Despite these efforts, the quicksilver remained visible in crevices and continued to give off vapors. Both ships had to be retired from service.

Whenever mercury is absorbed into the body in adequate quantities, it creates havoc. Many of those who routinely worked with mercury in manufacturing, particularly hatters of the nineteenth century, became agitated, delirious, and ultimately insane. This is where we get the phrase *mercurial disposition,* and it also explains how someone could become "mad as a hatter."

More recently, in 1996, Karen Wetterhahn, a forty-seven-year-old Dartmouth College chemistry professor, made a fatal error when handling the compound dimethylmercury under laboratory conditions. Despite having taken every recommended precaution—protective clothing, gloves and goggles, and a fume-ventilating hood—Wetterhahn spilled a few drops. It was enough to kill her.

As an expert in toxic metal exposure, Wetterhahn knew the dangers of dimethylmercury, one of the deadliest poisons on earth. The slightest skin contact is enough to fatally poison a human being. During her experiment, the drops of the chemical fell from a pipette onto her latex glove. Assuming she was protected, she first cleaned up the spill from her equipment before addressing her own gloved hand. What no one knew at the time was how easily dimethylmercury can permeate latex. Before she realized what had happened, she had absorbed a fatal dose, eighty times the toxic threshold. She died ten months later from a wasting condition with severe neurological complications.

Anyone over the age of sixty will recall being treated with mercury at one time or another during childhood, or even playing with it. Mercurochrome, the brand name of a topical mercury-based antiseptic whose active germ-killing ingredient is lethal to bacteria and to a much lesser extent to humans, was once widely available over the counter, and is still available in third-world countries. Merbromin, its generic name, was banned for sale in the United States in 1998 and shortly thereafter in Europe. But it is still used elsewhere because it is cheap and effective. It also happens to be toxic. Mercury-containing silver amalgam tooth fillings have raised overblown concerns, but have gradually been replaced with epoxy compounds. The mercury-based preservative thiomersal or thimerosal, once used in vaccines, has also been removed almost entirely from use, but here too, evidence of its toxicity, particularly as a cause of autism, was fabricated. Even beauty products such as mascaras, eyeliners, and skin-whitening creams, formerly made with mercury and providing a potential vector for its absorption by the body through the delicate tissues around the eyes, have been regulated in the United States. Yet imported mascaras, laden with mercury, continue to flow into this country, notably from China. Some FDA-approved cosmetics still contain trace amounts of mercury acting as preservatives and as antibacterials.

The problem with mercury is the same as with many heavy metals. They are very useful, they have a tactile appeal, and they are deadly. The intriguing heft and malleability of lead and the dazzling glitter and flow of liquid mercury are dangerous subterfuges. Once they are ingested, breathed, or otherwise invited into the human body, we have a devil of a time purging them through metabolic pathways. This gives them plenty of time to go to work, especially on the nervous system. How is it, then, that the crews of the *Triumph* and the *Phipps* could have been overcome so quickly, or Karen Wetterhahn's health compromised so completely by their brief exposures to what was once a ubiquitous metal, while the Mercurochrome generation managed to survive? The answer is twofold: it has to do with exposure levels and solubility.

Elemental mercury is a liquid metal at room temperature and is not easily absorbed by human tissue. This is why it can be handled for short periods of time with no ill effects. People used to drink it for "medicinal purposes," and it would pass through the body causing little damage while providing no benefits. When made into a compound such as mercurous chloride or the antiseptic Mercurochrome, the toxicity of the metal is significantly reduced by its insolubility in water and poor absorption through the skin.

The standard treatments for syphilis, going back centuries, included mercuryl iodide and mercurous chloride, also known as calomel. Both are organic compounds. They do not completely restrict the toxicity of the mercury, which is the entire point: the mercury is supposed to kill disease-causing microbes. Typically, it killed a lot more. These compounds were at first administered in the form of an inunction or salve, much like zinc oxide, and later in pill form or as an injection. The Swiss physician Paracelsus invented calomel in the early 1500s. He proposed that a little of what is bad for you can be good for you. What he didn't know is that mercurous chloride, when it encounters ammonia in the kidneys or lactose and sucrose in the gut, can convert to its far more toxic relative *mercuric* chloride. The result is precisely what Guy de Maupassant experienced when the euphoria of being diagnosed with syphilis wore off and he began taking calomel: bleeding gums, hair loss, migraine, and malaise.

In hindsight, the connection of mercury and syphilis to Maupassant's worsening condition and to his horrible death at the age of forty-two is obvious, although at the time it was not. It was still possible and quite common for a doctor to make a diagnosis of general paralysis and deny any syphilitic connection. Maupassant's loyal personal physician, Dr. Lacassagne, did this for the sake of the writer's family. "It pains me to speak in a journal," he wrote years later, "even a scientific one, of one of my clients, identified by name, especially when that client was my friend. But I cannot let it stand without saying that the idea does not conform with reality."

In the 1890s, no one had yet shown how a disease could cause someone to lose his or her mind, much less how a venereal disease could do it. It didn't make sense. However much scientists insisted on the brain as the organ of the mind, and despite the prevalent psychiatric view attributing insanity to brain disease, a dualistic conception of the mind and brain prevailed, and it still does. The mind creates itself, the mind rules itself, the mind keeps its own counsel. Perhaps it is ruled by a heart of darkness and the brain is merely the vessel. Of course, if the mind exists independently of the brain, if it ultimately has no material substrate, then there can be no such thing as a true *science* of the mind. Nor can there be a disease of the mind in the biological sense.

At the end of *Heart of Darkness*, Joseph Conrad tacked on a fairly maudlin scene. Upon his return from the Congo, Marlow, the man sent to fetch Kurtz, visits Kurtz's fiancée, his so-called Intended. He wants to tell her of Kurtz's final moments, to reassure her of his devotion and piety. To do so, he has to lie. Instead of relaying his true last words— "The horror! The horror!"—he tells her that her fiancé died with her name on his lips. The horror could refer to the depths of Kurtz's depravity, but just as well to his illness. A melodramatic gesture, perhaps, but something Marlow perceived as necessary. With syphilis, as Dr. Lacassagne demonstrated, the big lie was always necessary. One of the most commonplace diseases in the civilized world and one of the leading causes of death, it could not be acknowledged in polite company.

What killed Mr. Kurtz? Maybe it was his ambition. Maybe it was his venality. It would not have served Conrad's purpose to saddle him with a brain disease. If he had, the "heart of darkness" would have lost all of its suggestive power. Much better to make it an affliction of the soul, one capable of turning the sober and cultivated civil servant, a sensitive violinist and refined man of letters, into an unrestrained, murderous maniac. But are there diseases of the soul? In fiction, of course, there are. E. M. Forster made this quite clear in his *Aspects of the Novel*, when he wrote, "'The king died and then the queen died' is a story. 'The king died, and then the queen died of grief' is a plot." By that reasoning,

"Mr. Kurtz died of brain disease" is just a story, and not much of one, whereas "Mr. Kurtz died from a heart of darkness" is most definitely a plot.

For narrative purposes, the difference between a disease of the brain and a disease of the mind is very simple. The first is a story, as in "Bob had a stroke" or "We found a tumor in Mary's brain." The second is a plot, as in "Jealous of a particular sexual favor bestowed on her father by his mistress, Dora developed a persistent cough." One has no meaning; the other is driven by the need to know something more about the story. A story without a plot—without any hint of meaning—is merely a timeline, and not very interesting. Sigmund Freud understood this, and built a theory based on a metaphorical, rather than a medical, interpretation of all psychic distress. In doing so, he made neurosis compelling. Any good writer instinctively does the same. Conrad wisely chose not to reveal what killed Mr. Kurtz. There are several possibilities, but if the interested reader is looking for a strictly medical explanation, only one stands out.

CHAPTER 7

THE SOUL OF A NEW DISEASE

DONATIEN Alphonse François, Marquis de Sade, lived out his last days in the Charenton Insane Asylum, just outside of Paris, in solitary confinement. His multiple attempts to molest some of his fellow inmates had tried the patience of the asylum's director, Dr. Antoine Royer-Collard, beyond the breaking point. The marquis, having been declared insane after his publication of two notorious novels, *Justine* and *Juliette*, had been a thorn in Royer-Collard's side since his arrival in 1803. Within the comparatively posh confines of the newly reformed asylum, Sade wrote obsessively, and though he turned out some of his best work there, including plays he produced for his fellow inmates, he remained a corrupting influence. In his role as the Max Bialystock of Charenton, he relentlessly pushed the boundaries of decency, leading Royer-Collard to repeatedly petition for his removal to a prison. "He does not belong in a hospital," he wrote, "but in a secure place or a fortress. His madness is the perversion of others. Society cannot hope to cure him, and must subject him to the most severe sequestration. He enjoys too much freedom at Charenton." So into solitary he went.

We are in no position to say whether the Marquis de Sade was insane, disturbed, or merely undisciplined. To Royer-Collard, a deeply religious man, Sade was indeed an unrepentant malefactor, an immoralist unable to corral his urges. The reigning alienists of the era had

defined insanity as the inability to control one's passions. By this definition, Sade was a raving lunatic: he had violated and corrupted a female
servant, had committed sodomy, and had blasphemed. Yet his faculties
remained intact and undiminished. When Royer-Collard called him
"mad," he was speaking only in a figurative sense, and despite his best
efforts, Sade remained at Charenton in solitary confinement until he
died in 1814, and the question of his sanity went unanswered.

Four years later, into this cauldron of confusion over the nature of
insanity, a nineteen-year-old medical student named Antoine Bayle
strode through the gates of Charenton to report for his first day of work.
The marquis was long gone, though Royer-Collard still ruled the mad-
house. He would become Bayle's mentor and boss. Bayle brought new
ideas, informed by the emerging science of phrenology. Already a com-
petent anatomist, he had not yet written a dissertation, but he soon got
an idea for one. He began performing autopsies on patients who had
died, usually in their forties, of a highly characteristic and unprecedented
form of insanity, often accompanied by paralysis. Their illnesses at the
onset had been marked by unprovoked flights of madness involving ex-
travagant claims of world-changing self-importance, accompanied by
wasteful spending sprees. Without exception, euphoria and delusions of
grandeur had given way to a rapid descent into physical incapacity, leaving the victims unable to perform the simplest of tasks. Coma soon followed, then death. In the first six autopsies, Bayle found a common
feature: meningitis, an inflammation of the membranes surrounding the
brain. Such an abnormality, Bayle reasoned, could result in derangement
and incapacity. But in 1822 such an idea fell well beyond conventional
thinking. Perhaps, Bayle suggested, the inflammation had compromised
blood flow to the brain. He could not say what had caused the meningitis,
but this much seemed clear: in every one of the six cases he described,
a brain illness had produced insanity and not the other way around. "I
shall have attained the objective I set out for if this part of my work can
prove that *chronic arachnitis does exist and that it is a cause of a symptomatic
mental disturbance.*" But he couldn't prove it, and no one wanted to hear it.

Bayle had three things working against him. First, he was young,
just twenty-three at the time; his discovery was published as his doctoral

thesis. Second, he had no institutional support. Royer-Collard encouraged Bayle's theorizing, but let him go off alone to tilt at windmills. Third, he was going up against the previous generation of psychiatrists, notably Philippe Pinel and his protégé Jean-Étienne Esquirol. In 1814, Esquirol had flatly stated that "the opening of the body teaches us nothing with regard to the (seat of dementia) and all of the organic alterations of the brain belong less to insanity than to its complications."

Philippe Pinel in many ways was the very first psychiatrist. His involvement in mental illness began in the late 1700s when a close friend succumbed to what he described as a "nervous melancholy," devolving from there into mania and ultimately suicide. Pinel subsequently took a position at Paris's Bicêtre Hospital and immersed himself in the care of the insane. For his reforming efforts he is known as the father of modern psychiatry. But it was Esquirol, Pinel's successor (and eventually Royer-Collard's successor at Charenton), who turned insane asylums into mental hospitals, and in doing so established psychiatry as a branch of medicine. He set out not just to manage insanity, but to cure it.

As authorities in the field of institutional psychiatry, Pinel and Esquirol established a classification scheme of five types of insanity: lypomania (a state of depression), monomania (a persistent fixation or obsession in an otherwise rational mind), mania (a form of disoriented excitation), imbecility (today called developmental delay), and dementia. According to Pinel, unbalanced passion and rational thought coexist in every person, but when mental illness arises in the soul, it is due to an excess or imbalance. "A subject is mad or delirious," he wrote, "when his thoughts, judgments, and decisions are determined by passions, or can no longer be controlled by will." According to this theory, insanity does not originate in the biology or chemistry of the body, but in the spirit inhabiting it. It could not result from a disease of the brain any more than from a disease of the liver. By Pinel's definition, the Marquis de Sade was most definitely insane. Antoine Royer-Collard saw it differently, but not enough to stick his neck out for Bayle.

By the 1820s, psychiatrists had yet to reach a consensus on the causes of mental illness or the connection, if any, between insanity and a brain disease of the type Bayle described. "Its gravity," Bayle noted, "and its final results, nearly always tragic, and its wide social complications, deserve to have fixed on it the attention of the entire medical profession." He estimated that a fifth of all admissions to Charenton fit the profile. Bayle may have thought he was just doing his part, but for this impertinent reasoning he was attacked from almost every quarter. Academic psychiatrists did not see how insanity could cross from one descriptive category to another, from monomania to mania to dementia to imbecility. After following up his initial study with a report on a hundred autopsies, all showing the same pathology and trajectory, Bayle endured more personal attacks. Within a few years, he'd had enough. He quit his post and became a medical librarian. Even so, according to a pair of prominent medical historians, Bayle "may be considered as the father of the concept that a specific disease of the brain may be the cause of a specific mental disease."

Although Bayle did not give his disease a name, referring to it vaguely as "chronic arachnitis," a close colleague did it for him. Louis-Florentin Calmeil, another young intern at Charenton, wrote a 450-page book on Bayle's disease in 1826, and published it under the auspices of Royer-Collard. The volume—*Of Paralysis Considered Among the Insane*—succeeded where Bayle had failed. Calmeil not only legitimized the condition, but gave it a name: general paralysis of the insane. "I am aware that this locution sounds somewhat vicious," he admitted, "in that it conveys the idea of disordered mental function instead of conveying the material disorder giving rise to the condition." The material disorder is the inflammation of the lining of the brain, a chronic encephalitis. The disordered mental function had to be the consequence of it. Calmeil, with Royer-Collard's blessing, managed to nudge Bayle's theory to acceptance.

Like Bayle, Calmeil examined scores of cases and catalogued their similarities. The condition almost always began with a specific form of labored speech, at the time erroneously attributed to a minor paralysis of the tongue. Difficulties in fine motor movement soon followed, although strength in the large muscle groups seemed unaffected. These paralytic symptoms could precede, coincide with, or follow the onset of a characteristic florid manic insanity. As for the cause, Calmeil assembled what appear in hindsight to be a remarkably telling set of correlates. Men were afflicted at much higher rates than women were. Among men, retired soldiers were represented disproportionately, with no regard to status. "The malady afflicts men of every rank," Calmeil noted. "One sees the same infirmities in superior officers and simple soldiers. Is general paralysis in some way due to the influence of war fatigue?" He also noticed elevated rates among laborers. Finally, among other indicators, he noted how mercury alleviated certain symptoms, but he failed to make a connection with syphilis.

Although most physicians had shunned Bayle's theory, one branch of the profession came to embrace it and made it possible for Calmeil to produce his study. Asylum superintendents instantly recognized the symptom profile of general paralysis and even the brain pathology behind it. During the early 1800s they were seeing an increasing number of cases each month, all following the same downward spiral: delirium, elation, hallucinations, speech irregularities, monomania, delusions of grandeur, gradual onset of paralysis, dementia, raving, incontinence, coma, and death, usually within two years of the first symptom. Psychiatry in Bayle's era was not glamorous. It carried almost no respect within the medical community. Its practitioners, also known as alienists, had little or no medical training, and they functioned mainly as custodians, or effectively as jailers. In describing this odd but increasingly pervasive phenomenon, Bayle had given them a path to legitimacy. Before Bayle and Calmeil, asylum managers were charged with attending to a condition of the soul. Now they had something they could diagnose: a disease of the body, something seemingly new, something stereotyped enough to merit a name. The name Calmeil chose intentionally focused on the psychiatric rather than the neurological aspect of the condition, making it the first genuine psychiatric disease.

When the Marquis de Sade was packed off first to the Bicêtre asylum in 1801 and then to Charenton two years later, he joined a select group. There were only a few French asylums housing a relatively small proportion of the total population of the insane. The rest were sent to poor-houses or prisons. A century later, there were over a hundred asylums in France and over four hundred in Germany. This growth industry had been fueled partly by compassion and mostly by syphilis. It is impossible to know what percentage of psychotics had gone mad from heavy metal poisoning. Those who had gone mad as a hatter from inhaling mercury vapors, whether as an industrial contaminant or as a treatment for syphilis, would have been well represented. What distinguished general paralysis was the short life expectancy of its victims. Once diagnosed, they could expect to live only another few years.

General paralysis of the insane had to compete with a potent mythology. Historically, madness was thought to result either from demonic possession or from a defect of the soul. It was inextricably tied to notions of sin, guilt, blame, shame, bad bloodlines, and during especially paranoid eras, to witchcraft. Ironically, some twenty-five hundred years earlier, the Greek physician Hippocrates had been on the same track as Bayle when he ascribed mental illnesses to the body and not the psyche, specifically to the four humors. This idea held sway up to the Middle Ages, when the fixation with demonic possession returned. During the Enlightenment, the phrenological theories of Franz Joseph Gall, circa 1805, brought attention back to the brain as the basis of rational thought, of emotions, and of mental derangement. Bayle took it one step further when he associated a specific brain pathology with a coherent symptom profile. Once identified, general paralysis of the insane was found to account for about 20 percent of all asylum admissions. The beleaguered medical librarian had uncovered an epidemic, and his friend Calmeil had confirmed it. But neither man could say what had caused it.

In Bayle's initial study, he ascribed two out of his six cases of general paralysis to "excessive venery," but he did not pursue the connection. Calmeil, in noting the high incidence of general paralysis among military men and mercury users, failed to ask what else might be common to both groups. The syphilis connection made it into print only some thirty years later, in 1853, when Friedrich von Esmarch and Peter Willers Jessen, a surgeon and a psychiatrist, wrote: "It is striking that so little is to be found in the special psychiatric literature about syphilis and its relation to psychosis." They described three more cases, very similar to Bayle's, and attributed the mental illness directly to syphilis.

The name *general paralysis* emphasizes the symptoms of muscular weakness appearing in the limbs, tongue, and in the eyes. Yet unlike ALS, this was not a wasting illness. The muscles, although weakened, remained of normal size. Neurologists discovered something unique and vaguely disturbing about how the paralysis worked. In some cases, it was not caused by the loss of nervous connectivity from the motor cortex. Instead, the limbs became useless because of the loss of ability to organize movements, a problem now called apraxia. What sounds at first like a hysterical symptom along the lines of Maria Theresia von Paradis's blindness turned out to be something different. It was not an unconscious refusal to move, but a true incapacity. To acknowledge this, the head of the Malmö asylum in Sweden, a Dr. E. Salomon, suggested the name should be changed from general *paralysis* to general *paresis.* ("He who is generally paralyzed is certainly dead," he quipped.) A paresis is an incomplete or partial paralysis. Those who suffered from it were thenceforth known, primarily in America, as paretics. In Europe, the term *dementia paralytica* held sway.

Rarely does the common wisdom change on a dime. Even in the face of overwhelming evidence, there are always holdouts for the status quo. Bayle started the ball rolling for the possibility of a brain-based insanity. Calmeil nudged it along, as did Esmarch and Jessen. The heavy hitters finally weighed in when, in 1861, the highly respected German psychiatrist Wilhelm Griesinger famously declared: "Psychological diseases are diseases of the brain." According to Griesinger, insanity "is merely a symptom complex of various anomalous states of the brain." This took the mind out of the equation entirely, and it became the rallying cry for a field aiming at scientific respectability. Although a so-called Somatic School still existed and rebutted Griesinger by attributing insanity to disorders within the *body* (though not specifically within the brain), a turning point had been reached. Mental illness was now firmly rooted in brain illness. Psychiatry became a branch of medicine. Its calling card, the core of its legitimacy, was this alarming new phenomenon of the nineteenth century: general paralysis of the insane, or GPI, as it is still known.

"Psychiatry has undergone a transformation in its relationship to the rest of medicine," Griesinger wrote. "This transformation rests principally on the realization that patients with so-called 'mental illnesses' are really individuals with weaknesses of the nerves and brain. [Psychiatry] must emerge from its closed-off status as a guild and become an integral part of general medicine accessible to all medical circles." If Esmarch and Jessen were correct and syphilis turned out to be the root cause of general paresis, then it would no longer qualify as a psychiatric illness at all, but merely as an infectious disease with wide-ranging symptoms, the most dramatic and consistent being delusions of grandeur, some of them quite breathtaking.

"In the month of October he is Emperor Napoléon, he has immense wealth; forty thousand barrels of gold . . . he was going to build a château finer than the Tuileries and the Louvre . . . he has just bought Italy and is considering taking possession of Asia. When asked about his health he replies that he is fine." This particular delusion was quite common. An epidemic of Napoléons broke out in Paris when the emperor's remains were returned to the city in 1840. The Bicêtre asylum "recorded the admission of thirteen or fourteen emperors." This is not surprising. As the historian Laure Murat has noted, monomania followed a consistent pattern. "If male, he was usually the ruler of the world; if female, she was empress of the universe. Their fortunes amounted to billions, their armies were invincible, they could annihilate the earth in a single breath." Murat attributes most of these delusions to social and political anxieties—in other words, to hysteria. But general paralysis clearly accounted for the most serious cases. The disease was a kind of insidious Trojan horse. It could remain hidden for a long time, up to two decades, and then bring down its victim in just a few years. It seemed partial to soldiers and outdoorsmen, vigorous and active men. Maupassant was typical. He barely noticed his initial infection. It was little more than an inconvenience—a bad omen, for quite often the mildest cases at onset eventually reemerged as general paresis a decade or two down the line. By the time a patient received a definitive diagnosis, it was too late to do anything about it other than minister to his or her needs while mind and body fell apart. This fate befell several generations of men and women who drifted into madness at Charenton, the Bicêtre, the Salpêtrière, and probably even in the depths of the Belgian Congo. Once diagnosed, they were beyond help.

Today, the disconnect between neurology and psychiatry remains rooted in illnesses with both structural and functional indicators: schizophrenia, bipolarity, addiction, and so on. In the formative years of both specialties, as a consequence of evolving views of brain and mind, psychiatry claimed general paresis well before it was revealed to be a brain disease, and for good reason. As one of the definitive early textbooks on the disease stated, "Syphilis is in a sense the making of psychiatry and will go far to pushing psychiatry into general practice." Neurology, in the persons of Charcot and Freud, laid claim to hysteria before it was revealed to be solely a phenomenon of mind. Meanwhile, the treatment of syphilis, whose connection to both general paresis and hysteria was only suspected, was left to the dermatologists. If anything was to be done about the unabated spread of this scourge, they would have to be the ones to do it.

In the 1860s, Alfred Fournier surveyed the landscape of venereal disease and found it riddled with mistakes. A student of Philippe Ricord, he carried on his teacher's interest with a monomaniacal zeal. Fournier became France's leading expert on sexually transmitted infections, especially syphilis. Appointed head of the venereology service at l'Hôpital de Lourcine in 1868, he began lecturing on syphilis and gonorrhea. From there he became a *chef de service* at l'Hôpital Saint-Louis, then chair of syphilology and dermatology. In 1901, he founded the Society of Sanitary and Moral Prophylaxis, and through its auspices warned young women about the dangers of venereal disease while he lobbied for a ban on prostitution.

Early in his career, Fournier indulged in a bit of literary amateurism when he translated and annotated Fracastoro's poem about syphilis, calling it a serious medical treatise. "It is a veritable scientific monograph," he wrote in the preface, "in which central questions are seriously discussed, where symptoms are described, causes debated, and treatments formulated. . . . The basis of the work, its true subject, to which everything he writes converges, is the theoretical and clinical description of a disease." Fournier set out to update Fracastoro's catalogue. His main challenge was to make sense of signs and symptoms common to both syphilitic and nonsyphilitic patients. Which ones were caused by syphilis, and which ones were caused by another disease? Faced with this conundrum, Fournier came to view the world almost entirely through the lens of venereal disease, as though it were Valjean to his Javert. He was accused by one student of "seeing syphilis everywhere." According to another, he classified skin diseases as "syphilitic, parasyphilitic, syphiloid, and asyphilitic." Fournier responded brusquely, telling them he knew syphilis better than anyone else, and then pointed out the syphilitic connection to many conditions previously unexplained. Syphilis, said Fournier, is not just a disease of the skin, but of the entire body. It constantly fooled physicians who had not seen a sufficient number of cases to appreciate its sheer variety. Once the dermatological symptoms subsided, there was no telling where or when it would again surface, or if it would return at all. In the form of general paralysis, it could easily pass for any form of madness. But because neither general paralysis nor tabes dorsalis responded to the antisyphilitic treatments of the day, Fournier stopped short of attributing them directly to syphilis. He also could not prove their connection to each other, even though about 10 percent of tabetics ended up with general paresis, and at least a third of paretics eventually exhibited some of the signs of tabes. At the very least, he said, they were syphilis-*related*, or what he called *para*syphilitic. And they were not the only such diseases. By the time he was done, Fournier had tentatively grouped neurasthenia, hysteria, epilepsy, and hydrocephaly as parasyphilitic. He even threw in diabetes.

Fournier invented parasyphilis, though not in the way Charcot invented *la grande hystérie*. He based his description on statistical correlations with careful observation of the varieties of syphilitic disease, and on a theory of transmission and progression. Instead of focusing on the underlying cause, the identity of the offending germ, he emphasized the overall destructive potential of the disease, its pervasiveness, and the need to contain it through public awareness measures. He pointed out the dangers from a single case, passing from husband to wife, thence to child, thence to wet nurse. "I made myself a collector of syphilitic data," Fournier wrote, "just as a fad or special interest invites others to become collectors of paintings, of books, of Japanese articles, of autographs, of snuff-boxes. . . . Thanks to these notes, I was able first to convince myself and later to convince my colleagues of the pathogenetic relationship which attaches tabes and general paralysis and leukoplakia [flat white sores in the mouth] and the specific hereditary dystrophies to syphilis."

He also made explicit what Freud had merely implied. Syphilis was the driving force behind neurosis, behind hysteria, and behind the spectrum of unexplained ailments previously written off as psychogenic or neurasthenic. As long as the true nature of syphilis, its cause and possible cure, remained shrouded in speculation, it could play the role of a universal disease affecting rich and poor, civilized and uncivilized, corrupt and pure, vile and innocent. Fournier's critics may have ridiculed him for seeing syphilis everywhere, but it is impossible today, in a clinical setting, to imagine the parade of pathology that passed before his eyes, almost all of it syphilitic in origin, most of it disfiguring, disabling, dementing, and often fatal. The streets of cities teemed with syphilitics, some ambling with the "stamp and stick" gait characteristic of tabes, others with deformities, false noses, rashes, or hair loss, and still others raving and delusional. Viewing photographs of these patients today, we are inclined to regard them as oddities and rarities, like specimens in a pathology museum. But they were a commonplace in every village and town. Fournier saw syphilis everywhere because syphilis *was* everywhere.

CHAPTER 8

THE UNSETTLED TERRITORIES
OF THE MIND

According to Charles Baudelaire, poète maudit and author of *Les Fleurs du Mal*, syphilis is a bit of a lark. "On the day that the writer corrects his first proof," he wrote, "he is as proud as a schoolboy who has just caught his first pox." In time he would come to regret that statement. Gustave Flaubert also thought of the pox as a rite of passage, an obligatory waystation on the road to manhood. As noted, Guy de Maupassant practically exulted in discovering his own infection. Schadenfreude was invented for such types. Both Baudelaire and Maupassant died miserably of syphilitic insanity and paralysis in their forties. Flaubert would fight off crippling symptoms of syphilis and mercury treatments throughout his adult life, a full four decades of abject suffering.

The age of celebration did not last long. The American memoirist and three-time syphilitic Mabel Dodge Luhan referred to her infection as "this disgusting and ignoble disease that could never be ignored or forgotten." It was "a shameful accident to be hidden from the world." Venereal disease has always been accompanied by disgust and denial, from the naming of it after one's worst enemy to the false pride at catching it to the thinly veiled euphemisms (lues, paralysis, ataxia). The novelist D. H. Lawrence remarked that "the pox" was no joke to the Elizabethans. "They didn't think it funny," he wrote, "for by God it *wasn't* funny. Even poor Elizabeth's lack of eyebrows and her rotten teeth were not funny. And they all knew it. They may not have known it was the direct result of pox: though probably they did. The fact remains, that no man can contract syphilis, or any deadly sexual disease, without feeling the most shattering and profound terror go through him, through the very root of his being."

Physicians were aware of this terror and its residual effect on the family of the sufferer. They felt it too. "No man can look without a sort of horror on the effects of a sexual disease in another person," Lawrence added. "The fear and dread has been so great, that the pox joke was invented as an evasion, and following that, the great hush! hush! was imposed. Man was *too* frightened, that's the top and bottom of it."

Lawrence was one of the few public figures to openly acknowledge the big secret, the damage wrought by venereal disease on society, on the arts, on creativity, and on culture. His contemporaries, even the most adventurous and progressive, hid their thoughts from their own diaries, or opened up only in memoirs kept well hidden until after their deaths. Mabel Dodge Luhan, when dealing with the infection of her third husband, the sculptor Maurice Sterne, wrote in her journal about "ghastly secret things that were happening that must be concealed from people. There was always this nauseous accompaniment to our life . . . and we could not avoid our accompaniment of secret guilt and vileness." The specter of syphilis hung over the era like a sword of Damocles, as if even the mention of the word *syphilis* would cause the horsehair to snap.

In part it was simple ignorance. In the seasonal maelstroms of contagion raging across Europe, including plague, cholera, leprosy, malaria, gonorrhea, tuberculosis, and influenza, only syphilis, thanks to the sheer variety of its manifestations, evaded detection and correct diagnosis. Most victims wasted away in asylums and hospitals or in quiet desperation at home, hiding their disfigurement and the shame of insanity. Others carried on, asymptomatic and oblivious to their impending doom or the threat they posed to others. For the rich and famous who did succumb, they could take some solace in the conspiracies of denial usually well under way before the deathbed scene. For people of means, history would be rewritten. The cause of death would be recorded using some secondary feature of the disease—not technically a lie, but not the whole truth either.

The death of Lord Randolph Churchill, Sir Winston's father, followed this script. His life story is one of wealth, social position, advantageous marriage, political success, and brilliant oratorical skill. Educated at Oxford, he gravitated toward the sporting life—racehorses, rowdiness, drink, and women. Despite these distractions, he was elected to Parliament at the age of twenty-two. Exactly when he contracted syphilis is not clear. There are unverified tales, some involving a setup by friends, but the initial stage of the disease seems to have been fairly mild. As Fournier noted, these mild cases quite often progressed to either crippling tabes or the mania of general paralysis after a long period of latency. Churchill was forced to quit public life at the age of thirty-two, possibly to seek treatment. He returned and eventually rose to the post of Chancellor of the Exchequer. But in 1886 he suffered a noticeable decline. Mood swings, slurred speech, confusion, and other ominous signs pointed to a serious neurological disorder. His final speech at the House of Commons was a disaster, described in the London *Times* as "tragical." His health never recovered, pain set in, and he died on January 24, 1895. The cause of death was listed as general paralysis of the insane.

At the time, the syphilitic connection to general paralysis had not been proven, although most physicians sided with Fournier on the matter. Even so, in stating the cause of Churchill's death, the attending physician probably thought he was sparing the family any association with venereal disease, although even Lord Randolph's son Winston knew what it meant. Today, to judge from the official Churchill family website, a vigorous campaign to expunge syphilis from the record has succeeded. The original infection has been disputed and the cause of death has been revised to a brain tumor.

Lord Randolph Churchill, Charles Baudelaire, Édouard Manet, Friedrich Nietzsche, Oscar Wilde: it is impossible to say what killed them, but they were all rumored to have had syphilis. If it was not the direct cause of death, it was a facilitating one. Any man (for some unknown reason, men succumbed to general paresis at a much higher rate than women) who lived large and was then brought down in his forties or fifties by a paralytic, neurasthenic, or psychotic condition, it is safe to say, probably had syphilis. Any man who had a public manic episode, as Nietzsche and Van Gogh did, was also a good bet to have been a paretic. If we set aside the hundreds of thousands of anonymous victims of the disease, these well-known cases have led to speculation about the connection between madness and creativity, perhaps the sole hint of an upside in what otherwise seems a colossal waste of talent, if only it had been true. It is not. Moreover, unlike tuberculosis or cholera, syphilis never acquired any romantic connotations. There may well have been "love in the time of cholera," but there is no "love in the time of syphilis."

Sigmund Freud, unhindered by any false rectitude, provided some insight into this with his description of the young woman he called Dora in *An Analysis of a Case of Hysteria* (1900). The girl's father had contracted syphilis before marrying; Freud had treated the infection himself. Although he assumed he had cured it, most likely he did not. It either cleared up on its own (in 50 percent of infections, syphilis never progressed beyond the first stage) or had entered a latent phase. Freud acknowledged that even if the syphilis had been cured, the psychological effects of the disease lingered and had led to hysterical symptoms in the daughter. "Syphilis in the male parent," he noted, "is a very relevant factor in the etiology of the neuropathic constitution of children." In other words, according to Freud, syphilis was one of the principal causes of hysteria.

D. H. Lawrence, no fan of Freud's theories of sexuality, agreed on this one point. "The appearance of syphilis in our midst," he wrote,

> gave a fearful blow to our sexual life. . . . The very sexual act of procreation might bring as one of its consequences a foul disease, and the unborn might be tainted from the moment of conception. Fearful thought! . . . The fearful thought of the consequences of syphilis, or of any sexual disease, upon the unborn, gives a shock to the impetus of fatherhood in any man, even the cleanest. Our consciousness is a strange thing, and the knowledge of a certain fact may wound it mortally, even if the fact does not touch us directly.

Our *un*conscious is also a strange thing, at least according to Freud. The disease explained a lot of the misery he witnessed at the Salpêtrière. It probably explained Blanche Wittman's convulsions from the age of fourteen. She probably did not have syphilis, but like other women who had experienced abuse, she feared it, was traumatized by the idea of it, and had been repeatedly exposed to the threat of it in the most brutal way. It was all well and good to attribute neuroses to the absence of sexual fulfillment, to the need and desire for a regular orgasm, but what about the risk of seeking that satisfaction? The seriousness of this threat and the indelicacy of even alluding to it challenged the best fiction writers of the era.

In 1882, Henrik Ibsen wrote *Ghosts*, the tale of a young man who discovers he has inherited syphilitic insanity from his father. Not only can he not marry the woman he loves, but he is doomed. "The disease I have as my birthright," he says, pointing to his forehead, "is seated here . . . yes, it is seated here, waiting. And it may break out any day, at any moment." The play was a scandal. When it premiered in London in 1891, the reviewer for *The Daily Telegraph* described it as "an open drain; a loathsome sore unbandaged; a dirty act done publicly. . . . Gross, almost putrid indecorum. . . . Literary carrion. . . . Crapulous stuff."

Rudyard Kipling fared better in 1893 with "Love-o'-Women," a short story about a British soldier who fears the company doctor will discover his inability to stand upright with his eyes closed. He knew he would fail a Romberg test, the diagnostic assessment still used in hospital examining rooms and roadside sobriety tests. At the time of the story, a failed Romberg was a sure sign of locomotor ataxia, as tabes dorsalis was often called. Its cause was neatly summed up in the soldier's nickname. "They call it Locomotus attacks us," the doctor says in dialect, "ut attacks us like a locomotive . . . an' ut comes from bein' called Love-o'-Women." Kipling avoids ever mentioning syphilis by name, but readers at the time would have known exactly what he was depicting.

Arthur Conan Doyle's collection of medical stories, *Round the Red Lamp* (1894), directly confronts the threat of syphilis in the story "The Third Generation," when he describes the plight of a man who discovers his infection on the eve of his wedding, then kills himself. On an almost identical theme, Eugène Brieux's controversial play, *Les Avariés* (*Damaged Goods*, 1901), spells out the consequences of not killing oneself, but going ahead and getting married. Just as in Conan Doyle's story, days before he is to wed, a man is diagnosed with syphilis. He is advised to put off the wedding until he completes treatment, which will take a minimum of six months, possibly more. He succumbs to the promise of a quack doctor to cure him in a few weeks, then marries, and his first-born child becomes sick. The diagnosis is congenital syphilis. The doctor recommends the dismissal of the wet nurse lest the infection spread from the baby to her and then to other babies. The family pays her to stay, not telling her of the risk.

Ibsen's *Ghosts* and Conan Doyle's "The Third Generation," although medically inaccurate in suggesting that syphilitic insanity can be inherited, mirrored real life in one key respect: the landscape of sexual pleasure was mined with appalling risks. The idea that one might be doomed through no fault of one's own, or that one might go mad because of a single night's indiscretion, haunted several generations of young men and women. Degeneration theory did not make things any better. In some ways it made them worse by implicating entire families, making it impossible for a younger sister to marry if it became known that her older brother had died of syphilis. It had to be kept quiet.

Degeneration theory, a pseudoscientific reboot of the biblical notion of the sins of the father repackaged for the Darwinian era, is still with us in the entrenched medical term *degenerative brain disease,* and also in the word *degenerate* as used to describe a juvenile delinquent or a pervert. Unlike other technical terms of psychiatric origin, such as *idiot* and *moron*, the word *degenerate* made it through to the present virtually intact and without controversy, probably because people have forgotten what it meant. In its original sense, the word refers to a hereditary nervous condition that worsens with each generation, and it served as a portmanteau explanation for unexplained illnesses in the late nineteenth century. Charcot used it to explain hysteria, but the theory was not new with him. Its origins went back to the 1850s, and grew out of a sense of futility in treating the insane, fueled by religious and moral prejudices.

Bénédict Morel, a psychiatrist of the Salpêtrière Hospital, Viennese born but French educated, saw degeneration in the asymmetrical faces, misshapen ears, and pointy skulls of inmates of the Maréville asylum in Nancy, where he had once worked. He assumed there had to be a connection between twisted bodies, deformed crania, and misbegotten thoughts. The explanation now seems a little too pat. Environmental toxins from the slums, self-inflicted toxins in the form of alcohol and drugs, moral toxins of the brothels—according to Morel, all of these evils triggered disturbances in the nervous system, leading to an incipient weakness or susceptibility to various forms of neurosis. From there, the effect was multiplied in a hereditary cascade, swollen by additional tributaries in successive generations, all fed by accumulating moral weakness. The second generation inherited neurosis and from it developed mental illness, the third generation imbecility, the fourth generation sterility, and from there, the line died out. Neurosis, hysteria, mania, moral insanity, imbecility, criminality, and sterility—this was degeneration. The principal selling point of the theory was its implicit argument for racial purity and the maintenance of class distinctions.

Driven by fears of miscegenation, immigration, rapid urbanization, immorality, and the imminent collapse of civilized society, criminal anthropologists and social scientists used degeneration as the scientific justification for the eugenics movement, and ultimately, for genocide. It had a good deal of curb appeal. It was moralistic, nationalistic, and in a time before DNA sequencing, irrefutable. Not surprisingly, anthropologists and other natural scientists in Germany, France, and England gravitated to it, and used it to establish the racial superiority of the German, French, and English races, respectively. Degeneration allowed those at the top of the social and racial pecking order to justify their place there and to hold on to it. Horrific in hindsight, but less malignant in its original context, Morel's theory attempted to explain insanity and mental illness in the light of recent discoveries in the emerging field of neurology. It was one of many ideas thrown against the wall at the time, and it managed to stick. But even ideas that did not stick could be influential in their way. One of them, conceived by a disciple of Morel's, attempted to get at the very mechanism of degenerative nerve disorders by using artificial means to journey to the land of the insane.

The Hôtel Pimodan on the Île Saint-Louis in the center of Paris dates back to the time when the saltpetery gave way to the Salpêtrière asylum. Four stories tall, with gilded interiors in the Louis XIV style, it is not a hotel in the modern sense but rather a *hôtel particulier* in the Parisian sense of a stately urban residence, one later divided up into apartments and rented out to artistic types. The poet Charles Baudelaire leased several rooms there in the 1840s. It was where he began work on *Les Fleurs du Mal*. His friend, the poet and playwright Théophile Gautier, also rented an apartment, and strange happenings began to occur in its salon. All it would take, as Gautier recalled, was a spoonful of green paste.

They called their monthly gatherings the Club des Hashischins, or the Hashish Eaters Club. Their supplier, a Dr. X, treated it as a controlled scientific experiment, while the rank and file, a who's who of the French arts scene including Baudelaire, Gérard de Nerval, Alexandre Dumas, and Eugène Delacroix viewed it as an exploratory séance. Hashish was something new in Paris, a mind-expanding hallucinogen as opposed to popular but mind-narrowing depressants like morphine, chloral hydrate, or opium. Its novel feature, crucial for Dr. X, was the mind's retention of awareness under its influence. Hashish eaters preserved the memory of the experience, and men of letters like Gautier provided florid descriptions of the sensation.

"It seemed that my body was dissolving and becoming transparent," he reported. The "intangible essence" of his soul was changed in an instant. "I could clearly see in my chest the hashish I had eaten in the form of an emerald glowing with a million sparkles. My eyelashes grew to infinity and like golden threads wound around little ivory spindles that spun themselves with dazzling speed."

Dr. X recorded these episodes of "artificial insanity," as he called them, as faithfully as he could, using them as data in an attempt to understand the experience. Dr. X was not merely an observer. "In order to know how a madman loses reason," he wrote, "one must have lost reason oneself." In essence, Dr. X did with hashish what Charcot tried to do with hypnosis and hysteria: to artificially produce the symptoms of a mental illness. The only difference was Dr. X's insistence on trying it on himself.

Dr. X had a name: Jacques-Joseph Moreau. Born in 1804, the son of a future Battle of Waterloo veteran, educated at the College of Tours, he would later style himself as Moreau de Tours, as he is now known in the literature. In 1826, after finishing his medical studies, he arrived at the Charenton asylum as an assistant physician. The new director, Antoine Royer-Collard's replacement, was Jean-Étienne Esquirol, the very man who had coined the term *hallucination*. In the few years since Antoine Bayle had described general paralysis of the insane, Esquirol had warmed to the idea of a biological basis of mental illness. His mentoring of Moreau and their joint study of mania would lead directly to the young man's psychotropic experiments with hashish.

At the time, two methods of treatment of the insane vied for acceptance. The "medical" treatment entailed the punishment of bad moral habits—notably masturbation—with cold baths, restraints, and other corrective measures. The "moral" treatment, pioneered by Philippe Pinel among others, focused on psychological well-being. Both Pinel and his student Esquirol designed asylums featuring open spaces in which inmates could interact with one another and with nature. With his wealthier patients, Esquirol even recommended extended travel in the company of a junior associate. He sent Moreau to the Middle East with one such client. Moreau returned a few years later with an appreciation for the culture, its rich history, and one mind-altering ritual. His first experiences with hashish, a greenish paste of cannabis ingested in walnut-sized dollops, gave him some insights into the phenomenon of mania. It caused him to rethink everything he thought he knew about the "true and essential nature of madness."

When he returned to Paris, Moreau enlisted his friends at the Hôtel Pimodan to help document the experience. "There is not a single, elementary manifestation of mental illness," he wrote, "that cannot be found in the mental changes caused by hashish, from simply manic excitement to frenzied delirium." He tried to write down his own thoughts while under the spell of the drug, and he had his friends record their own reactions. Moreau then posited a theory of insanity somewhere between the so-called somatic school, which attributed mental illness to illness in the body outside of the brain, and the physiological school, which pegged it to physical lesions within the brain.

Moreau knew that Philippe Pinel had failed to find any sign of pathology in over 250 dissections he had performed on the brains of insane patients. "Does psychosis," he wondered, "like all other illnesses, depend upon organic lesions, or is it rather a purely functional disturbance of the intellect?" He was aware of the limitations of investigative methods. Just because Pinel could not find anything did not mean there was nothing to be found. On the other hand, from his experiments with hashish, he could see how the drug acted "directly on the faculties of the mind without the mediation of the organs," so that "the mind can be profoundly changed without affecting the body." The Hashish Eaters Club provided Moreau with data in the form of imaginative, sometimes ecstatic prose, yet it failed to illuminate the nature of insanity. Perhaps, he mused, it had to do with changes in blood circulation in the brain. This was the extent of what Moreau could offer. He failed to demonstrate that hashish had any therapeutic benefits for his mental patients. His primary contribution to the literature was to explore the effects of psychotropic drugs on symptoms of mental illness over a century before Timothy Leary and, perversely, the CIA resurrected the same line of inquiry. Moreau also promoted the idea of a functional (or dynamic) lesion of the brain, later taken up by Charcot, and he supported the hereditary origins of mental illness, also later taken up by Charcot. This left psychiatry and neurology in an uncertain place.

In 1876, the Paris Faculty of Medicine established the first academic chair for the study of insanity. They awarded it to a relatively unheralded alienist named Benjamin Ball. Officially the chair was created for mental pathology and diseases of the brain. In other words, it was a chair in psychiatry as psychiatry was understood at that time in Paris. Charcot was a natural choice and had made his interest clear, but he was deemed too political, perhaps too showy, and too anticlerical. The far less talented Ball was the safe and uncontroversial choice. Besides, Charcot was a neurologist, not a psychiatrist. Six years later, in 1882, Charcot would be offered a chair created especially for him, a chair in diseases of the nervous system, implying anything having to do with constitutional health. In other words, Charcot the neurologist would deal with minor mental illnesses such as anxiety, depression, neurasthenia, and of course, hysteria. Ball the psychiatrist would cover the major mental illnesses, including psychosis, mania, dementia, and general paralysis—which is to say, all forms of insanity. A serious problem with this division of labor did not escape Ball's notice.

"One is insane or one isn't," he wrote, is "totally false and made to please those inclined to view only one side of things." At the time, asylum superintendents wanted nothing to do with anything short of verifiable insanity. Epilepsy merited special treatment; hysteria none. Ball saw the risk in such a strict dichotomy, and to illustrate it he drew upon a neat analogy.

Half a century earlier, in 1833, King Louis-Philippe had instructed one of his generals, the Count de Larue, to negotiate a treaty with Morocco to determine the Algerian border. In the end, the border was drawn straight from the Mediterranean to the point where the Western Saharan desert began, then left imprecise, with both sides conceding that the land was uninhabitable. "The astuteness of the Moslems," Ball wrote, "trumped the French negotiators that day, since we know today that in this supposedly uninhabitable territory there exists a population of 600,000 souls." In other words, Larue had been had. "The case is the same," Ball went on, "in the region situated on the frontier between sanity and insanity, one which we believed to be deserted, but which contains not 600,000, but many millions of inhabitants."

Neurology and psychiatry, in these early years, played the roles of Algeria and Morocco, but with negotiators on neither side fully appreciating the layout of the terrain. Charcot's work on hysteria edged neurology away from the clinical and neuroanatomical investigations of brain illness and set the stage for Freud. The psychiatrists on his team, notably Charles Féré, helped to bridge the gap, but with Charcot's death, a chasm opened up between the two fields. Psychiatry, paradoxically, claimed biologically based insanity, including general paralysis, while neurology, by default, inherited hysteria and hypnosis.

If Ball had been cleverer, he would instead have crossed two axes to create four quadrants. In the upper right quadrant would be *mens sana in corpore sano*—a sound mind in a sound body. In the lower left, an unsound mind in a sick brain, the very definition of insanity. The other quadrants were fuzzier. The quadrant of sound minds in unsound bodies would have contained epileptics, tabetics, and if Charcot's theory held, hysterics. Who, then, would inhabit the quadrant of unsound minds within healthy brains? Does this quadrant even exist? Did Moreau de Tours visit this place while hallucinating on hashish? In other words, were neurosis and hysteria diseases of the body or afflictions of the psyche? The answer was up for grabs, and Ball's analogy was right. Someone was bound to come along, conquer this territory, and claim it as his own.

In 1885, two years removed from finishing his medical degree, Sigmund Freud won a fellowship to travel to Paris and study with Charcot at the Salpêtrière. Any aspiring neurologist of the time made the rounds of the laboratories and clinics run by the big names—Charcot in Paris, Theodor Meynert in Vienna, John Hughlings Jackson in London, and Rudolf Virchow in Berlin. Although he was supposed to be studying neuropathology, Freud could not resist the gravitational pull of Charcot's Tuesday demonstrations of hysteria. In announcing his intention to sit at the feet of the Master in Paris, Freud knew he would be burning his bridges with the neurological community in Vienna, especially with Theodor Meynert, his boss at the time, who viewed Charcot's foray into hypnotism as a gimmick. Freud went anyway. It was a difficult time for the penniless student. Years later, he recalled how he "walked about the streets, lonely and full of longing, greatly in need of a helper and protector, until the great Charcot took me into his circle." Still, he kept looking homeward. Vienna was not only where his fiancée awaited, it was also where a fascinating cold case he had been following for five years begged for some form of resolution. The patient was a handsome young woman, the case involved sex, and it had the potential to usurp the practice of psychiatry and the concept of the mind for the next century and beyond.

CHAPTER 9

THE DIFFICULT CASE
OF ANNA O.

Bᴇʀᴛʜᴀ Pappenheim was born into a household and a culture in which, as she would later say, women were considered of secondary importance to men. She would spend much of her adult life trying to remedy that situation. The year was 1859; the place, Vienna, Austria. The household was a turbulent one. Bertha's oldest sister had died before Bertha was born; the next oldest sibling died of tuberculosis. Her father, a wealthy Jewish merchant, then contracted pleurisy. She herself suffered from a variety of health problems, her treatment proving both controversial and consequential. Today she is known for two things: first, as a writer, poet, and pioneering feminist; and second, as Patient Zero of the therapeutic technique and theory of mind known as psychoanalysis. In the first of these roles, as Bertha, she is a rather significant historical figure, a crusader for women's rights, a champion of orphans, and a thorn in the side of male-dominated Orthodox Judaism. In the second, as Anna O., she provided the source material for a heroic origin story, one later revealed to be a carefully crafted myth. Although Bertha Pappenheim was a real person, a woman of great interest beyond her regrettable and counterproductive run-in with Sigmund Freud, Anna O. is an entirely fictional character created to fit a narrative. In the chasm between the biography of Bertha and that of Anna O. lies the birth of the twentieth century's most controversial yet persistent theory of mind.

Bertha was placed on a collision course with Freud in mid-July of 1880, when her father took ill while on a family vacation. The twenty-one-year-old Bertha reacted in a visceral way. She reported having hallucinations and muscle spasms. She developed coughing fits, anemia, and eating disorders. Her mental condition went downhill along with her father's physical one. In November, back home in Vienna, her father summoned the family doctor, Josef Breuer, not for himself, but for Bertha. For half a year she remained bedridden with headaches, mild paralysis, eye squint, anesthesia, hallucinations, an inability to speak, and somnambulism. Confronted with what he believed to be a psychogenic condition rather than a real disease, Breuer saw few options beyond simply listening to his patient. In an era when bloodletting, purgatives, rest cures, and water cures were testing the limits of the Hippocratic dictum to do no harm, it was a novel and sensible idea.

At first he asked Bertha to tell him a story, any story. This is how it began, with Bertha deciding to speak to Breuer exclusively in English, without ever explaining why. She would later refer to this as her "talking cure," or sometimes as "chimney sweeping." By either name, it seemed to work. She left her bed in April; then her father died and her symptoms returned. She hallucinated and refused to eat; she became difficult, uncooperative, inconsolable, unreachable. In June of 1881, Breuer packed her off to a sanatorium at the start of an extremely hot summer. She developed hydrophobia and refused to drink water. This lasted six weeks, after which Breuer resumed his treatment and managed to cure her hydrophobia by adding a twist to his method. He asked Bertha to tell him a specific story, to try to recall the precipitating incident. In order to find out what had made her so averse to drinking water, he hypnotized her in order to break down her resistance to reliving the memory. Under hypnosis, she recalled seeing a dog lapping water from an ordinary drinking glass. It disgusted her, but the very act of recalling her disgust and seeing its cause in such a mundane thing, or perhaps simply the awareness of her access to the source of a previously hidden feeling, made the symptom go away. Breuer asked her to tell more stories, each time singling out a particular symptom, sometimes using hypnosis. As Bertha revisited each precipitating incident, one by one the symptoms would disappear. During this process, she reported a sensation of being split between past and present, between real and evil. Two years after taking up her case, Breuer abruptly terminated her treatment. The reason emerged much later from a warren of secrets and lies, and it cast a shadow over the entire enterprise of psychoanalysis.

During Breuer's treatment of Bertha, he constantly violated patient confidentiality by reporting the details of her situation to his friend Sigmund Freud. To make matters worse, Freud relayed them to his fiancée, Martha Bernays, an intimate of the Pappenheim family. Therein lies the rub: Freud himself never personally treated Bertha, and his account of her case relies entirely on Breuer's recollections. Freud was fascinated, and he decided "that it was not any kind of emotional excitation that was in action behind the phenomenon of the neurosis, but habitually one of a sexual nature, whether it was a current sexual conflict or the effect of earlier sexual experiences." Breuer countered that the girl's sexual side was "extraordinarily underdeveloped." The two men fell out over this. Freud thought the sexual angle might appeal to Charcot, but "the great man showed no interest in my first outline of the subject." Freud also believed that he alone could trace the source of Bertha's troubles to her unresolved and unfulfilled sexual feelings for her father. "I had an impression," he wrote, "that it accomplished more toward an understanding of neuroses than any previous observation."

In Breuer's account, Bertha returned home and gradually recovered. Ten years later, when Freud and Breuer began to write up the case in what was to become the kernel of psychoanalytic theory, they changed Bertha's name by moving her initials back one letter in the alphabet. Bertha Pappenheim became Anna O. In their monograph, published in 1893, and in their subsequent book *Studies on Hysteria* (1895), Freud and Breuer pronounced her treatment a "complete success." But was any of it true?

According to records and correspondence, Bertha did not recover when her sessions with Breuer ended in June of 1882. She entered a sanatorium again on July 12 and stayed almost through November, stricken with a neuralgia brought on by an addiction to the morphine Breuer had been prescribing for her. Breuer had also sedated her with chloral hydrate, a dilution of trichloroethanol, the active ingredient in knockout drops. Chloral was a hypnotic and addictive antianxiety sedative popular with the upper and middle classes. At the sanatorium, all efforts to end her addictions proved unsuccessful at first, and Bertha continued to display neurological symptoms, leading to recurring stays at the facility over a five-year period, each time with a diagnosis of unremitting hysteria. In short, Bertha came out of Breuer's care far worse off than when she had entered it. Instead of being the complete success Breuer would later lay claim to, his interventions had been a disastrous failure. As Freud wrote to Martha Bernays, "Bertha is once again in the sanatorium in Gross-Enzersdorf, I believe. Breuer is constantly talking about her, says he wishes she were dead so that the poor woman could be free of her suffering. He says she will never be well again, that she is completely shattered." Ten years later, though, both Breuer and Freud would blithely refer to Breuer's treatment as a "cure."

There are conflicting accounts of why Breuer ended Bertha's treatment. At one session, Breuer supposedly found "Anna" in a state of distress, suffering from acute abdominal pain. When questioned, she said, "Now the child I have from Dr. Breuer is coming." Breuer fled the scene, fobbed off his patient on a colleague, and took his wife on a holiday to Vienna, where they conceived a child. Anna had apparently developed passionate feelings for Breuer. Freud was right: the emotional excitation behind her neurosis was sexual.

This story got a great deal of mileage over the years, going a long way toward discrediting Breuer and making Freud seem like a savant. It had one drawback: it never happened. There was no affair, and the pregnancy was purely hysterical. Breuer did not flee in a panic, and his daughter was born three months before the alleged incident took place. The pregnancy scare, the almost slapstick flight for the nearest door— all of it was a gaudily embellished fiction authored by Freud himself, and disseminated by his biographer Ernest Jones. It was a deliberate and self-serving lie, concocted to bolster the theory of the sexual origin of neurosis and to discredit Breuer.

But the deception goes even deeper. All of the symptoms Breuer recorded, leading up to Bertha's institutionalization, went unnoticed by anyone else in her family. Breuer personally witnessed none of them. The paralysis, the eye problems, the inability to speak, the fainting, even the blindness—all of them were merely reported by the patient to Breuer. In 1882, he conceded as much, saying, "I recount the matter as I learned it from her." Her only witnessed symptom was a persistent cough: "I first visited the patient at the end of November on account of her cough. It was a clear case of *tussis hysterica*; however, I classified the patient immediately as mentally ill on account of her strange behavior."

Breuer was a poor Svengali. Freud was a brilliant one who did not have to manipulate his patients; he only had to manipulate their stories. He would develop his theories of the Oedipus complex, infantile sexuality, penis envy, repression, and transference, all based on case histories of patients in his Vienna practice, and much as he did with Bertha Pappenheim, he would alter facts to suit the theory. In doing so, he would leave behind his neurological training to promote mind over brain in his interpretation of mental phenomena. Oscar Wilde once remarked that there was no fog in London until J. M. W. Turner painted it. In the same way, there was no unconscious or preconscious in Vienna until Freud described them.

Freud kept a copy of André Brouillet's *A Clinical Lesson* in his examination room in Vienna, and later in his London office. Though he had studied with Meynert in Vienna and with Virchow in Berlin, he said of Charcot, "No one else has affected me in the same way." Freud refined Charcot's theory of hysteria to avoid the ridicule heaped on the Paris School, and he adopted the method of free association in place of hypnosis (or mesmerism). He eventually dropped the terms hysteria and hystero-epilepsy, substituting neurosis and psychoneurosis in their place. As for degeneration theory, he never had any use for it, not surprisingly given his own second-class status as a Jew within the Viennese medical establishment. In his otherwise laudatory eulogy of Charcot, Freud felt obliged to point out one shortcoming: "So greatly did Charcot overestimate heredity as a causative agent that he left no room for the acquisition of nervous illness. To syphilis he merely allotted a modest place among the 'agents provocateurs.'" This was in 1893, well before the connection of syphilis to psychosis was an established fact, and it reveals the essential incompatibility of Charcot's degeneration theory and Fournier's belief in the syphilitic origins of insanity. Yet Freud never quite abandoned Charcot's belief in a "dynamic lesion," nor did he completely reject the role of heredity.

"Generally speaking," Freud wrote, "our civilization is built up on the suppression of instincts." An unavoidable side effect of this suppression comes in the form of two nervous disorders, distinguishable only by careful clinical observation. One of them is neurosis, the other psychoneurosis. By neurosis, Freud meant various forms of mental and physical unease previously grouped under the term *neurasthenia* by the American neurologist George Miller Beard. Though the condition appears toxic, to use Freud's term, it is merely a societal by-product and not hereditary. In other words, neurosis is not an organic illness. The symptoms, Freud wrote, point to triggering events in the patient's sexual life—or lack of one. "We may therefore regard the sexual factor as the essential one in the causation of the neuroses proper," he concluded. Freud's psychoneuroses differ very little in appearance from the neuroses. The symptoms, including hysteria and obsessive compulsion, are mostly psychogenic. They arise in "unconscious complexes" of a sexual nature. "They spring from the sexual needs of people who are unsatisfied and represent for them a kind of substitutive satisfaction." But psychoneuroses are not generated entirely within the mind, according to Freud. They are inherited and thus are of the body. This is how Freud slyly revived Charcot's notion of a dynamic or functional lesion. Psychoneuroses are organic, not purely psychogenic. "We must therefore view all factors which impair sexual life, suppress its activity or distort its aims," he concluded, "as being pathogenic factors in the psychoneuroses as well." The distinction betrays his debt to Charcot, and also a disinclination to share credit with him.

Freud attributed neuroses to "a quota of affect and a sum of excitation." He claimed that this quota "possesses all the characteristics of a quantity (though we have no means of measuring it), which is capable of increase, diminution, displacement, and discharge, and which is spread over the memory-traces of ideas somewhat as an electric charge is spread over the surface of a body. This hypothesis . . . can be applied in the same sense as physicists apply the hypothesis of a flow of electric fluid. It is provisionally justified by its utility in coordinating and explaining a great variety of psychical states." Here Freud conjures a vague somatic source of neurotic symptoms, justifying it solely on the basis of its utility in explaining everything, obviating the need for either verification or the search for alternative and verifiable explanations.

Whenever you read about Freud, you will find no middle ground. Those who write about him either believe he was a genius who made some mistakes, yet still reshaped psychiatry and our awareness of the human psyche permanently for the better, or consider him a great and persuasive writer who nonetheless was a scientific bumbler, a prevaricator, and an appallingly abusive physician. He is credited with demystifying hysteria by providing it with an etiology and a cure. In reality, he did neither. When he turned away from neurology to pursue psychotherapy, and in particular to delve into the neuroses of an urban upper-class clientele, he left behind the search for the structural causes of mental illnesses and entered a realm in which the scientific method did not—indeed, could not—apply. Freed from the burden of scientific proof, he theorized freely, much as Franz Joseph Gall did about the localization of brain function when he correlated the behaviors of individuals with the phrenological bumps on their skulls. Gall got some things right—brain function is indeed localized—and so did Freud—sex is indeed a factor in neurosis. But empirical proof is less interesting than metaphors, origin stories, heroic tales of discovery, and therapeutic breakthroughs.

In proposing a "sexual factor" in the origins of neurosis, Freud hardly went out on a limb. When we consider all of the possible causes of self-doubt, self-loathing, second-guessing, and anxiety in the human condition, sex is an obvious candidate. But over time, the concomitants of sex have changed dramatically, with death and disease no longer looming over the enterprise as they once did. In Freud's era, in almost all cases of neurosis, and notably in the cases of hysteria he wrote about, syphilis loomed large. It provided a compelling justification for the suppression of natural and even salutary sexual behavior, and this internalized dread, at least according to Freud, erupted in the form of neurological symptoms and abnormal behavior. Freud was generally careful to limit his clientele to patients with disturbed minds in otherwise healthy bodies—with one exception. He could not avoid syphilis, because as Fournier had already discovered, syphilis overshadowed everything, even insanity.

CHAPTER 10

THE DEVIL AND
ADRIAN LEVERKÜHN

*I take it, no fool ever made a bargain for his soul with the devil:
the fool is too much of a fool, or the devil too much of a devil—I
don't know which.*

—Joseph Conrad, *Heart of Darkness*

To Gustav Mahler's dismay, the Austrian premiere of Richard Strauss's opera *Salome*, featuring the erotic Dance of the Seven Veils, a suicide, a beheading, necrophilia, and some other unseemly plot turns, with Strauss himself conducting, proved too steamy for the burghers of Vienna and had to be relocated to the provincial city of Graz. Faced with such prudishness, Mahler, the director of the Vienna Opera, wondered if he could stand to keep the job much longer. Yet the relocated production came off beautifully. All of the big names in music were there—Arnold Schönberg, Giacomo Puccini, Alban Berg, and a young composer named Adrian Leverkühn.

In many ways, Leverkühn was the most important of the group, although his presence was something of an accident. He had stopped off in Graz en route to a brothel in Bratislava, then known as Pressburg, with the sole purpose of contracting syphilis from a woman named Esmerelda. On his way, he seized the opportunity to see the incomparable Strauss conduct his new work. Leverkühn dreamed of one day standing on the same podium, and he was taking the steps to make it happen. After Salome declared her love to the severed head of John the Baptist and was crushed to death under the soldiers' shields, Leverkühn went off to lose his virginity to a prostitute. It was May of 1906. The date is important.

Strauss's *Salome* was rooted in scandal. The story concerns Herod's daughter, who as a reward for performing a dance for the high officials of Galilee is granted a wish. Fulfilling a grudge held by her mother, Salome asks for the head of John the Baptist on a platter. The biblical version is sordid enough, but Strauss chose to adapt from Oscar Wilde's controversial 1891 play instead of from scripture. Wilde had spent two years in Reading Gaol for homosexual acts, and had himself contracted syphilis from a prostitute while a student at Oxford. He died in 1900 at the age of forty-six from cerebral meningitis caused by an inner ear infection, although at the time the death was attributed to syphilis. Whatever the truth, the stigma remains: Wilde was an artistic genius who suffered from an incurable disease, and it cut him down in the prime of life. Not so coincidentally, this was precisely the fate to which Adrian Leverkühn aspired, and in the end it was the one he achieved.

Leverkühn was aiming for the jackpot of neurological conditions: general paresis of the insane. He harbored no illusions. He knew how Maupassant and Baudelaire had died. Why would he want to suffer the same fate? Why would anyone? We know the answer because we have a record of Leverkühn's internal dialogue on the matter—because Adrian Leverkühn is not a real person, but rather the protagonist of Thomas Mann's *Doctor Faustus*, a retelling of the Faust legend repurposed as an allegory of Germany's twentieth-century decline and self-destruction.

The origins of *Doctor Faustus* are detailed in Mann's notebooks and in a retrospective work called *The Story of a Novel*, in which he freely reveals his source material for the life of Leverkühn. The visit to the brothel, the seemingly intentional courting of syphilis, the bursts of creativity, and the ultimate descent into madness—all come from the biography of Friedrich Nietzsche. Nietzsche wrote most of his major works during the late 1880s, three of them in his annus mirabilis of 1888, all the while contending with migraine, toothaches, and digestive problems. This astounding period of creativity ended in catastrophe. As the story goes, Nietzsche rushed to the defense of a horse being whipped in the central square of Turin, then collapsed in a state of delirium and was whisked off to an asylum. He was diagnosed with general paralysis, but lived another ten years, casting some doubt, at least in retrospect, on that diagnosis. What had inspired and nourished Nietzsche's high-level productivity in the midst of debilitating, humiliating physical anguish? Mann thought he knew. For him, Genius was a small, remote, wind-buffeted, and sparsely populated island in the middle of a sea of Madness.

According to Plato, artists must be out of their minds when the muse speaks through them. "A poet," he wrote, "is a light and winged and sacred thing, and is unable ever to indite until he has been inspired and put out of his senses, and his mind is no longer in him; . . . it is not they who utter these words of great price, when they are out of their wits, but that it is God himself who speaks and addresses us through them." In time, poets and artists tired of being regarded as empty vessels. For Marcel Proust, the gods had nothing to do with it. Confining himself to bed with illnesses imagined and real, he insisted that "infirmity alone makes us take notice and learn, and enables us to analyze processes which we would otherwise know nothing about." Guy de Maupassant simply stated: "Great minds that are healthy are never considered geniuses, while this sublime qualification is lavished on brains that are often inferior but are slightly touched with madness."

Mann wanted to have it both ways. "What was it," he wrote in his notebook, "that drove Nietzsche into the uncharted wastes of thought, that whipped him upward into those heights in torture and made him die an agonizing death upon the cross of thought? It was his fate—and that fate was his genius. But this genius has yet another name. That name is: disease." Mann had already delved into the murky depths of disease in *The Magic Mountain* (tuberculosis) and *Death in Venice* (cholera). But this novel would be different. The disease would be an active character in the story, an abetting agent of the Devil, and the Fifth Business in a dramatic allegory. In order to create a convincing portrait of this character, Mann would have to learn everything there was to know about one particular disease, circa 1940. He had to get the dates correct in order to use Leverkühn's life as a parable. *Doctor Faustus* would not only be a bildungsroman of the life of Adrian Leverkühn, but a bildungsroman of syphilis itself.

Readers in 1947, when the novel was published, would have been better prepared than the average reader of today to fully appreciate it. A passing familiarity with music theory helps, but an intimate knowledge of medical history, in particular the succession of events leading to a cure for syphilis, is essential. These events unfolded over the span of a remarkable decade, not coincidentally the most important decade of Adrian Leverkühn's life.

Leverkühn contracts syphilis in 1906, seeks treatment in 1910, and has a dialogue with the Devil in 1912, during which he enters into a Faustian bargain. He agrees to forswear love in return for twenty-four years of artistic genius. He then goes on to reshape the world of classical music. After a gradual deterioration of his health, he succumbs to syphilitic madness, much like Maupassant, and dies in 1940. These dates correspond closely with key events in the history of syphilis. In 1905, its cause was isolated and identified. In 1906, a blood test was developed. In 1910, the first cure for syphilis was marketed, and in 1912, the year of Leverkühn's meeting with the Devil, neurosyphilis as a diagnostic entity was born when general paresis of the insane was proven to be a late-stage syphilitic infection.

It is impossible to understand the structure of the novel without appreciating these developments in some detail, or the singular event that made them all possible: a chance discovery by an eighteen-year-old chemistry student, briefly home from college on Easter break. This remarkable discovery would produce several seemingly unrelated outcomes, including a revolution in fashion known as the Mauve Decade, a synthetic drug to treat malaria, an antidote to cyanide poisoning, and the very first chemotherapy, which also happened to be a cure for syphilis.

In 1853, William Henry Perkin spent his Easter vacation in the laboratory he had built in the attic space of his parents' East London home, continuing an experiment assigned by his teacher at the Royal College of Chemistry, August Wilhelm von Hofmann. In attempting to develop a synthetic version of quinine, the cure for malaria, von Hofmann had been tinkering with a derivative of coal tar called aniline. Quinine, like most remedies that had to be carefully extracted from naturally occurring substances, was labor intensive and quite expensive to produce, and greatly in demand. A synthetic version of it would have been a godsend. Coal tar, by contrast, a combination of carbon, oxygen, hydrogen, nitrogen, and a little sulfur, is an abundant industrial by-product. It contains naphtha, the substance used by Charles Macintosh to create the first waterproof fabric for the raincoat that now bears his name. Naphtha also contains benzene, and this gives rise to aniline. Aniline has the unique property of yielding vibrant colors when mixed with other compounds, and over that Easter weekend, young Perkin managed to produce a brilliant purple while testing the solubility of aniline. Quite accidentally, he came up with a reliable and stunning dye for textiles. Years later, he reflected back on the fateful day:

> I was endeavoring to convert an artificial base into the natural alkaloid quinine, but my experiment, instead of yielding the colorless quinine, gave a reddish powder. With a desire to understand this particular result, a different base of more simple construction was selected, viz. aniline, and in this case obtained a perfectly black product. This was purified and dried, and when digested with spirits of wine gave the mauve dye.

Recognizing the importance of the discovery, Perkin built a lab in his backyard to keep von Hofmann off the scent, patented his formula, and explored ways to mass-produce the stuff. He called the dye mauve, after the flower, and named the color Tyrian purple. Scientists called it mauveine. It was the first synthetic dye, and it became wildly popular.

Perkin and Sons dye works opened in 1857 in West London. It would spearhead the emergence of a thriving dyeing industry in England and would make Perkin a rich man. But a lack of foresight by

British lawmakers, specifically their failure to protect and enforce patents for hundreds of new synthetic chemicals, led to a collapse of the industry in England and its rebirth in Germany two decades later, spearheaded by scientists who had learned their techniques while working for Perkin. This would have far-reaching effects well beyond the textile industry. In 1865, a German company got a contract to provide gas street lighting to the Grand Duchy of Baden. As a by-product, the company found itself with an abundance of coal tar. It soon diversified into the dyeing business as BASF, the Baden Aniline and Soda Factory. Today it is the largest chemical manufacturer in the world.

Experimentation with coal tar derivatives, meaning aniline-based compounds, led to important applications beyond dyeing blue jeans. It led directly to the invention of urethane and polyurethane, as well as herbicides, antioxidants, and even painkillers such as Tylenol (acetaminophen). Other by-products included fertilizers and rocket fuel. Aniline dyes were also found to have an affinity for human tissue. Different dyes seek out different kinds of cells, and this facilitated the discovery of the neuron and of the cell layers of the cerebral cortex in the 1870s, both previously invisible under a microscope. Rather fortuitously and unexpectedly, dye compounds made from aniline were also found to be toxic to certain microorganisms. One of the more lethal dyes, methylene blue, turned out to be the antimalarial drug von Hofmann had been searching for, and the benefits of aniline dyes did not end there.

In 1905, two German scientists, a protozoologist named Fritz Schaudinn and a dermatologist named Erich Hoffmann, using a variant of methylene blue, discovered a tiny corkscrew-shaped bacterium of the genus *Treponema* in tissue samples taken from syphilitic patients. Protozoology is the archaic term applied to the study of protozoa, primitive one-celled creatures (the current term is protistology). Schaudinn had been on the hunt for malaria-causing organisms for years. He believed he was zeroing in on a particularly nasty malarial germ when he was called away from his research to verify the work of one of his underlings. The man claimed to have found the bug responsible for four infectious diseases, including syphilis. This had been a holy grail in protozoology for decades. The challenge was twofold: first, isolate a candidate microbe; then prove it alone had to be the right pathogen. Such a bug had been hypothesized for syphilis, but in the teeming world of microorganisms, it had eluded dozens of pursuers. This new claim was no different, Schaudinn discovered. It was another dead end, but while looking for this chimera in his colleague's samples, he saw something else.

It appeared under the microscope as little more than an apparition, a wormlike shadow almost indistinguishable from its background. Most of his colleagues had missed it, but Schaudinn recognized it as belonging to the genus of spiral-shaped bacteria: *Treponema*. A similar type of organism, as it happens, causes leprosy and Lyme disease. But this one was different. He called it a *spirochete* because of its corkscrew shape; also *Treponema pallidum*, or the pale treponeme. In *Doctor Faustus*, Thomas Mann refers to these shadows as "the flagellants," because of their whiplike tails. He also personified them as the "small folk." Schaudinn found them in abundance on samples from syphilitic skin chancres with no exceptions. But open sores contain lots of microbes, so this proved nothing. He had to look deeper to see if he could find spirochetes in the swollen lymph glands of fully developed cases. Hofmann provided the tissue samples, and Schaudinn tried every dye at his disposal. His unique talent consisted of rooting through a landscape of microorganisms and picking out the shapes of things that did not belong in healthy tissue. He found one.

In 1905, Schaudinn presented his evidence to the Berlin medical society. He claimed to have found the grail, but his audience was not impressed. The president of the society brought the proceedings to a premature end by saying, "Herewith the discussion is closed until *another* cause of syphilis is brought to our attention." But Schaudinn soon had the last laugh thanks to a recent technological advance: dark-field microscopy. It works in the way the morning sun, streaming at a low angle through a window, will reveal a coating of dust particles on a polished floor. In normal lighting, they would go unnoticed. In the same way, if a bright light is shone almost horizontally across a microscope slide, many things previously undetectable are revealed by their shadows. Using dark-field microscopy, anyone could see Schaudinn's spirochetes, even with a classroom microscope, and his claim was quickly confirmed. In every slide preparation of syphilitic tissue, the spirochetes stood out as plain as day. When the two researchers returned to the medical society a few weeks later, they received a standing ovation.

The discovery of the spirochete explained everything. It allowed teams of researchers to narrow their sights on the same target. With the cause of syphilis now revealed, research into the disease fell into step behind typhus, cholera, and tuberculosis, and onto the next big challenge: having identified its cause, how could you tell whether someone was a carrier? With syphilis, this was especially important, because it almost always entered a latent, non-symptomatic phase in which the patient could delude himself or herself into thinking it had simply gone away. But whether the mind is aware of the presence of the disease or not, the immune system will react in a very specific way. It "knows" in the sense that it automatically mounts a defense through a system of killer cells. Immunologists at that time were just discovering the existence of these cells, and just how ingeniously evolution had equipped mammals to ward off infection through them.

In 1901, a Belgian bacteriologist named Jules Bordet discovered an important property of blood. It involved something called serum, the part of the blood left over when the white and red cells, along with clotting agents, are removed with a centrifuge. The remaining liquid is mostly water along with a few other special things having special properties. Bordet uncovered a curious fact: the serum of one animal can break down red blood cells belonging to an animal of a different species. The process of bursting the walls of these red corpuscles is called *hemolysis*, a reaction caused by a protein in the serum known as *complement*.

Going further, Bordet and Dr. Paul Ehrlich of the Pasteur Institute showed that complement goes hand in hand with antibodies to bind up antigens (anything recognized by the immune system as an invader). Antigens goad the immune system into concocting a specific cocktail of complement and antibodies to fight off the infection. This discovery provided the basis for blood tests, still in use, to identify various bacterial infections. Specifically, it led to the Wassermann blood test for syphilis.

The original version of the test, as developed by the bacteriologist August von Wassermann in 1906, required a great deal of technical skill to execute properly and was far from perfect. Red blood cells from an animal (at first guinea pigs were used) were added to a patient's serum. In the presence of syphilis, the extract in the serum fixes the complement, meaning it binds with the remaining complement and prevents hemolysis from occurring. If the complement did not become bound up by the extract, it would be able to break down the red blood cells, and the mixture would turn pink. In the presence of antibodies to syphilis, it would stay blood red.

Although the test fell short of always detecting the *presence* of syphilis, it more reliably indicated its *absence* (a "negative" Wassermann test). This was crucial. Wassermann also applied his test to cerebrospinal fluid as a way to confirm the presence of syphilis organisms and associated antibodies and to make a diagnosis of general paresis. Medical science now had a reliable blood test, one capable of distinguishing a mental illness caused by a brain disease from one brought about by psychic distress. The repercussions of this went far beyond the treatment of infectious disease, because syphilis, unlike tuberculosis or malaria, could produce neurosis, psychosis, and mania—behaviors previously written off as hysterical. A blood test for general paresis of the insane gave psychiatry a firm foothold in medicine. It was its one and only true diagnosis. The Wassermann test also acted as a springboard for Sigmund Freud and his small but very active society of psychotherapists. By leaving all nonsyphilitic psychoses untethered to objective observation, it gave Freud the leeway he needed to lay down a psychosexual theory of human behavior rooted in the unconscious. The gap between neurology and psychiatry began to widen.

In the wake of Schaudinn's brilliant discovery, the investigation of the spirochete continued at a rapid pace. Paul Ehrlich, having pioneered complement fixation tests, now set aside his research into vaccines to delve further into the properties of aniline dyes, and in particular one called methylene blue.

Methylene blue was first synthesized in 1876 by Heinrich Caro, a German chemist who learned his trade by making mauveine in Manchester, England. One of his other discoveries was the first synthetic indigo dye. But methylene blue was more than just a dye. It later turned out to be an effective antimalarial drug, a treatment for psoriasis, and a cure for urinary tract infections. Used as a stain in microscope preparations, it revealed the axon tails of neurons, opening up the field of cellular neuroscience. It also had an uncanny ability to seek out selected cells and in some instances destroy them. Ehrlich decided to see whether he could find other dyes capable of seeking out specific pathogens and delivering a toxin directly to the target. In the tradition begun by William Perkin, he started with aniline as a base and ultimately chose arsenic as the toxin. He mixed hundreds of compounds and tested them on rabbits inoculated with spirochetes. It took months of failed attempts, followed by retrials of failed attempts, before one compound, the sixth chemical in the sixth series he tested, passed muster. He called it compound 606 and marketed it under the trade name Salvarsan. A highly unstable yellow powder intended to be carefully mixed into an injectable solution, it was the first antibacterial chemotherapy, and it quickly became the most prescribed drug in the world. It was dubbed Dr. Ehrlich's Magic Bullet.

The discovery of the cause of, a diagnostic test for, and a cure for syphilis, all within a five-year period, constitutes one of the most profound accomplishments in the history of medicine. Over the course of four centuries, syphilis had been a widespread and deadly scourge. Unlike plagues of influenza, cholera, or Black Death, which come and go like comets, syphilis was a constant and insidious presence. By some estimates, it affected a tenth, maybe up to almost a fifth of the population at any given time. It didn't kill everyone who got it. Sometimes the immune system could fight it off. Only 20 percent of cases progressed as far as tabes or general paresis. Now it could be detected and stopped at the first sign.

In 1912, six years into his infection, Adrian Leverkühn's tertiary-stage syphilis symptoms begin to appear. "Afflicted creature that I am," he writes, "I had lain in the dark all the day with tedious head ache, having often to retch and vomit, as comes with severe visitations." Somewhat delirious, he becomes aware of "a piercing cold, as if one sat in a room warmed against winter and abruptly a window burst open upon the frost." And with that cold wind, like Marley's ghost, the Devil himself enters the room.

Faustian bargains have a rich literary history, as do fantastical intellectual dialogues plopped into the middle of wide-ranging tales. In Mann's novel, the give-and-take centers on genius, madness, and illness. "You, dear boy," says the Devil, "knew well enough what you lacked, and held true to your German nature when you made your journey and, *salva venia*, caught the French measles." To close the deal, he says, the composer need only agree to give up something—hardly anything, really. Just love. In return, the Devil will offer twenty-four years of inspired musical creativity, punctuated only by the indisposition attendant upon his disease. Leverkühn will die mad, but he will achieve glory.

Forswearing love had its literary heyday in the 1800s, often in characters motivated by nobility of the soul. In real life, the motivation was often based on a healthy respect for contagion. Guy de Maupassant, the unrepentant womanizer who once, wanting to impress Flaubert, brought a witness to a bordello to certify ejaculation in six consecutive couplings within the span of an hour, consulted his own doctor about the prospect of marrying his cousin. Because of his active syphilis, the doctor advised against it. In the end, he never married.

"You may in time eliminate it from your system," says the doctor in Sir Arthur Conan Doyle's "The Third Generation," to a man due to be wed in a few days, "but many years must pass before you can think of marriage." The same advice goes out to Georges Dupont in Eugène Brieux's play *Les Avariés* (*Damaged Goods*). "This disease, even when it is all but suppressed, still lies below the surface ready to break out again.

Taken all around, it is serious enough to make it an infamy to expose a woman to it in order to avoid even the greatest inconvenience." But in the story and the play, cautionary tales both, the doctor's advice is ignored, and love is not forsworn. In Conan Doyle's story, the man commits suicide; in Brieux's play, a plague descends on the man's family. In that light, what did Adrian Leverkühn have to lose?

"The proper planets met together in the house of the Scorpion," the Devil tells him, "just as a most well-instructed Master Dürer drew it for his medicinal broadsheet, and there arrived in German lands the small delicate folk, living corkscrews, our dear guests from the Indies, the flagellants . . ." Here Mann alludes to ancient history, the return of Columbus's ships with spirochetes on board. "I mean the flagellates, the tiny imperceptible sort, which have flails, like our pale Venus—the *spirochaeta pallida*, that is the true sort." Mann employs the spirochetes to establish the framework for a key episode in the novel. Leverkühn visits two doctors in 1910, the first year of the availability of Dr. Ehrlich's compound 606. Before he has a chance to follow up on his initial consultation, the first doctor dies mysteriously, and the second one is hauled off by the police. Leverkühn, suspecting nothing and lacking the motivation to find yet another doctor, gives up. Later the Devil explains how he had disposed of both men. "Dispatched, dispatched . . . once they had set matters on the right path. . . . In no case could we permit the provocation by quick- and quack-salvery to continue." The reference, far more obscure today than it was when Mann wrote it, suggests that Leverkühn had started on a regimen of vigorous rubbing of syphilitic sores with mercurial ointments and the very painful injections of Ehrlich's Salvarsan. Mann's contemporaries would have understood the reference. An editor today would insist on a footnote.

In the year of Leverkühn's meeting with the devil, Hideyo Noguchi, a Japanese bacteriologist working at the Rockefeller Institute for Medical Research, set out to find a cure for yellow fever. He failed. He also tried to develop a skin test for syphilis similar to the tuberculosis skin test. He injected an extract of syphilis just under the skin of five hundred subjects, many of them in institutions for the developmentally delayed. Facing criticism and outrage over human experimentation, the institute pointed out that Dr. Noguchi had tested the procedure on himself first. Noguchi later tested positive for syphilis. A careless and impatient researcher, he tended to fail at most things he attempted—with one notable exception. In the same year of 1912, Noguchi detected the presence of spirochetes in the brains of patients with general paresis of the insane.

The finding produced a seismic change in psychiatry. Antoine Bayle and Alfred Fournier had been right all along. As had long been suspected but was until now unproven, insanity could indeed be brought about by a true brain disease. Maupassant and Gilles de la Tourette had died of syphilis; perhaps Mr. Kurtz had as well. With this singular discovery, the degeneration theory of neurosis as well as Alfred Fournier's parasyphilis gave way to a newly named entity: *neurosyphilis*, a spirochetic infiltration of the brain and nervous system. It also brought Noguchi's life and career to a somewhat pathetic end. He died insane in 1928, having never bothered to seek treatment for his self-inoculation with syphilis. The spirochetes had gone into his brain.

Had Thomas Mann not become a writer, he would probably have become a physician. He read the medical literature very carefully, consulted with several physicians while researching his novel, and put together a timeline tracing the history of syphilis from the Old World to the New. Some of the medical and historical details Mann wedged into his novel were common knowledge in his time. Much of it, though, was arcane and jargon-laden; a neurology resident or infectious disease specialist at a top hospital today would have a difficult time following the Devil's allusions. Still, the accurate details of neurosyphilis Mann places in the Devil's mouth are worthy of a textbook of neurology. So is the description of Leverkühn's insane gaze: "I realized that it was caused by the pupils, which were not perfectly round, but somewhat irregularly lengthened and always stayed the same size, as if they were not subject to the influence of any change in light." These are the Argyll Robertson pupils characteristic of neurosyphilis. To write his novel, Mann had to become a philologist, a musicologist, and a syphilologist. To understand his novel, his readers would have to do the same.

Mann was both conscientious and imaginative about medical details. In *Doctor Faustus*, he imparts intentionality to the vector of a disease. Insentient spirochetes become willful actors. "I do assure you that it is indeed as if some certain of these small folk may have a passion for the uppermost," the Devil says, "a special estimation for the region of the head, the meninges, the dura mater, the tentorium, and the pia." The insinuation is difficult to dismiss: syphilis germs have minds of their own, they are devious and conniving, and they sometimes disguise themselves via a clever imitation of other germs. And in syphilis he chose a glorified precursor of artistic genius, one combining suffering and sensuality, love and death.

Mann knew something else in 1940 no one could have known in 1912: once syphilis had invaded the depths of the nervous system to produce a diagnosis of tabes dorsalis or general paresis, Salvarsan was of no use. In fact it could be lethal. He also knew of a possible remedy, a fever treatment discovered in 1917, but he left any mention of it out of his novel. After all, once Leverkühn had tasted the rewards of his pact with the Devil, he was too intent on artistic creation to worry about his health. He was not looking for a way out of the deal he had made, even though by the 1920s there was one available to him.

In 1884, a year before Sigmund Freud set off for Paris to have his life changed by Charcot, he slogged through tedious workdays in the clinic of Professor Max Leidesdorf in Vienna, doing the drudgework at this exclusive spa, and compensating for his dimming prospects with an increasing dependence on cocaine. He shared the experience (but not the cocaine) with a close colleague, Julius Wagner-Jauregg. The two had a lot in common. They had been born a year apart, attended the University of Vienna, and studied medicine with an interest in psychiatry. For a brief time they even worked together in the same lab at Salomon Stricker's Institute of General and Experimental Pathology. When Freud left for Paris, Wagner-Jauregg remained at the Leidesdorf Clinic and eventually became first assistant. Three years later, with Freud back in Vienna and floundering in his private practice, Wagner-Jauregg had his first breakthrough: a woman whose psychosis was cured by a high fever. Wagner-Jauregg was not the first person to notice the curative potential of fever, or the first to induce fever as a treatment, but he would be the first to use malarial fever specifically to target syphilitic dementia. He called it pyrotherapy.

Before he tried malaria, Wagner-Jauregg experimented with tuberculin, an extract of the tuberculosis bacilli. With little to lose, he used it on paretics as early as 1900, well before the discovery of the spirochete, and when a diagnosis of general paresis was a death sentence. His treatment induced a raging fever, and in too many cases the patient died. His breakthrough had to wait until 1917, when he ran into a colleague who was treating a soldier struggling with vivax malaria, one of the five kinds of malarial bugs afflicting humans. The fever it produces recurs on a forty-eight-hour cycle, precisely the predictability and control Wagner-Jauregg was looking for. He asked for a sample of the soldier's blood. He then inoculated nine paretics, knowing he could bring them out of the fever cycle using quinine, but also knowing the spirochetes would kill them within a year or two if he did nothing. As a chaser to the quinine, he added a supplement of Neosalvarsan, the second generation of Ehrlich's compound 606. In the follow-up, one patient died, six improved, and two went into hospice, probably doomed. Of the six best cases, four relapsed, but the other two were cured and discharged. This set Wagner-Jauregg onto a series of trials, with no shortage of subjects. At the time, general paresis accounted for 10 percent of all asylum admissions, and the asylums could offer nothing in the way of a cure. He published his results in 1921. Out of two hundred cases of general paresis treated with malarial fever, about a quarter were cured, discharged, and eventually went back to work.

Julius Wagner-Jauregg wandered into the realm of biological psychiatry when he took a leap of faith back in 1899, with no confirmation of the syphilitic origin of general paresis and without any proof that syphilis was a bacterial infection. For his efforts, he was awarded a Nobel Prize in 1927, one of only three ever granted to a psychiatrist. The prize committee acknowledged his additional realization that treating general paresis would require not just one fever, but a succession of them. Once the malaria was set in motion, the patient merely had to outlive the spirochetes and the malaria for a week to ten days. The fever cure, using the same strain of malaria Wagner-Jauregg first employed during World War I, would remain in use for three decades, only to be rendered obsolete by the ultimate magic bullet, the medicine that would replace Neosalvarsan.

Not long after the publication of *Doctor Faustus*, a chance discovery presented the means of ending syphilis once and for all, but in a sad commentary on a peculiar strain of Calvinist sentiment that had settled over the industrialized world, it would not be the end of syphilis.

CHAPTER 11

SEX AND THE NEW WOMAN

Mabel Dodge, heiress from Buffalo, patroness of the arts, and a supporter of the infamous Armory Show of 1913, was depressed. This was not unusual for her. Alternately fidgety and faint, she wondered how to get out of yet another mess she had gotten herself in. Freshly married to a successful architect, Edwin Dodge, newly installed in a lavish apartment on lower Fifth Avenue, just twenty-three years of age, with all of the benefits of privilege, she still agonized over the cards she had been dealt, and in particular her choice of a husband. Her track record had not been stellar. After graduating from college, she married a man who did not meet her parents' approval. Then she began an affair with her father's physician, a prominent Buffalo surgeon, from whom she contracted a case of the clap. "I had never heard this word before, and I have never heard it since," she confessed. Her parents packed her off to Europe to put an end to her affair, and she made the acquaintance of an artistic circle including Gertrude Stein, Alice B. Toklas, and André Gide. She had a son by her husband, but the husband died soon after, stranding her in Europe. After two halfhearted suicide attempts, she returned to New York, married Edwin, and regretted it by the time the ink on the thank-you notes was dry. Pathologically bored and still borderline suicidal, she consulted a psychiatrist. Naturally, she chose the best one in town.

Bernard Sachs, or Barney to his friends, came of the same family that created the firm of Goldman Sachs. His credentials were impressive. A graduate of Harvard University, he studied medicine in Strasbourg, France, and then made the rounds of the most prominent clinics in Europe, including a stint with Charcot in Paris and with Theodor Meynert in Vienna, where he shared a lab bench with Sigmund Freud. Sachs and Freud coauthored two research papers on neuropathology, and they remained in touch, albeit infrequently, for the rest of their lives. Sachs went on to achieve the kind of success Freud despaired of ever attaining. He set up a successful private practice, consulted at various Jewish hospitals, and discovered Tay-Sachs disease, a genetic neuro-destructive disorder with a high incidence among Ashkenazi Jews. By the time Mabel Dodge called upon him, he was the president of the American Neurological Association, the publisher of *The Journal of Nervous and Mental Disease*, the head of a neurology inpatient clinic at Mount Sinai Hospital, and the most celebrated psychiatrist in all of New York.

Sachs was in his fifties when he met Mabel, and he was strictly old school, meaning he had hung out a shingle as a neuropsychiatrist with a specialty in neurological disease, but not necessarily in neuroses per se. As well as anyone at the time, he understood the mind's relationship to the brain, but not to any other organ. In other words, he was not a sexologist. His prescriptions for his highly neurotic clientele eschewed the exotic and clung to simple common sense. "Take long vigorous walks," he said to Mabel, "and eat plenty of beefsteaks." Not that it mattered to Mabel, who wanted something else, something very specific. She needed Sachs to prescribe a holiday from Edwin, to say to him, "Leave your wife alone for a while." Sachs did, Edwin complied, and he never came back. As Mabel confided to her diary: "Edwin had flowed out and stayed out."

Despite his warm regard for his old colleague Freud, Barney Sachs bristled at the growing influence of psychoanalysis on American psychiatry, along with its overemphasis on sex. Sachs was no puritan. He appreciated Freud's openness in regard to human sexuality and its role in everyday life, but he strongly warned his colleagues to avoid using psychoanalysis on children. "The trouble with Freudians," he wrote, "is that they insist that your mind is always filled with nasty thoughts or that you are trying to hide something." Mabel, on the other hand, was open to anything. She epitomized the New Woman, having had affairs with many men, perhaps most famously with the journalist John Reed, and also with some women.

The "beefsteak" suggestion paints a clear picture of Sachs as a psychiatrist. He had little patience for catharsis, abreaction, the unconscious, or the alleged oral, anal, and phallic stages of sexual development. His suggestions were concrete and straightforward: eat something and get out of the house, stay busy. Mabel did. By donating money to the organizers of the 1913 Armory Show, the one featuring Marcel Duchamp's *Nude Descending a Staircase,* she took credit as one of the driving forces behind modern art. She soon was hosting "evenings" at her Fifth Avenue apartment, and her modest salon began to attract the artistic and literary stars of the modern era. She even invited Sachs, despite his suspicions of the bohemian crowd. According to Mabel, "He thought it would be advisable for some of those artists themselves to apply for admission to the psychopathic ward: that the exhibition at the Armory was the best evidence of mental derangement flaunted in public he had ever seen and he advised me to keep out of it." Instead, having gotten what she wanted, she drifted away from Sachs and took on a different therapist, the psychoanalyst Smith Ely Jelliffe, described by Dodge's biographer as "a man of prodigious intellect." Although he later became a Jungian analyst and split with Freud, Jelliffe handed Mabel the American version of psychodynamics—all mind and no brain.

Presented with these two irreconcilable world views, Mabel embarked on psychoanalytic sessions with Jelliffe three times a week, expense be damned. She had by now remarried, and her third husband, the painter Maurice Sterne, voiced his support at first, but soon became skeptical. He volunteered to remove himself from her company, much like Edwin had, until she completed her therapy. This effectively ended marriage number three, but not before he left her with a memento, her second syphilis infection.

In the two decades following Charcot's death, neurology as a therapeutic discipline had been moribund. Its great breakthroughs had occurred in the realm of mapping the cerebral cortex and identifying the cellular structure of gray matter. Hysteria and hypnosis had proven to be dead ends. Psychiatry, meanwhile, had produced the very useful Kraepelinian dichotomy of dementia praecox and manic-depressive illness, a classification scheme still in place today in the guise of schizophrenia and bipolar illness. As for therapeutic measures, psychiatry continued to focus on the body and its problems rather than on the mind and its demons. Rest cures, water cures, dietary measures, and tranquilizing drugs dominated the bill of fare at the spas. Into this landscape of psychoses, neuroses, and the psychopathology of everyday life, Freudian analysts provided some refreshingly novel explanations and answers. It is not surprising that someone of Mabel's disposition chose Jelliffe over Sachs.

Sachs may have represented the old school and Jelliffe the new, but one awkward fact flew beneath the radar. Sachs had an encyclopedic knowledge of general medicine, while Jelliffe and most of his cohort did not. Jelliffe had trained in neurology and psychiatry, but had concentrated his intellectual efforts on writing, editing, and publishing, with an emphasis on psychoanalysis. He may have had a prodigious intellect, but not as a clinical diagnostician or medical researcher. He represented everything Sachs railed against: self-promoting celebrity physicians, the sexualization of every aspect of human relations, and the elimination of the brain from considerations of the mind.

Like Freud's famous first patient Dora, Mabel Dodge suffered from anxiety rooted in the threat posed by syphilis. Her own father, like Dora's, was treated for it. In her memoirs, she also acknowledges having married three men even though she knew they had the disease, and having aborted a pregnancy conceived with Edwin out of fear of congenital syphilis. She struggled to understand her purpose in life while pursuing relationships in which she subordinated herself sexually and intellectually to men. She quit therapy with Jelliffe after he insisted she see no other therapists, and then began seeing Jelliffe's teacher, A. A. Brill, who encouraged her to write. She began with a Hearst newspaper column, and continued the journal she had begun with her sessions with Jelliffe, all while in the throes of anxiety and depression. To make matters worse, she also had to seek treatment for her syphilis infection. Like Freud's early patients, she exhibited symptoms of two conditions, hysteria and syphilis, but by this time, syphilis had legitimized psychiatry. It had brought sex and all forms of mental illness into the same sphere.

In 1917, Mabel and Maurice Sterne moved to Taos, New Mexico, and established an arts colony in the desert. Their marriage hung by a thread. Now a writer of some fame, Mabel attracted artists and writers, including Ansel Adams, Georgia O'Keeffe, Marsden Hartley, D. H. Lawrence, and Aldous Huxley, for extended visits. Maurice eventually left, and Mabel married her fourth husband, the Native American Antonio Luhan, who, like Edwin and Maurice, infected her yet again with syphilis. She and Tony underwent an arsenical cure together, entailing a series of injections of Dr. Ehrlich's Neosalvarsan over months. At this point she stopped having sex altogether, wondering, "Is there really that much syphilis in the world?"

At the time, yes, there really was that much syphilis in the world. By some estimates, at least 10 percent of the urban population had it, with a larger percentage of the military afflicted. Improvements in general public health, the availability of the Wassermann test, and antisyphilis treatments had reduced mortality, but the available remedies were still risky, inconvenient, painful, and had a low rate of compliance. Mabel's case indicates why.

Ehrlich's first commercial version of compound 606, Salvarsan, had the disadvantage of being extremely unstable when exposed to air, and it had to be carefully dissolved in distilled water. Despite Ehrlich's explicit instructions, many doctors were not up to the task, and side effects from improper preparation included kidney failure, seizures, rash, infections at the injection site in the buttocks or around veins—even death. A full arsenical treatment consisted of twenty injections over a period of eighteen months, with supplements of mercury injections and creams, or bismuth injections in the form of a solution of sodium bismuth tartrate. Adherence to the regimen required a great deal of self-discipline and a willingness to put up with the discomfort and consistent side effects, including vomiting, diffuse pain, and headache.

In 1910, the first year of commercial production, 65,000 doses of Salvarsan were administered to some 20,000 patients as part of a clinical trial. By 1920, 2 million doses were administered each year in the United States alone, mostly in the form of Neosalvarsan, a more stable second-generation version of the drug. Mabel privately rued the inconvenience and shame associated with the treatments. She recalled watching as husband Maurice "skulked down the street to Dr. Bergman's office." On one such visit, the doctor's wife ran to the Sterne apartment and burst into Mabel's living room, telling her something had gone horribly wrong. They rushed back to the doctor's office to find Maurice "lying on his back on a couch choking and clawing the air, his brown eyes rolling up." Maurice eventually came out of it, and when Mabel asked what had happened, the doctor replied, "I think I got a bubble of air in my hypodermic!"

"He did not seem at all embarrassed," Mabel wrote later. "Now that it was over he looked a little annoyed at Maurice. 'Well, I think you may go home now.'"

Syphilis does not discriminate by class. Still, no one wanted to talk about it. Mabel, like her contemporary Karen Blixen, another famous syphilitic and the author of *Out of Africa*, left all mention of it out of her published memoirs. As much as she thought of herself as a liberated New Woman, Mabel lived quietly with the shame of her venereal infections, and revealed them only in her posthumously published "suppressed" memoirs.

When Salvarsan had first hit the market, Ehrlich himself had faced pushback from several quarters. He was accused of encouraging promiscuity and prostitution. The Russian Orthodox Church came out squarely against any form of treatment for syphilis, citing the disease as God's punishment for the sin of lust. Ehrlich might have faced even greater pushback had it not been for congenital syphilis, the inherited form of the disease. Any pregnant woman with untreated syphilis would almost certainly pass it along to her child. In about 40 percent of those cases, the child would be stillborn. Those who survived often had birth defects such as sunken noses and pointed teeth, mental retardation, failure to thrive, and a short life expectancy. In 1917, an estimated 20,000 still-births in England were attributable to syphilis. This meant approximately 30,000 children were born with the disease and had to struggle with its crippling effects. Whatever objections Salvarsan faced at first, they soon evaporated in the face of such dire statistics. But Salvarsan was not a permanent solution. Given the difficulty of administering it, not to mention its toxicity, something better was needed. Like many medical breakthroughs, it came about by a series of fortunate accidents.

Alexander Fleming's lab in London's St. Mary's Hospital was a study in organized chaos. Barely a square inch of his desktop lay uncovered. Jenga-stacked petri dishes containing miniature metropolises sprawled across his lab benches. Colonies of staphylococci flourished in the cultures, the fate of the budding Whovilles hanging in the balance. Fleming was not a tidy man, and his workspace reflected it.

Back in 1923, in the first of his happy "accidents," he had let fall a nasal drip onto a culture dish teeming with bacteria. Something in the drip, a naturally occurring product of the human immune system, killed the bacteria. He isolated it and called it lysozyme. The human body, he observed, manufactures its own antibiotics, and deploys them in nasal mucus and tears. Moderately effective against minor infections, these lysozymes cannot compete with major ones, but this small discovery primed Fleming for his next big one.

Five years later, Dr. Fleming's annual vacation had come around. He packed up the family and left his burgeoning pile of bacterial creations unattended. While he was away, a tragedy on a small scale befell one of them. He had forgotten to place a preparation dish in the incubator, and a mold spore contaminated the culture. At its browned edges, the staphylococci had died off. Something in the fungus had killed the bacteria. Fleming's reaction, perhaps apocryphal, and not half as iconic as "Eureka!," was simply to remark, "That's funny!"

Fleming then set out to replicate the effect. He grew the mold again, isolated a substance within it, and applied it to various bacteria, again to lethal effect. He called it "mold juice" at first, later settling on a more proper Latinate term, *penicillin*, after the genus *Penicillium*, the name of the mold that had contaminated the plate. "When I woke up just after dawn on September 28, 1928," he reflected much later, "I certainly didn't plan to revolutionize all medicine by discovering the world's first antibiotic, or bacteria killer. But I suppose that was exactly what I did."

Fleming was born in 1881 in Ayrshire, Scotland. He went to St. Mary's Medical School, London, finished in 1906, and immediately began to specialize in vaccine therapy. He appreciated what Paul Ehrlich had accomplished with the release of Salvarsan, and in 1910 he took part in its first large-scale clinical trial. When Ehrlich sent out the initial 60,000 trial doses, the London shipment went to Fleming at St. Mary's. At the same time, Fleming was serving as a private in the London Scottish Regiment of the Territorial Force, the volunteer reserve component of the British Army. He became adept at administering Salvarsan, to the point that his fellow volunteers had dubbed him "Private 606" (Salvarsan had not yet acquired its trade name, and was still known as compound 606). He developed a method of intravenous injection to replace the extremely painful practice of injection in the buttocks, and made a lucrative side business out of administering the shots to well-heeled Londoners.

Despite his knack for administering compound 606, Fleming believed in vaccines over chemotherapies. Better to build the body's immune system and prevent infection rather than to flood it with toxic chemicals. By the time of his big discovery, Fleming had already done extensive work on antisepsis and on influenza vaccines. He acknowledged a problem with all topical antiseptics such as carbolic acid (another coal tar derivative): they killed off protective white cells before they could reach the deeper source of the infection. An effective germ killer, he knew, would have to come from within the body.

The story of the accidental contamination of the petri dish sounds like a tale made better through many retellings. It is probably partly apocryphal. It is also self-effacing and perhaps falsely modest, crediting fate over insight, chance over effort. It is important to note that Fleming found, allegedly by accident, precisely what he had been searching for over the course of two decades. A year later, he published the results of his experiments with penicillin in the *British Journal of Experimental Pathology*, an obscure academic publication. He claimed success in killing the bacteria responsible for a number of infections, including scarlet fever, typhus, and diphtheria. Oddly, he did not think to test it on syphilis.

The response in the scientific community to this breakthrough was tepid. It was one thing to kill a germ in a petri dish, another to kill it in a human body. Besides, it seemed impractical to make enough penicillin to kill off an infection in a living being. After struggling to mass-produce his mold juice and find a way to administer it, Fleming eventually gave up and moved on to other things.

Ten years later, in 1939, two Oxford scientists, Howard Florey and Ernst Chain, took on the very serious problem of infectious disease in wartime. Facing daunting statistics of lost manpower during the Great War, they searched through the literature for any promising leads and happened upon Fleming's paper. Penicillin sounded like the stuff they were looking for, but they first had to make enough to test it on human subjects. They turned their Oxford laboratory into a penicillin manufactory, and by 1941 had enough to treat a nasty infection. Their first patient, a forty-three-year-old policeman, had scratched his cheek on a rosebush thorn. The scrape had developed into a series of abscesses as infection spread. Penicillin halted the progress of the infection, but the test supply ran out before the sepsis could be overcome. The policeman died. From then on, Florey and Chain limited their tests to children, who did not require such large doses. Satisfied they were on the right track, they turned their attention to their biggest challenge: how to mass-produce something that fermented on the surface of growth mediums.

With the war effort taking up too many resources in England, Florey made a dangerous transatlantic passage to drum up support from research labs in the United States. The Department of Agriculture's Northern Regional Research Laboratory (NRRL) in Peoria, Illinois, took up the challenge of increasing the yield of the fermentation process. By a happy accident, as an accelerant in any process, the lab routinely tested corn-steep liquor, a by-product of corn milling. In this instance, it increased the yield of penicillin tenfold. Further refinements, including the use of a mold sourced from a rotten cantaloupe found in a Peoria fruit market, further increased yields, and the major drug companies, prodded by appeals to their patriotism from the federal government, took up mass production using the Peoria method. Initial human trials on staph infections commenced in 1942, and penicillin proved effective against staph, strep, and gonorrhea. As word began to seep out to the public, supplies of the new wonder drug had to be rationed.

By war's end, penicillin had spared more lives than were saved by the Bletchley codebreakers. In all previous wars, deaths from disease and especially from infection had far outnumbered combat deaths. Due to penicillin—which is to say due to Fleming, Florey, and Chain—the ratio was reversed in World War II. The three men received the Nobel Prize in Medicine in 1945 for their wonderful discovery, though just how wonderful it was had yet to be fully demonstrated.

CHAPTER 12

WINNING THE BATTLE
AND LOSING THE WAR

Government ain't good for nothin' but giving you syphilis and flu shots.

—*Barbershop: The Next Cut* (2016)

In 1934, the New York state commissioner of public health, Thomas Parran Jr., went to the studios of CBS Radio to deliver a stern warning to a national audience about a public health crisis. Told at the last minute he could not utter the words *syphilis* or *gonorrhea* over the airwaves, or even mention his goal of a war on syphilis, he walked out of the studio in disgust. He shouldn't have been surprised. In the years since the end of World War I, moral indignation had made a comeback. A wartime awareness campaign inspired by an epidemic of syphilis afflicting potential draftees, along with funding for prevention and cure of venereal diseases, had both dwindled to almost nothing. Parran was now fighting a war on two fronts. With the onset of the Great Depression, syphilis had returned to its traditional role of a well-deserved scourge tormenting the sinful and the poor. The word on the street once again was that it "did not happen to nice people." Parran tried to point out the toll it took. It was cheaper to prevent than to treat. But he would have to go it alone in order to get the point across. In the end, his walkout at CBS got the result he wanted. Fifteen major newspapers printed the text of his speech in full.

Thomas Parran Jr., the son of a Maryland tobacco farmer, almost succeeded in wiping out syphilis, but in the end, the relentless power of moral rectitude would win out over the public good. A cure in the form of Fleming's mold juice had existed since 1928, although its ability to kill spirochetes, even in late stages of the disease, would remain unknown until the mid-1940s. The war effort further delayed the discovery by preventing the diversion of penicillin to clinical trials when it was desperately needed on the front lines. Despite Parran's campaigns and other public health measures, the bureaucratic will to end a devastating plague would ultimately collapse in successive generations for a simple reason. Syphilis, unlike smallpox, *means* something. To a significant and influential segment of the population in any generation, disease exists for a reason.

Parran began his career in 1917 as a rural health services emissary for the U.S. Public Health Service. It was his first real job. Out in the field, he found an overabundance of venereal disease, especially syphilis. He recognized it largely as a problem of awareness. Hardly anyone knew what it was or what it could do. In 1926, he was promoted to head the Division of Venereal Diseases of the U.S. Public Health Service. Five years later, Franklin Roosevelt, then the governor of New York, appointed him as his public health commissioner, and in 1936, Roosevelt, now president, made Parran the surgeon general of the United States. It was a meteoric rise. But despite his important role in government, he still could not say the word *syphilis* on the radio.

To win hearts and minds, Parran wanted to change the very name of venereal disease in order to downplay its association with sin, to make syphilis a medical problem rather than a moral one. For the most part, thanks to the censors at CBS, he succeeded. *Time* magazine, in a profile of Parran, said, "To break down this taboo in the U.S. and tackle syphilis scientifically rather than morally is the high and burning purpose in the official life of Surgeon General Parran." The American Medical Association eventually got on board. "One of the principal obstacles to the conquest of syphilis," stated their editorial, "has been squeamishness about facing the problem and the unfortunate classification of syphilis as a venereal disease. It is, of course, only a venereal disease in part."

The term *venereal disease*, originally *morbus veneris*, dates to the mid-1600s. It is an unfortunate term because it is a loaded one. If it had been simply an allusion to Venus, the goddess of love, it would be fairly benign. But the name also connects with the deadliest of the seven deadly sins, venery. The name is also a judgment: the sin of sexual excess leads to syphilis; God judges those who transgress; whoever gets it cannot be innocent. Many state boards of censors banned not only the word *syphilis*, but even the mention of venereal disease. So did the Hays Code, the original guidelines for decency in motion pictures. The attitude has been persistent, counterproductive, and unavoidable. Syphilologists struggled against it for over a century and won a small victory with the adoption in the 1970s of the term *sexually transmitted disease*, or STD, and the more recent STI, *sexually transmitted infection*. But not all cases of syphilis are the result of venery, nor is syphilis always sexually transmitted. Husbands infect wives, wives infect husbands, mothers pass the disease to their babies, and babies pass it to their wet nurses, who in turn pass it along to more babies.

Alfred Fournier, in his 1907 book called *The Treatment and Prophylaxis of Syphilis*, tells of the gift of a trumpet to a child. A young uncle demonstrates the instrument and passes it to the mother, who tries it, then passes it to the child. "The young uncle had numerous mucous patches in his mouth. The result was that both mother and child were infected, and the child a few years later succumbed to general paralysis." He also noted the high frequency of syphilis among glassblowers. It was conveyed "during the operation of blowing bottles by the tube being passed from mouth to mouth." Other vectors of contagion included speaking tubes, pens, cigar stubs picked up and smoked by children, postage stamps, toothbrushes, and even money. "Dr. Castel observed a case of buccal contagion in an omnibus conductor, who developed a chancre of the lip from holding money in his mouth."

Before Schaudinn and Hofmann came along, the microscopic world was an esoteric and remote place, visited only by a select few. Bugs too small or too pale to be detected by schoolroom microscopes were suddenly revealed thanks to aniline dyes and dark-field microscopy. Few people at the time knew what a virus or a bacterium looked like, but by the 1920s any educated person could recognize a spirochete. No other disease has a comparable symbolic representation, almost a logo. Diego Rivera even painted them into his fresco for the lobby of the new Rockefeller Center in 1933. Not only was the spirochete a character in Thomas Mann's *Doctor Faustus*, a conniving accomplice of the Devil himself, but elsewhere it was portrayed as a predatory animal, an opportunist, a graffito, lurking in back alleys and hanging around houses of ill repute. The play *Spirochete: A History* by Arnold Sundgaard, a hit in Chicago where it premiered in 1938, covered the major events leading up to Schaudinn and Hofmann's discovery. Sundgaard's play was in effect a public service message, an adjunct to Parran's national campaign, which culminated in May of 1938 with a huge victory over the moralists via the passage of the National Venereal Disease Control Act. Congress finally stepped in and not only uttered the previously unspeakable and unprintable name of the disease, but effectively declared war on the spirochete.

It was one thing to inspire an act of Congress, to win a tactical victory over ignorance, and quite another thing to implement it. Parran faced a number of daunting logistical and tactical hurdles, including identifying carriers, standardizing treatments, getting the infected into treatment, and then getting them to stick with it for eighteen months. Parran also had to get doctors and nurses on board. At that time, the treatment of sexually transmitted diseases occupied the low-status end of the medical profession. Few doctors specialized in it, and general practitioners dispensed a chaotic array of remedies, including arsenicals, mercury, bismuth, and potassium chloride, guided mostly by personal preference and instinct. Prophylactic measures and morning-after precautions ranging from antiseptic scrubbing to urethral flushings felt more like punishment than prevention. Those who delayed treatment and reached the tertiary stage faced the prospect of two weeks of Wagner-Jauregg's malarial fever cure. As a result, less than 20 percent of those with positive Wassermann tests completed the regimen.

Parran came up with a five-point program. He set up free screening centers, instituted Wassermann blood test dragnets in areas of high incidence, had public health workers track down sexual partners for testing and treatment, urged states to adopt mandatory blood tests as a requirement for marriage licenses, and launched a massive and often-ridiculed public awareness campaign involving posters, films, advertisements, and a series of books, beginning with *The Next Great Plague to Go*, in 1936. The notion that nice people don't get venereal disease was a smoke screen, he said. In the Scandinavian countries he had visited, they treated syphilis as just another disease, and had achieved remarkable results with no deterioration of the moral order. It could be done here, but time was of the essence.

By the time of Pearl Harbor, according to the Centers for Disease Control, syphilis affected a half million U.S. citizens. Three percent of new military recruits, including over 200,000 known tertiary stage cases, had tested positive. By 1943, the number of citizens infected with syphilis had risen to 575,593, an alarming .4 percent of the population. Parran mounted a propaganda campaign warning soldiers about the dangers of careless and casual sex. He teamed with Warner Bros. to produce the 1940 film *Dr. Ehrlich's Magic Bullet*, starring Edward G. Robinson. Because of the delicate subject matter, the filmmakers had to negotiate with the Hays Code board and its explicit prohibition of any depiction or mention of "sexual hygiene and venereal diseases." A waiver was granted, and the picture went on to earn an Oscar nomination.

Moral outrage followed each of these successes. According to *Time* magazine, the War Advertising Council, which was responsible for war bond drives, withdrew its support from Parran's campaign in 1944, calling it "shameful, sinful." At times it seemed as though this kind of rectitude was the only thing standing between Parran and the eradication of a plague he referred to as a "shadow on the land." But the means of solving the problem was at hand. By 1941, penicillin had been proven to cure infections. It had yet to be tested on syphilis and gonorrhea.

Although Parran faced censure for uttering the name of the problem he was trying to solve, psychoanalysts had already cornered the market on talking quite openly about sex. They brought intercourse, sexual deviancy, and sexually transmitted disease into the medical mainstream.

They could discuss syphilis all they wanted. After all, in their world view, syphilis was the engine that drove the neuroses. Without it, there would have been nothing to psychoanalyze.

The German psychiatrist Richard von Krafft-Ebing had kick-started the science of sex in his *Psychopathia Sexualis* of 1886. In it, he coined the terms *sadism* and *masochism,* construed homosexuality as a degenerative mental illness, and pointed out the ubiquity of sexual pathologies. The English physician Havelock Ellis, in his *Sexual Inversion* (1897) and the multi-volume *Studies in the Psychology of Sex,* continued the discussion. Ellis considered homosexuality a heritable but not a pathological condition. Through these and later works, Ellis explored in frank terms sexual preferences and various forms of sexual arousal. Freud followed with *Three Essays on the Theory of Sexuality*, a prelude to his theory of psychosexual development, in which he cites sex as the basis of all neuroses and perversions. Like Ellis, Freud did not consider homosexuality to be pathological, but rather an arrested stage of sexual maturity. He placed sex at the center of almost all functional disorders, and eventually began to attribute organic disease to the somaticizing effects of sexual anxiety and the repression of sexually traumatic memories. Sexology, the term that emerged to describe the scientific consideration of sexual behavior, quickly acquired a certain cachet. Sex was both a problem and, in its fulfillment, a cure.

This is what women like Mabel Dodge wanted to hear: a theory explaining their anxieties in terms of their sex lives, a nonjudgmental appraisal of sexual experimentation rooted not in terms of degeneration, germs, and disease, but in natural and healthy needs and urges, with suggestions on how to live a fuller sexual life. No moralizing, no patronizing, but an alternative to a world view mired in squalor. Mabel believed she could purify her body and uplift her mind by purifying her soul. The key could be found in her unconscious. Yet her desire for sexual and intellectual fulfillment and her ability to access her subconscious ran headlong into the reality of her syphilis infection and the degrading treatments it entailed. Mabel was convinced she had only herself to blame. Why did she marry men who she knew had syphilis?

It is difficult today to imagine what it was like to live with the constant fear not just of infection but of the very real possibility of dying insane. Every era has its existential threat, and some people run headlong toward it. Before there was the bomb, there was syphilis. A cure for it had its own Manhattan Project, and it would be headed by Thomas Parran.

As early as 1927, Parran oversaw the commissioning of officers to work on venereal disease research and treatment. The center of this effort was the Venereal Disease Research Laboratory of the Public Health Service. Its director, Dr. John Friend Mahoney, also served as director of the Marine Hospital on Staten Island, the last of a chain of institutions for the care of seamen in the merchant marine. It was a perfect place to study the disease up close. Mahoney's story is embedded in a long line of military struggles with massive upsurges of venereal disease during wartime. The problem was not one of morals, but of the loss of frontline fighting men to gonorrhea and syphilis after they had sex with prostitutes. When young men are sent into battle, they have no incentive to exercise sexual restraint. Prostitutes followed armies as part of their supply chain. New recruits were carrying gonorrhea into the service and escalating the numbers of infected soldiers.

Mahoney traveled to Europe between the wars to confer with his fellow venereologists, and he returned to Staten Island armed with some ideas for treating gonorrhea using newly available sulfa drugs. Recently synthesized as yet another medicinal coal tar derivative, these drugs were the first widely available antibiotics prior to penicillin. They worked with gonorrhea, but syphilis would prove to be more intractable. The spirochete, known to be unique in its structure and surface proteins, did not respond to antibacterial sulfonamides in the same way as conventional bacteria, notably staph and strep. In 1940, Mahoney's lab acquired its first cache of penicillin, a precious commodity. His technicians tried a small amount of it in petri dishes filled with spirochetes, and seeing no effect, almost walked away. But Mahoney was astute enough to try penicillin again, on infected rabbits this time. He knew that sulfonamide's antibacterial properties emerge only after it metabolizes within living tissue, and he intuited that penicillin had to circulate in the blood to be effective. It cleared up all of the syphilitic lesions and ridded the animals of the disease.

Penicillin had already been tested on standard infections, but Howard Florey and Ernst Chain had not tested it on spirochetes, probably because unlike staphylococci or streptococci, they are impossible to grow in the lab, and thus very difficult to study. They had, however, provided the Americans with some idea of the dosages required for the treatment of sepsis. In 1943, Mahoney launched his landmark study of four patients, all men recently infected with syphilis. After eight daily treatments of injected penicillin, the blood tests came back negative for all four. This was too small a sample to be certain of a complete cure, and Mahoney did not rule out the possibility of the reemergence of the disease in a later stage, possibly even as general paresis. Nevertheless, when he presented his results at that year's meeting of the American Public Health Association, one observer called it "probably the most significant paper ever presented in the medical field." By the following year, penicillin had become the treatment of choice for syphilis. *Time* dubbed it the "New Magic Bullet."

During the final years of the war, the diversion of penicillin from treating wound infections to treating venereal disease caused some controversy. Sulfonamides had saved thousands of front-line soldiers, but could do nothing for syphilis, and Colonel Edward Churchill, chief surgical consultant for the North African theater of operations, said that penicillin should be used to first treat soldiers "wounded in brothels." By his calculation, this would return more soldiers to the front lines than treating battlefield injuries would. It took three months in 1944 for the army to liberally roll out penicillin. Along with a rapid cure and a reduction in the number of infections came social commentary. As in the past, moralistic skeptics worried that the ease of treatment would lead to greater promiscuity and a paradoxical increase in VD.

Initially, some physicians held out for the old remedies. The fever cure remained in use through the 1950s, employing the same strain of malaria used by Wagner-Jauregg in his first trials. Arsenicals, mercury, and bismuth all took time to die out. But Parran and Mahoney had won their battle. In the aftermath, Mahoney quietly and modestly climbed the ladder of the Public Health Service, becoming commissioner of public health for New York City and later director of the Public Health Laboratories until his death in 1957. For the introduction of penicillin to treat syphilis, he was one of the first winners of the Lasker Award, a coveted medical equivalent to the Nobel Prize. New Yorkers who were around in the 1950s can recall his bold and idiosyncratic introduction of street-corner mobile units offering walk-in blood tests for syphilis, complete with loudspeakers and pamphlets describing the dangers of forgoing treatment.

Thomas Parran Jr. retired from the Public Health Service in 1948 and went into university administration and philanthropy. He died in 1968. The following year, the University of Pittsburgh's Graduate School of Public Health, where Parran had served as the first dean, renamed its headquarters Parran Hall. The American Sexually Transmitted Disease Association named its lifetime achievement award after Parran. A few years later, revelations about both men began to cloud these legacies, if not the triumphant aspect of the struggle to end syphilis.

Today the story of Parran's and Mahoney's efforts to cure venereal disease gets scant attention, and the sexual nature of the disease explains why. We remember the accomplishments of Jonas Salk and Albert Sabin in conquering polio, a disease of innocent children. Syphilis, more widespread than polio and affecting far more children, could not escape its associations. In that sense, the antisyphilis campaign failed. Congenital syphilis was never publicly discussed, before or after penicillin. It could not compete with polio, cerebral palsy, or muscular dystrophy for the hearts and minds of philanthropic Americans. With the war over, the public refused to acknowledge the extent of the problem. The CDC declared the United States polio-free in 1994, and the disease has since disappeared in almost all other countries. Syphilis, on the other hand, has not only not gone away but has become associated with two of the most notorious public health scandals in history, both carried out under Parran and Mahoney.

In 1932, the U.S. Public Health Service, with Parran's blessing, initiated the notorious Tuskegee syphilis study. Mahoney commissioned the lesser-known Guatemala syphilis experiment in 1946. Tuskegee tracked 399 syphilitic men who were told they had "bad blood," a euphemism of the time for syphilis. The plan was to observe the course of untreated syphilis in a rural population. Instead of running for six months, as initially intended, the experiment ran for forty years, during which time the subjects, all black sharecroppers, were denied a cure, even after penicillin became widely available. Forty of them infected their wives, and seventeen children were born with congenital syphilis. Either Parran or Mahoney could have ended it at any point. It took a reporter's exposé to bring the experiment to the attention of Congress in 1972. Back in the planning stages of the Tuskegee experiment, Parran is remembered for writing: "If one wished to study the natural history of syphilis in the Negro race uninfluenced by treatment, [Macon] county would be an ideal location for such a study." The memory of Tuskegee still taints Parran's legacy with the Public Health Service.

Perhaps more damning but less well known is the Guatemala syphilis experiment. The U.S. Army command was anxious to find effective ways to prevent syphilis after sexual exposure, and wanted to see whether penicillin worked as well as or better than arsenicals did. Their goal was to create an anti-venereal field pack to issue to the infantry. Seven hundred Guatemalan soldiers, prisoners, and institutionalized mental patients were inoculated with syphilis in different ways, including having sex with prostitutes provided by the researchers. Of these, 427 became infected and at least 369 were treated with high doses of penicillin, although it was not known if the doses were adequate to eradicate the disease, or how many subjects, if any, were actually cured. Surgeon General Parran was fully aware of the ethical issues. None of the participants was informed of the nature of the experiment, and consent was not obtained from the soldiers, prisoners, or orphans. After they had been infected, not all of them could be tracked down. The work was haphazardly conducted, the follow-up blood tests were erratic, and little of practical value was learned. The existence of the study was not revealed until 2005, and it led to a formal apology by President Barack Obama to the Guatemalan government for "crimes against humanity."

In light of these revelations, the American Sexually Transmitted Disease Association renamed the Parran Award as the ASTDA Distinguished Career Award. The University of Pittsburgh, forced to confront the gravity of the charges against him, chose to emphasize the immense good done by Parran, while acknowledging his ethical lapses and, despite a vociferous campaign by students, has not renamed Parran Hall.

With the discovery of a cure for syphilis, many questions were left unanswered. Did mercury or bismuth treatments also cure syphilis? What led to the virtual disappearance of tabes dorsalis between the two world wars? Did infections with relatively mild first stages have a greater chance of progressing to general paresis? How many of the neurological symptoms attributed to neurosyphilis were the product of mercury treatments? With the advent of penicillin, none of these questions mattered anymore, and the answers were not forthcoming. We still do not know. What mattered to Parran, Mahoney, and the public health community was the total eradication of syphilis. But it takes more than the discovery of a cure to wipe out a disease. Through Mahoney's efforts, by 1950 the number of cases of syphilis was halved from its 1941 level, down to 217,558, and it continued to decline through the 1970s to unheard-of low levels of about 50,000, before swelling again to almost five times that number in the early 1990s, in parallel with the emergence of AIDS. The number of late-stage cases, including neurosyphilis, stayed constant at around 20,000 throughout that period, until a bump in the late 1990s, as might have been expected ten years after the peak of the HIV epidemic. Cases of congenital syphilis were also down to a few hundred in the 1970s and 1980s, from ten times that number in the 1940s.

It has been suggested that a variant of "herd immunity" brought about the decline of syphilis after World War II. If enough people were treated, the idea went, it would diminish the reservoir of spirochetes able to perpetuate the infectious chain. Some bacteria are indeed inadvertently wiped out of the population by the casual use of antibiotics, but this is also unlikely to eradicate syphilis. The *Chicago Tribune* at one point suggested every man, woman, and child in the United States receive penicillin to prevent syphilis, an idea wisely ignored by the CDC. It takes a very high dose of penicillin, much higher than the dose for a simple infection, to cure a case of syphilis. Fortunately, the spirochete has not become resistant to antibiotics, and it remains a stable target from a bacteriological point of view. Find it, treat it with high doses, and it's gone—at least until the patient gets reinfected.

Parran and Mahoney also included as part of their campaign the elimination of reinfection. By 1950, most states mandated a blood test before a marriage license would be granted. The ostensible reason was to prevent transmission of the disease to offspring, but Parran and Mahoney had bigger designs. They hoped to use this contrivance to stamp the disease out altogether by exposing and treating it. A decade later, many states had rescinded the requirement. By 2002, only eleven states in the United States still required the test. The last to have the requirement was Mississippi, which dropped it in 2012, but still recommends syphilis testing on its public health website. With the decline of mandatory blood test surveillance, the disease has made a quiet comeback.

CHAPTER 13

THE PSYCHIC INTERPRETATION
OF DISEASE

Before Charcot, asylums provided an occasionally safe but more of-ten brutal home for the insane, if not a convenient dumping ground for undesirables who had merely been *declared* insane. After the reforms of Pinel and Esquirol, asylums for the well-to-do began to look more like spas and less like prisons, though they served essentially the same func-tion. The rationale for locking people up was simple: We do not know what is wrong with them, we cannot cure them, but we need to pacify them somehow. We justify doing this by declaring them insane, by call-ing insanity, effectively but not definitively, a disease. This is how the Marquis de Sade ended up at Charenton.

Despite early reforms, conditions at asylums for those of limited means remained miserable. John Conolly, a physician working at the Middlesex County Asylum in the 1840s, described the situation as one of "a barbarous system of coercion and restraint . . . founded on a fal-lacy," specifically the fallacy of a purely psychological illness. In his opinion, insanity was "a state of unsound, physical health—a state of functional disease—in the great majority of cases capable of a cure, under appropriate treatment; capable also, under injudicious treatment, of being rendered permanent and incurable." Yet the nature of the func-tional disease causing insanity remained a mystery. Psychiatry had no diagnosis it could claim as its own until Antoine Bayle described general paralysis of the insane in 1822. It had no identifiable bodily illness to treat until Noguchi discovered the spirochete in the brains of paretics in 1912. Well into the twentieth century, absent scientific evidence, psychiatrists leaned on observation and induction, as well as invasive remedies such as insulin coma, convulsive therapy (via the drug metrazol, later via electroshock), and eventually lobotomy. All of these were discovered and implemented by trial and error. John Romano, a neuropsychiatrist and historian, recalled the state of affairs in the 1930s, during his internship at Milwaukee County General Hospital, with a kind of nostalgic fondness mixed with horror:

> We were involved in the therapies enthusiastically proposed at that time, with *dauerschlaf* [prolonged narcosis] and insulin, with pentavalent arsenicals [Neosalvarsan] and the Kettering hypertherm [fever therapy] used to treat patients with neurosyphilis. We used chloral and bromides and the barbiturates as wisely as we knew how, and we practiced the various types of insight and supportive psychotherapies then available. Sulpha had arrived but penicillin was yet to come, and we would wait another 20 years before chlorpromazine became available. Later in our stay, metrazol was used, and ECT was on the horizon. We seemed to have an endless number of acutely disturbed patients, and along with the nurses and attendants we responded to their emergency needs with the gusto of seasoned fire horses.

Neurology, meanwhile, having cornered the market on the treatment of hysteria, thanks mostly to Charcot, managed to sidestep both the biological basis of insanity and its treatment, concentrating instead on paralysis, sensory loss, seizures, and the localization of brain function. American psychiatrists of the early twentieth century, most of whom had trained in Europe, followed Freud and Charcot in focusing on neuroses and personality disorders instead of the more incapacitating psychiatric conditions. As a result, according to the historian Charles E. Rosenberg, much of our century's most influential psychiatric writing has consisted of general statements about the human condition, in the form of hypothetical etiologies of particular personality types and related modes of behavior. . . . Rather less attention has been paid to the great and dismayingly intractable clinical burdens of age, grave illness, and deviance which have traditionally filled our state hospitals.

Psychiatry, he concluded, has "become a kind of residual legatee for the attempt to solve some of society's most intractable problems." The driving force behind this social engineering, the link connecting neurology and psychiatry, and the product of neurology's dalliance with hysteria, was psychoanalysis.

In 1895, the year Freud published his study of Anna O., he attempted to place his psychoanalytical theory, his updated mesmerism, on a firm biological footing. He gave up in frustration and never published it, but returned to the subject in a late and controversial work he did publish, *Beyond the Pleasure Principle*. In this essay Freud suggests that individual cells have minds of their own. The cells in question are egg and sperm. They require a libido, he writes, "as a reserve against their later momentous constructive activity." But the idea of imparting intentionality does not stop there. The destructive activity of cancer cells and infectious organisms is also intentional. "The cells of the malignant neoplasms which destroy the organism," he writes, "should also perhaps be described as narcissistic in this same sense: pathology is prepared to regard their germs as innate and to ascribe embryonic attributes to them." The malignant neoplasms he cites would also include spirochetes. This kind of fantastical theorizing tested the patience even of Freud's most ardent followers, but it had the advantage of being impossible to disprove. It was, in essence, novelistic. It paved the way for Thomas Mann to give Adrian Leverkühn's infection a conscience, and make it a conniving accomplice of the Devil.

Orthodox psychoanalysis was built upon untestable theories. Freud's close friend and confidant, the Hungarian analyst Sándor Ferenczi, went so far as to place the blame for the manic delusions of general paresis on narcissism. "No one of course would dream of underrating the significance and the primordial role of the purely physical symptoms of paresis," Ferenczi states. "It is also agreed that a large proportion of the disturbances of the mental functions must be regarded as pathological deficiencies or as the effects of pathological irritation, i.e. as the direct effects of the organic process." Nevertheless, unable to let it go as a purely biological brain disease, he adds, "The manic-megalomanic phase of general paralysis (which often appears to be the primary phase) is a step-by-step regression of the narcissistic libido to superseded stages of ego development. From the psycho-analytic viewpoint *paralysis progressiva* is in reality *paralysis regressiva*." Here it may be useful to recall the scene in Stanley Kubrick's masterpiece, *2001: A Space Odyssey*, when the memory banks of the computer HAL are serially dismantled. In psychoanalytical terms, the result, to use Ferenczi's interpretation, would be "a narcissistic psychosis; its symptoms are the mental expression of the great injury and loss of libido which the patient's ego has suffered by the loss or devaluation of an ideal with which it had completely identified itself. The depression is unconscious mourning over this devaluation." Not even the most fervent Freudian believes this anymore.

Psychoanalytic theory also promoted the untestable notion that repressed desires and feelings can bring about changes in cellular structure. Mabel Dodge's first analyst, Smith Ely Jelliffe, gave her a taste of this in their initial sessions:

> Dr. Jelliffe told me his fascinating theories on disease and his belief that nearly all bodily illness is a failure of the spirit expressing itself at the physical level, just as disorders of the brain represent, at the symbolic level, the inabilities of the psyche. . . . Tumors, cancers, and so on appeared to him to be manifestations in the flesh of one's unsublimated hatreds for people or situations outside oneself whom one regarded as parasites and whom one was unable to successfully deal with. Most of the insanities that were not of organic origin were, he thought, due to one's own inability to cope with oneself.

Neuropathologists, immunologists, and infectious disease specialists fought to delegitimize these ideas for decades, ultimately banishing them from academic medicine, but not from popular culture. The psychic interpretation of all disease is still alive and well.

Thomas Szasz called Freud "a moralist in the guise of a scientist," someone who "conquered what is in effect the human condition by annexing it in its entirety to the medical profession." He accused him of founding "a sort of secular religion which has had immense influence on popular contemporary thought and life." He railed against not only the highly coercive methods of psychoanalysts but also the pathologizing of everyday life. The psychoanalyst pronounced a summary judgment on each patient, recommended intensive therapy sessions, usually four times a week, often lasting several years, or until the therapist deemed the mission complete. The patient had little say in the matter and had to be prepared to spend thousands of dollars. Such abuses drove Szasz to write a series of books attacking Freud's legacy.

The analysts struck back. Lawrence Kubie, speaking for the Freudians, took on Szasz's arguments in a paper called "The Myths of Thomas Szasz." Kubie had established a reputation in New York as a celebrity analyst. He had treated George Gershwin, Tennessee Williams, and the Broadway playwright and theater director Moss Hart. A volatile man, deeply neurotic by his own admission, Kubie was brilliant but undisciplined. He tended to clash with anyone who questioned his judgment or his integrity. As a leading theoretician of his craft, he had helped devise the U.S. Army's policy on homosexuality prior to World War II, declaring it a mental illness and grounds for barring from the service. He also advocated and employed gay conversion therapy.

Kubie was sympathetic to Szasz's views on the overreach of institutional psychiatry. As for the "myth" of mental illness, he countered with an organic definition. "The process of mental illness," he claimed, "is initiated when anything freezes behavior into forms that can no longer change." This unbreakable pattern of obsessive behaviors can be easily recognized when pathological behaviors persist. What Kubie suggested, more elegantly than Freud or Jelliffe did, was a brain-physiological explanation of mental illness based on the tendency of unconscious thoughts and the emotions they summon to produce real changes in brain function. This became a leitmotiv of psychosomatic medicine in the 1940s, and a passing fad in academic circles for a time. Psychosomatics insisted that unresolved inner conflicts precipitated *all* illness, not just mental illness. "Preconscious coded signaling," according to Kubie, "is the instrument by which experience is processed within us on the psychological level and can be translated into somatic changes, or conversely, somatic experience into psychological change." The end result is disease. "I maintain," writes Kubie, "that whenever the processes which produce any pattern of behavior pre-determine its automatic repetition, becoming repetitive irrespective of arguments and exhortation, rewards and punishments, success or failure, even of satiation of instinctual needs, a process has been set in motion which is the process of illness."

Unconvinced, Thomas Szasz kept writing books, and found himself increasingly marginalized professionally, lumped in with a counterculture that had rejected all institutional authority. But contrary to what many of his attackers claimed, Szasz was not anti-science or anti-psychiatry. Instead, he worried that science had drifted off its moorings. He was right. The psychosciences *had* slipped off their moorings, and they would continue to drift, always on the lookout for the next big idea, whether it meant ignoring the brain or trying to tie brain function directly to the measurable output of brain processes. Where Freud had tried to read minds, the new neuropsychiatrists would try to read brains. Szasz anticipated this:

> The mathematicians, neuroscientists, and philosophers who offer these seemingly super-sophisticated accounts of the relationship between mind and brain claim that they are laying the foundations of a new science of the mind. Perhaps so, but I doubt it. I believe they are writing science fiction. . . . Why? Because the writers illustrate their stories with striking images of the brain obtained by high-tech scanners, analogize

and equate the mind with the brain, use incomprehensible mathematical symbols or give ordinary terms novel, idiosyncratic meanings, and promise to bring closer a brave new world of Mental Health.

By the 1950s, there were half a million patients confined to state and county mental hospitals in the United States. The number had increased more than twofold in just a few decades, and looked as if it might double again before the end of the century. Instead, from the 1960s onward, the asylum population declined to its pre-1910 levels and has remained relatively stable ever since. This miracle was wrought not by neurologists, psychiatrists, or psychoanalysts, but by chemists. Penicillin almost wiped out neurosyphilis within twenty years of its approval as an antisyphilitic, eliminating the source of 20 percent of asylum admissions. Antipsychotic drugs—notably chlorpromazine—then replaced electroshock and lobotomy by turning inpatients into outpatients, and paved the way for the deinstitutionalization movement of the 1960s. Around the same time, hospital administrators finally tired of the psychoanalysts and started purging them from departments of psychiatry, where they had racked up a miserable track record of cure. Freud, Kubie, and the psychosomaticists had lost their audience by the 1970s. This still left the fundamental question unanswered: What is the difference between a brain disease and a mental illness?

The discovery of the spirochete in the brains of paretics overturned centuries of misconceptions about the nature of insanity. Until then, heredity could conveniently be blamed for most of the debilitating mental illnesses. Every family carried its own original sin from some debauched ancestor. Insanity was a standard diagnosis in its own right, not merely a symptom of something else. It was simply "in the blood" or "all in one's head." Noguchi changed all that. Instead of a disease, syphilitic insanity became the consequence of a disease, potentially curable, ultimately explainable, and definitely nonheritable from the father. With the resulting emergence of *neuro*syphilis as a legitimate disease entity, the word *degeneration* shed its original sense of a heritable and constitutional weakness. References to the "sins of the father" also receded into the background. Although *degeneration* remains in current use to describe the natural or pathological deterioration of nerve cell structures—as in *degenerative* nerve diseases such as ALS or Huntington's chorea—it no longer has any connection to hereditary vulnerability of the nervous system.

Before the identification of the spirochete, the perception of general paresis mirrored the perception of autism or schizophrenia today. Speculation as to its cause was rife. But like tuberculosis, cholera, pellagra, and poliomyelitis, it then underwent a natural progression: observation and description, discovery of etiology, exploration of treatments, and the development of a cure and its deployment. It is a great medical success story, but so far an isolated one. Schizophrenia, bipolar disorder, addiction, attention deficit and obsessive-compulsive disorders also present highly specific symptom profiles, as general paresis originally did, except with no objective reality, nothing to see in the brain. Yet their symptoms do respond to exploratory treatments—specifically to antipsychotic, antianxiety, or antidepressant drugs. It is then natural to ask whether the response alone qualifies these conditions as true diseases. In other words, is response to treatment a valid marker of organic disease?

In the no-man's-land between brain disease and mind disorder, a tentative answer can be found in an unusual condition studied by Charcot, and regarded by him, along with hysteria, as a true neurological disease. Its reemergence as a named disorder distinct from hysteria occurred in the late 1940s, and its response to a new generation of drugs distinguishing it from purely psychic phenomena occurred two decades later. To name it, researchers resurrected the man who first described it: Georges Gilles de la Tourette.

CHAPTER 14

A BEAUTIFUL NAME FOR
A HORRIBLE DISEASE

SHE was a twenty-four-year-old Italian American New Yorker, "pleasant, likeable, and attractive," according to her physician's notes, at least during brief intervals between her highly distractive compulsions—neck jerks, tongue protrusions, soft intermittent barks—none of them under her control, all of it starting from age ten, with the proximate cause, the temporal explanation, being a series of hay fever injections, totally circumstantial and impossible to prove. The onset was slow at first, the twitching of one arm, migrating to the neck and eventually the head. Her classmates, in the grips of their own insecurity (it was 1968), started to call her "Twitchy."

Things gradually got worse. At age twenty-two, she began to emit sudden involuntary, sometimes obscene utterances, but only at home. She could suppress the cries and the barks in public, but at the cost of other tics such as the darting tongue (cruder than William F. Buckley's reptilian one), the constant clearing of her throat, and the occasional low woof, all of it exacerbated by tension, all of it absent whenever she was alone or asleep. Various doctors had been consulted, treatments suggested and attempted, but nothing worked. She had become, not surprisingly, shy and withdrawn, a bit depressed. As a last resort, despairing of the neurologists and their ineffective treatments, she dropped in on Dr. Arthur K. Shapiro, a psychiatrist at Cornell University Medical School.

It was not his specialty, but then it wasn't anyone's specialty. It was too rare, too obscure, something out of a daguerreotype era. But there she was, and there *it* was—a rare problem in need of a clever solution. After getting a patient history and conducting a clinical exam, Dr. Shapiro delivered his verdict. She suffered, he said, from an unusual condition, one first described some eighty years earlier. He called it an organic brain dysfunction and assured her that it did not interfere with thinking or other functions. Then he told her what it was.

"What a beautiful name for such a horrible disease!" she replied.

Georges Albert Édouard Brutus Gilles de la Tourette is a cumbersome handle to carry through life, even if it does strike most people as singularly beautiful. Shapiro probably told the young woman she suffered from *la maladie des tics de Gilles de la Tourette*, an upsetting affliction for some people, a fairly benign one for others. Shapiro could find only fifty cases in all of the medical literature, the first nine owing to the landmark study published by Gilles de la Tourette, at Charcot's urging, in 1884. Little progress had been made since, though the number of confirmed cases had recently grown, along with the notoriety of the condition and the loosening of diagnostic criteria. But even with increased awareness, the disease, if disease it was, posed little urgency and generated hardly any interest within mainstream neurology or psychiatry.

Shapiro decided to challenge what he saw as lazy received notions about ticcing disorders by taking on not only this one patient, but the condition itself. He had no tolerance for the classic Freudian interpretation of ticcing as a narcissistic ejaculatory impulse. Nor was he convinced it was purely imitative, a variety of hysteria. If it did have a localized source in the brain, a new generation of drugs might help him find it or at least treat it. So he opened the medicine cabinet and contemplated the therapeutic armamentarium at his disposal.

Jean-Martin Charcot and Georges Gilles de la Tourette regarded hysteria as an organic illness with no clear correlate to visible pathology, even under the microscope. Unable to pinpoint it, they blamed it on a "dynamic lesion." So it is not surprising they thought the same about *la maladie des tics.* Like hysteria, ticcing appeared to imitate organic neurological disease, notably epilepsy and seizure disorders, too well to be purely psychogenic. Charcot had a simple litmus test: Could he imitate the symptoms? If he could convincingly reproduce them in one of his famous Tuesday demonstrations, it was unlikely they could come straight from unconscious and inaccessible impulses via the motor cortex. The difficulty of producing individual tics, combined with the effort of keeping it up all day long, eventually convinced Charcot he was dealing with a true disease.

Almost any gesture can crystallize into a lightning-like fragmentary microcosm of a tic: tight closing of the eyelids, nose wriggling, mouth opening, rotation of the shoulders, a sharp upward or sidelong glance. These often begin as nothing more than bad habits. People either grow out of them or adopt them. Ticcing syndromes, however, go well beyond habits. They cannot be broken. They usually first appear in childhood and get worse over time. The average age of onset is five or six, and the movements usually peak in intensity and variety at about age ten. Most tics in children, if they are going to clear up, disappear by midadolescence. By the age of eighteen, according to one large study, about half of all patients diagnosed with a ticcing disorder are free of their tics. It is rare for ticcing to commence in adulthood, and if it does, it is advisable to look for causes other than Tourette's, such as prescription medications, illicit drugs, or rare genetic conditions.

The current edition of the *Diagnostic and Statistical Manual of Mental Disorders*, or *DSM-5*, lays out three possible diagnoses: a provisional tic disorder, a persistent vocal or motor tic disorder, and full-blown Tourette syndrome. The first involves an onset of ticcing lasting less than a year, the second a chronic verbal or motor disorder of more than a year's duration. Full-blown Tourette's involves both motor and vocal tics with onset before age eighteen, and with no connection to another medical condition. The *DSM* is mute on what sorts of conditions these are—brain-based or psychogenic. For the purposes of diagnosis and treatment, it doesn't matter. What does matter is the presentation of the condition and its severity. Tics can grow in number and complexity to become almost choreographed. Bending forward in a bow, brushing one's hair with a hand, jumping, touching, and head tossing—all can be suppressed momentarily, but only through considerable effort, and the very ability to resist the compulsion, to stifle the action, distinguishes tics from neurological signs associated with other brain disorders. Huntington's chorea is perhaps the most devastating example.

Whether ticcing is a purely neurological disorder or a functional psychiatric one, in the final analysis it reflects an inability to resist impulses, so it reasonably belongs to both fields. Neurologists have never known what to make of it, psychiatrists even less so. They have come up with colorful names for its more bizarre manifestations—*coprolalia,* for compulsive cursing, combining the Greek word for feces and the Latin for tongue, and *copropraxia,* similarly derived but misapplied to the grabbing of one's own genitalia or other lewd gestures—but no cure. The verbal behaviors constitute a stereotype rather than a uniform feature of the disorder. In some reports, only about 10 percent of Touretters exhibit copralalia. The content of these compulsive utterances may in fact be culturally conditioned. According to some studies, Japanese ticcers do not curse as profusely as American ones do, perhaps because of social norms. Boys are diagnosed with Tourette's more often than girls are by a margin of three to one. These statistics hint at a cause, but no one has been able to prove anything. If someone were to discover a genetic marker, it might establish Tourette's as a true disorder of the brain, but for now it remains a notional one. There is absolutely nothing for the neuropathologist to see at a brain autopsy.

Because Touretters usually report the urge to unleash their disruptive gestures or curses as initially resistible but ultimately overwhelming, the disorder is tentatively called neuropsychiatric. Embedded in it is a form of compulsion, frequently paired with an obsession. True compulsions are unquenchable urges to perform physical acts such as touching a doorknob or a person, or arranging and rearranging objects just so. Obsessions well up when ideas cannot be dislodged from the mind and are played over and over again. In their most complex forms, obsessions and compulsions combine to form specific rituals such as rubbing the finial of a newel-post at each passing, avoiding stepping on any crack in a sidewalk, or opening and closing a screen door four times on the way in or out. Some children seek a kind of relief from hidden urges by repeating these sorts of movements and rituals until, as they usually say, it "feels just right."

There have always been people living at the mercy of uncontrollable thoughts and actions, and historically they were assumed to be possessed by evil spirits. This state of affairs lasted until the nineteenth century, when medical science chased away the spirits. The possessed then became patients, and a few of them achieved the dubious honor of becoming famous first cases. If patient zero is the source of an epidemic, then patient alpha is its archetype. Medicine has patient zeros, psychiatry and neurology have patient alphas, each of whom has wielded a disproportionate influence over our current understanding of mental illness. Blanche Wittman was one, little Maria Theresia Paradis was another. Tourette syndrome has three.

As Georges Gilles de la Tourette scanned the newspapers in the summer of 1884, he would have kept tabs on the cholera epidemic in Marseilles and the German microbiologist Robert Koch's efforts to find the cause of the disease. Elsewhere, the French colonial forces, after their incursions into Indochina, had set off a war with the Chinese. Jules Ferry, the French prime minister, citing the duty of the superior races to "civilize the inferior races," had established a French colony in Tunis. Even Gilles de la Tourette himself made the news that summer with accounts of his experiments involving the commission of crimes under hypnotic suggestion. The "murderer" he had manipulated, of course, was Blanche Wittman, whose name by now was familiar to readers of *Le Temps* and *Le Constitutionnel*. He had induced her to serve a supposedly poisoned beer to a man during a demonstration. This was reported as a salvo in the well-publicized skirmish between Charcot's group and the Nancy School led by Hippolyte Bernheim, all part of the hysteria over hysteria. Could a hypnotist induce an unwitting subject to commit a crime? Gilles thought not. He turned the page, and an obituary caught his eye: the Countess Picot de Dampierre had just passed away at the age of eighty-four. Obituaries in the French dailies were generally reserved for the military, the polity, and the nobility—the celebrities of the day. The countess's name struck a chord. Wasn't she the ticcing woman first seen by Dr. Itard in 1825?

Look up any reference to Tourette syndrome and the "Marquise de Dampierre" will show up as the first recorded case of the illness. Never identified beyond this vague and incorrectly assigned title, a minor elevation of her actual rank, she is the most famous of all Tourette sufferers, yet no one within the Tourette community seems to have any idea who she was. Effectively anonymous, she is the perfect cipher on which to hang an origin story. Her involvement with Tourette syndrome emerges through two levels of hearsay, and her true diagnosis is uncertain. Her fame rests on a two-page summary of her case by a Dr. Itard, in which she is referred to simply as "Mme de D . . ." It was not the first time Itard had named a famous patient.

Jean-Marc-Gaspard Itard has three claims to fame. He is known as the father of special education for his work with the deaf, as the first physician to describe a case of Tourette syndrome, and as the teacher who tried to civilize the wild boy of Aveyron. Also known as Victor of Aveyron, the wild boy was a twelve-year-old found living in the woods in the South of France. Assumed to have been abandoned at the age of six, possibly because of mental retardation, the boy could neither speak nor understand spoken language. Itard gave him a name, took him into his home, and attempted to socialize him in what was the ultimate nature-versus-nurture experiment. It would be immortalized on film in director François Truffaut's *The Wild Child*, in which Truffaut himself portrays Itard. The film's upbeat ending glossed over what turned out to be an educational failure. Victor learned to verbalize just two thoughts—"milk" and "Oh, God!" He never mastered basic social skills or developed the means to live independently. He died in the home of his caretaker at the age of about forty. The events of his early life and his true mental condition will never be known.

Two decades after abandoning Victor's tutelage, Itard took over as head physician at France's Royal Institution for Deaf-Mutes. In 1825, another extraordinary patient came to his attention. In his brief summary of her case, Itard provided almost everything known about her today. Mme de D . . . first developed rapid involuntary movements of the arms and hands at the age of seven. At first written off as mischievousness by her family, these odd movements graduated into something more troubling. They spread to her neck and face, resulting in extraordinary grimaces and strange, nonsensical utterances, but with no sign of mental impairment. As a teenager, she was sent to a specialist in Switzerland, who recommended milk baths. The mountain air seemed to do her good because her symptoms went away completely, allowing her to return to an arranged marriage in Paris. After the wedding, all went well for about eighteen months; then the tics and vocalizations reappeared. By this time her grunts had taken concrete shape in the form of rather crude outbursts, usually in the midst of dignified social gatherings. Itard does not quote her, but according to Charcot, who encountered the woman decades later, her stock phrases were *merde* and *foutu cochon*, loosely translated as "shit" and "fucking pig."

What makes her story memorable, almost iconic, is the contrast between the dignity of her social station and her inability to resist turning decorum into farce. It was as though Margaret Dumont had switched brains with Groucho Marx. Were she not of the nobility, Tourette syndrome would undoubtedly have had a different patient alpha.

Who was Mme de D . . . ? The obituary Gilles de la Tourette read belonged to Émilie Ernestine Prondre de Guermantes, the Countess Picot de Dampierre, niece of a Napoleonic general and aunt to a commanding officer of the Franco-Prussian War. Both men died gloriously in battle. "Countess" and not "Marquise," she was lauded for her charitable works. Her dates of birth and marriage seem to match those given by Itard for Mme de D . . . , but his description better fits Eulalie, Émilie's half sister, known for her *écarts de langage,* meaning her flagrant departures from standard discourse, a habit apparently beyond her control. Whoever Mme de D . . . was, she is an odd choice for the standard-bearer of Tourette syndrome. There is no clinical description of her in the final sixty years of her life, yet Gilles de la Tourette's inclusion of her case as the first observation in his landmark publication of 1885 heavily informs not only his own description of the affliction bearing his name, but also the one given in the current edition of the *DSM*.

It is only natural to wonder, given her remarkable recovery in Switzerland and the subsequent return of her symptoms after a year of marriage, whether Mme de D . . . had a functional illness or whether she had a brain disease. Her first odd movements at age seven could have been the result of Sydenham's chorea, or St. Vitus's dance, an autoimmune condition set off by rheumatic fever and involving rapid and uncontrollable movements in the feet, hands, and face. Charcot and Gilles de la Tourette knew the symptoms of Sydenham's intimately, having differentiated the various choreas into categories, distinguishing them from cases of hysteria. A simple test, according to Gilles de la Tourette, consisted of asking the patient to lift a full glass of water to her lips. A true choreic, unable to control the spasms, will spill the water. A ticcer will suspend the tics long enough to complete the motion without spilling. Similarly, a choreic vocal outburst can occur without the limb or neck being affected. This is not the case when ticcing patients blurt out their obscenities. Firsthand observation of the patient, then, is crucial. Relying on accounts of contemporary observers reporting their impressions can lead to armchair neurologizing. Does Boswell's account of the lexicographer Samuel Johnson make him out to be a Touretter? Was Mozart a ticcer? It seems absurd to ask, although the same can be said for the three canonical cases on which the clinical description of Tourette syndrome depend: first Mme de D . . . , then a certain Monsieur O., whose case was described in detail by two of Charcot's students, and finally Arthur Shapiro's famous first ticcing patient, the young Italian woman. All three should be disqualified due to insufficient evidence. Their persistence in the medical literature attests to the power of a good story over good data.

Georges Gilles de la Tourette's original interest in tic-like movements was piqued when he translated a work by the American neurologist George Beard. In "Experiments with the 'Jumpers' or 'Jumping Frenchmen' of Maine," Beard describes a geographically isolated group of people who startled violently in response to various stimuli. Today we call all these conditions hyperekplexias. Gilles also examined two related phenomena. The first, unique to Indonesia and called latah, involved a hodgepodge of startle responses to unexpected stimuli, mainly affecting women. The other, occurring only in Siberia and called miryachit, involved not only jumping, but vocal outbursts and imitations, all beyond conscious control. With Charcot's encouragement, Gilles de la Tourette published his breakthrough article, and called it "A Study of a Nervous Disorder Characterized by Motor Incoordination with Echolalia and Coprolalia." Satisfied with the result, Charcot named the disorder after his assistant. Its defining characteristics, outlined in the paper's conclusion, include motor incoordination in the form of involuntary and repetitive convulsions, combined with vocal outburst, often obscene, imitative, or socially inappropriate, with no sign of physical or mental impairment. The condition was not life threatening, did not progress into dementia, but seemed to be heritable and incurable. As with hysteria, Charcot attributed it to a dynamic lesion, and Gilles de la Tourette grouped jumping, latah, and miryachit into the same category as "analogies of the affliction we have observed and described." Struggling with the absence of any visible pathology in the brain, he asked, "As for the essential nature of the affliction, what can one say in the absence of any anatomo-pathological facts?" He meant it rhetorically. He had no answer.

In 1902, Henry Meige and Eugène Feindel, two of Charcot's former students, picking up where Gilles de la Tourette left off, produced a 500-page study entitled *Tics and Their Treatment*, in which they reviewed every recorded case of ticcing disorders, focusing on one patient in particular: a Monsieur O., fifty-four years of age, a robust former athlete in good overall health who kept a detailed journal throughout most of his life. Meige and Feindel reproduced large portions of the journal in their book. Monsieur O. noticed his first tic at the age of twelve—a simple grimace accompanied by a headshake. "I always felt an urgent need to imitate," he confessed. He would imitate actors on the stage, their pronunciation, their intonations and turns of phrase. One day he saw an old man grimace and he replicated the expression involuntarily, then picked up more mannerisms by observing friends and acquaintances, all consciously imitative, as he freely acknowledged, though the urge to imitate seemed unconscious and irrepressible. By his own description, he makes it sound almost like a hobby. "The initial motivation becomes lost to sight," note Meige and Feindel, "the movement repeats itself to no end." How it began is irrelevant; the subject is unable to stop it, and it becomes second nature.

Monsieur O. may not have been a Touretter. He could have been imitating one. The classical disorder associated with the name of Gilles de la Tourette, according to Meige and Feindel, "should be reserved solely for those cases involving progressive evolution of ticcing resulting in generalized involuntary convulsions accompanied by coprolalia, and occasionally by echolalia." The onset of facial tics should typically occur at the age of six or seven, and progress to contortions of the shoulders and head, eventually involving the larynx, at first in unintelligible grunts, but later in quite intelligible and socially awkward ones, always involuntary. The description fits Mme de D . . . , yet many ticcing cases did not hit all of these markers. For those cases, Meige and Feindel postulated the existence of a degenerative susceptibility to imitative behavior, evolving into bad habits. Citing Charcot, they placed heavy emphasis on hereditary predisposition, and in doing so supplied lethal ammunition to the eugenics movement. "It has lately been fashionable to say," Meige wrote, "that a ticcer has a neuropath for a father, a hysteric for a mother, an epileptic for a brother, or even a general paralytic for a grandfather." Unfortunately for the entire Paris School founded by Charcot, degeneration theory was in the process of being ushered out the door by the Freudians. Monsieur O. had a lot to do with it.

Sándor Ferenczi, Freud's imaginative Hungarian disciple, conjured up the official psychoanalytic explanation of Tourette's ticcing disorder, basing it mostly on Monsieur O. Because Meige and Feindel failed to preserve the patient's complete journal, the patient profile is limited. Still, it provided enough evidence for Ferenczi to declare Monsieur O. a classic narcissist. His ticcing exposed either an inability or an unwillingness to repress his masturbatory impulses. Where Charcot and Gilles de la Tourette had seen degeneration at work, Ferenczi saw only immaturity and a lack of willpower. This narrow and judgmental opinion had the effect of stigmatizing two generations of ticcers before it was discarded along with such Freudian notions as the Oedipus complex and his seduction theory. Freud himself, following Charcot, viewed ticcing as psychoneurotic, meaning organic. Ferenczi agreed, but thought the organic component by itself, though necessary in producing a susceptibility to the syndrome, was not sufficient to bring about the full-blown symptoms. Succumbing to the availability heuristic, he placed great weight on one other case besides Monsieur O.—in particular on a patient he referred to as "an obstinate onanist."

> [He] never ceased to carry out certain stereotyped actions during analysis. He kept on smoothing his coat to his figure, frequently several times to the minute; in between he assured himself of the smoothness of his skin by stroking his chin, or he gazed with satisfaction at his shoes, which were always shining and polished. His entire mental attitude, his self-sufficiency, his affected speech couched in balanced phrases to which he was his own most delighted listener, marked him out as a narcissist contentedly in love with himself, who—impotent with women—found his most apposite method of gratification in onanism. He came for treatment only at the request of a relative and fled from it in haste at the first difficulties.

What he fled from was Ferenczi's proposed treatment of "systematic innervation exercises with enforced quiescence of the twitching part." Roughly translated: trigger the tics and then have the patient try to control them, ideally while looking in a mirror. This proved to be an abject failure.

Ferenczi's theory may have been flawed, but his method had some merit. It prefigured what would later be known as exposure and response prevention techniques. Invented by Victor Meyer, a former RAF fighter pilot and prisoner of war turned experimental psychologist, the technique involved confronting obsessive-compulsive subjects with the precise triggers that set off their repetitive behaviors. But instead of taunting them with mirrors and appealing to their vanity, Meyer employed intensive coping strategies. His first two subjects had both failed to respond to psychotherapy or even psychosurgery. After undergoing his behavioral therapy, they became functional, not entirely cured, but not totally obsessed with handwashing in one case, and with sex in the other. Meyer's technique has remained the go-to method of behavioral intervention, though it would soon be augmented by a more remarkable, less labor-intensive remedy pioneered by Arthur Shapiro.

The introverted young woman who consulted Shapiro in 1968 sparked the first real therapeutic advance in the treatment of Tourette syndrome, and the only empirical attempt to understand the nature and cause of the disease. For half a century, psychoanalysts had succeeded only in stigmatizing the condition, in the process making it worse. Shapiro decided it was time to put an end to their involvement.

According to her psychological profile (the Minnesota Multiphasic Personality Inventory, or MMPI), Shapiro's patient was "a naïve and immature woman of low average intelligence and extreme emotional inhibition." Shapiro found her to be "unaggressive, dependent, passive, and depressed." He considered using hypnosis, but found her to be a poor candidate for the technique Blanche Wittman had mastered so artfully. She also rejected individual psychotherapy, group therapy, and Meyer's exposure and response prevention therapy, leaving Shapiro with only one other option. Antianxiety and antipsychotic drugs were hitting the market, fresh off clinical trials, with off-label experimentation being the order of the day. Shapiro, with his patient's permission, decided to see whether any of them could reduce or remove her symptoms. Maybe he could trace her problem to a chemical imbalance.

He decided to test thirty-six drug combinations over a period of a few months, repeating each one two or three times, with unimpressive to nonexistent results in all but one instance, a new drug called haloperidol. The response was immediate. At the lowest dosage, her symptoms disappeared on the first day of treatment. "Acquaintances looked oddly at her; relatives spontaneously shook her hand in congratulation. The patient felt less nervous, shy, and self-conscious, as though she had a new lease on life. No longer were stares a constant companion. Her mother reported that previously the patient had appeared 'depressed, dazed, and scared. Now she socializes, dances, and is calm but lively, just wonderful.'"

It was not quite the complete and instant recovery it appeared to be. The treatment lasted eleven months, while Shapiro tinkered with dosage levels and even worked in a placebo experiment. He then tried the drug on two other patients, a fifteen-year-old and an eleven-year-old boy, both suffering with extreme twitching, grunting, and in one case, self-striking behaviors, along with psychotic tendencies and depression. Haloperidol eliminated not only the repetitive behaviors but also the psychosis and depression. At least it seems to have done so. "Improvement," Shapiro cautioned, "might have been due to psychological reaction to alleviation of symptoms, placebo effects, and my reassurances that the symptoms were organic and not psychological."

Haloperidol, known by the trade name of Haldol, had been discovered in 1958. The Food and Drug Administration approved its use in the treatment of acute psychosis in 1967, a year before Shapiro's experiment. During his trials, it had the status of an investigative drug, its full effects and side effects unknown. The sheer number of drugs tested by Shapiro would seem to rule out a placebo effect, although these initial experiments were not carefully controlled. The immediate goal was the reduction of symptoms, and while it seemed to have worked, it cannot be conclusively attributed to Haldol.

Shapiro began to keep meticulous records on a parade of Tourette's patients who sought out his specialty clinic. He developed several scales by which to gauge the severity of symptoms, starting with a sample of 145 cases. Through word of mouth within the Tourette's community, nearly every TS-diagnosed patient in the United States eventually made the trip, and Shapiro ultimately amassed records for 1,610 of them. These included clinical examinations, birth records, medical and psychiatric records, X-rays, CAT scans, and EEGs. He administered either the MMPI (for adults) or the Child Behavior Checklist (for identifying problem behavior in children and adolescents), and he took a complete personal history.

Contrary to the eugenic claims of Meige and Feindel, he failed to find any evidence of psychopathology in the families of patients with TS, nor did he find higher rates of schizophrenia, psychosis, obsessive-compulsive traits, hysteria, or maladjustment in the Tourette's group compared to a control group. In fact some of the MMPI results suggested the opposite: better social adjustment among Touretters than among other psychiatric patients. In addition, when he did find psychological disturbances in his TS patients, he deftly attributed them to the unpleasant and socially ostracizing aspects of the illness rather than to a fundamental part of its biology.

"It is likely that the aetiology of Gilles de la Tourette's syndrome is organic pathology of the central nervous system," Shapiro concluded. He recognized the intellectual bankruptcy of attributing ticcing to narcissistic tendencies and the suppression of masturbatory impulses, calling Ferenczi's musings a "wastebasket diagnosis." Yet his own success with haloperidol sounded almost too good to be true.

The skeptic's case for Tourette's as a purely hysterical disorder is superficially compelling if anecdotal evidence is allowed. Mme de D . . . , at the age of seventeen, saw the remission of all symptoms for over a year after her spa treatment in Switzerland, only to see them return in full after a year of marriage. Monsieur O. freely admitted his obsession with imitation, how it gave him a kind of psychic thrill. Even Shapiro's first case, according to her family members, exhibited no symptoms while alone at home.

Shapiro's data would seem to weigh heavily against a diagnosis of hysteria, but there is much to fault in his measurements, in particular the vagueness of claims such as "at least 50 percent improvement" and "at least 70 percent improvement," with no indication of precisely what improved, on what scale, and from what baseline. It is not clear whether tics were reduced (although, based on case descriptions, they probably were), or to what extent obsessions or compulsions were mitigated, or whether social functioning—the ability to return to school or work—improved. Shapiro was careful to note the doses of the drug he used, but he admitted his inability to explain the precise mechanism behind ticcing, or why it subsided with Haldol.

Still, there is a strong argument to be made for Tourette's as a true brain disorder. Touretters have many nonspecific neurological correlates, including EEG abnormalities, minor or subtle neurological findings on the clinical examination, higher than normal proportions of left-handedness or ambidextrousness, and a higher ratio of male to female diagnoses. Numerous other factors have been brought to bear on the side of a brain disease: the premonitory symptom of the urge to have a tic, the tic itself, and the act of trying to suppress a tic all have correlates in functional imaging. But none of these clinical or imaging features is consistent, and in any case, they simply reflect the activity at a moment—a snapshot, not a disease. The high rates of attention deficit hyperactivity disorder, up to 60 percent in Touretters, and rates of depression over the patient's lifetime of up to 10 percent, are held out as additional biological markers. Similar correlations have led to ascribing a neurological basis for other borderline syndromes such as ADHD, adolescent adjustment reaction, and drug addiction. Viewed in modern terms, however, these conclusions are soft.

Tourette's ultimately did gain acceptance as a true brain disorder, and not merely a syndrome, in part by analogy with other movement disorders possessing plausible explanations in neurophysiological processes. The word *syndrome* remains attached to it out of historical continuity, but the promotion to a disorder, a halfway mark to disease, is significant. Lightning-fast involuntary movements show up in a variety of diseases involving damage to the region of the brain known as the basal ganglia, deep clusters of nerve cells functioning, according to physiologist Derek Denny-Brown, as a start-stop switch for all brain activities. Something in the basal ganglia initiates highly overlearned motor and mental routines, bypassing the momentary delay required for the switch to engage. Denny-Brown intuited that the switch also controls mental routines, and if left open, would create obsessional and impulsive behavior. The basal ganglia seem to be the best bet for the seat of Tourette syndrome, as evidenced by aspects of the disease itself, but also because drugs like cocaine, having their primary effect on neurons in that region, specifically on the neurotransmitter dopamine, can produce or inhibit such behaviors. The impulsive behaviors are different from similar derangements caused by damage to the frontal lobes. Excessive movements initiated in the basal ganglia are repetitive, unpredictable, and leave insight intact, whereas in frontal lobe disease, the loss of insight itself is inseparable from the impulsive and inappropriate behavior.

Another intriguing aspect of tics is their relationship to rheumatic fever and streptococcal infections. This is embodied in a controversial entity called PANDAS, or pediatric autoimmune neuropsychiatric disorders associated with streptococcal infection. Researchers noticed how patients who developed rapid movements in their limbs after strep infections also acquired obsessive-compulsive traits. PANDAS shares many characteristics with Tourette syndrome, notably tics, OCD, and attention deficit hyperactivity disorder, but for now it is only a theoretical disorder, one perhaps attracting more traffic on the internet than may be merited by the data.

When the discovery of the spirochete turned general paresis of the insane into a model for all mental illness, it initiated a search for organic factors in all functional disorders. But neurosyphilis is an unsuitable model for anything clearly unrelated to infection or inflammation in the frontal and temporal lobe regions. Like neurosyphilis, Tourette syndrome was first written off as a neurodegenerative problem in which symptoms dominate signs. It emerged out of a morass of indistinguishable sensorimotor afflictions previously attributed to insanity. The symptoms appeared to be imitative, possibly hysterical, likely hereditary or even syphilitic in origin. Unlike neurosyphilis, Tourette syndrome has not yet been solved, and may also turn out to be a special case, another neuropsychiatric unicorn.

Ticcing disorders, OCD, and even schizophrenia are not contagious, not germ-based diseases, and cannot be cured using antibiotics or prevented with vaccines. They seem to arise on the level of neurochemistry and neurophysiology. Haldol, it turns out, is not unique in its ability to reduce ticcing. It can even make the symptoms worse. The current explanation of this assigns blame to dopamine receptors in a specific part of the basal ganglia, making the relief of symptoms a matter of finding the right chemical balance.

This leads back to the question of whether the existence of a pharmaceutical remediation of a nagging neurological symptom is sufficient to distinguish it as a disease. Could it simply be that the drugs equally raise or lower all boats regardless of the patient's condition? (In general, they do.) Arthur Shapiro's drug treatment and Victor Meyer's exposure and response prevention techniques come down on opposite sides of the essential question of brain versus mind. Both have limitations. Meyer's talk therapy is inconsistent, it does not work for all ticcers, and when it does work, the effects do not always last. It tends to be more effective at treating phobias. It also has no objective metric to judge success. What does "improved" even mean? Shapiro's observations were similarly vague, and his experiments lacked the rigor of contemporary trials. Haldol works only while patients are on it. It suppresses rather than eliminates the underlying condition. It is in a class of drugs known as neuroleptics, and these will calm anyone, sick or not, indicating that the drug works on the brain rather than the mind. Yet Haldol did not clinch the argument for brain over mind. The prospect of a treatment in the form of a pill, something capable of providing immediate relief from symptoms—even if it falls short of a cure and even if it fails to answer the essential question of "What is causing this?"—has an overwhelming appeal, and it has driven a neuropsychiatric approach to mental illnesses that sidesteps the question.

Haldol was merely a bellwether. Other drugs, more potent and more focused on psychotic illness, were in the works well before Shapiro's experiment, and these would precipitate a neuropharmacological revolution extending far beyond the psych wards. Just as psychoanalysis did for over a half century, this revolution would divert everyone's attention from the real issue—where should neurology and psychiatry converge in the investigation and treatment of mental illness?

CHAPTER 15

MEDICINAL LOBOTOMY:
THE INVENTION OF THORAZINE

In the 1940s, the French pharmaceutical company Rhône-Poulenc re-vived the exploration of aniline dye compounds derived from coal tar, picking up where Paul Ehrlich had left off three decades earlier. They were looking for an antihistamine to preempt allergic responses to sur-gical anesthetics and to revive people from shock. In doing so, they came up with a family of chemicals called phenothiazines, organic com-pounds of no apparent use beyond making other compounds, notably methylene blue, the antimalarial stain first synthesized in 1876. One derivative of phenothiazines gave rise to diphenhydramine (Benadryl). Another variety also blocked histamines, but did something else, some-thing much more profound. It had a unique calming effect. They called the compound promethazine.

A few years later, Henri Laborit, a French naval surgeon working at the Hôpital Maritime in Bizerte, Tunisia, experimented with promethazine as an adjunct to anesthetics in order to prevent surgical shock. He noticed how relaxed, unconcerned, and even detached the patients were after surgery. Laborit then looked for corroboration of this effect. "I asked an army psychiatrist to watch me operate on some of my tense, anxious Mediterranean-type patients. After surgery, he agreed with me that the patients were remarkably calm and relaxed." As an anti-shock agent, promethazine appeared to be safe and effective, and

Rhône-Poulenc went to work synthesizing a more potent version. They came up with the compound chlorpromazine, better known by its trade name of Thorazine.

Laborit began to use phenothiazine derivatives routinely as a surgical anesthetic, and while speaking at a medical conference he happened to make an offhand remark suggesting they might also be used in psychiatry as a "medicinal lobotomy." Someone took him up on it. The first drug treatment of a case of psychosis occurred in Paris at Laborit's suggestion. A twenty-four-year-old man in a greatly agitated psychotic state, most likely schizophrenic, was given repeated intravenous doses of Thorazine, and he immediately calmed down. After twenty days he was, according to his doctor, "ready to resume normal life." By 1952, Parisian psychiatrists were administering Thorazine to psychotic patients rather than lobotomizing them, and the practice spread first throughout Europe, and later to America. As one French psychiatrist noted,

> By May 1953, the atmosphere in the disturbed wards of mental hospitals in Paris was transformed: straitjackets, psychohydraulic packs and noise were things of the past! Once more, Paris psychiatrists who long ago unchained the chained, become pioneers in liberating their patients, this time from inner torments, and with a drug: chlorpromazine. It accomplished the pharmacologic revolution of psychiatry.

The impact of Thorazine in the United States was impressive. Francisco López-Muñoz and his colleagues, in an article in the *Annals of Clinical Psychiatry*, relate how in 1955, the year before Thorazine was rolled out, psychiatric patients occupied half of all hospital beds. The number of patients admitted to psychiatric hospitals in the first half of the twentieth century had exploded from 150,000 to 500,000. But by 1975, two decades after the introduction of Thorazine, this had decreased to fewer than 200,000. Deinstitutionalization, made possible by the discovery of promethazine and its derivatives, commenced in the 1960s, and continued at a rapid clip. By 1996, inpatients at overburdened public psychiatric hospitals had fallen by 89 percent from the peak years.

Thorazine not only provided a medical breakthrough in the treatment of schizophrenia, but its success changed theories on the causes of psychosis as well. It marked the return of what had been known in the 1920s, prior to the Freudian takeover, as biological psychiatry. By providing the first reasonably accurate clinical studies of the effects of Thorazine on patients with manic psychosis, Heinz Lehmann, a German-born psychiatrist working in Montreal in the 1950s, struck the first blow against the creeping influence of psychodynamics. "Psychiatry," he noted, "needed a big contribution to show that the psychoanalysts were wrong." The new psychotropic drugs would provide it:

> Up to the early 1950s, the teaching in most American universities was that it is simplistic to believe that there's any kind of organic substrate to schizophrenia; that most psychoses . . . could only be treated with psychoanalysis, and that any other treatment than psychoanalysis was anachronistic and just simplistic. We had to show that there was a physical cause, a physical substrate, a physical pathophysiology for the major mental disorders. And the only way to show this, and therefore to help patients to get the right kind of integrated treatment, was by proving that with a pill you could remove hallucinations. Having shown that, the analysts had to admit that there was a physical cause, and we could begin to use the biopsychosocial model that we have now.

Thorazine was to psychosis what Haldol was to Tourette syndrome. By mitigating the worst symptoms of psychosis, it established a biological basis for something historically written off as either a psychogenic problem at best or a degenerative condition at worst. This was enough to end the romance between the medical schools and the Freudian analysts, but drug response by itself has not fully legitimized the medical diagnosis of schizophrenia and other psychiatric disorders or fully established their biological basis.

Xanax, Klonopin, Valium, and the rest of the benzodiazepines are exceedingly popular medications. They reduce anxiety as advertised, with few side effects. But does that make anxiety a biological disease? Thomas Szasz insisted it does not. Schizophrenia, Tourette syndrome, and social anxiety disorder also respond to medications. Does that make them true diseases of the brain, or are they merely, as Szasz would say, "problems with living"? The question goes back to the Marquis de Sade's stay at the Charenton asylum. We cannot tell whether he was insane or simply "out of control." A true test would be to see whether out-of-control psychotic and stressed-out nonpsychotic subjects react the same way to Thorazine, or whether its calming effects work only with truly diseased patients.

In the 1950s, a British researcher discovered an unexpected organic chemical in deep regions of the human brain, and recognized it as 3,4-dihydroxyphenethylamine, or dopamine for short. A year later, the Swedish neuropharmacologist Arvid Carlsson found a way to measure dopamine levels in brain tissue, and he discovered high levels of it in the basal ganglia. Studies of the basal ganglia had revealed their role in initiating normal movements. The next step was to connect insufficient dopamine levels in the basal ganglia to the symptoms of Parkinson's. This was confirmed by the Austrian biochemist Oleh Hornykiewicz, who developed and tested a drug called levodopa (or L-dopa), which reversed the slow motor responses characteristic of the disease. Experiments with L-dopa and Thorazine confirmed a crucial discovery made back in 1921. Although neurons had originally been thought to communicate with one another via electrical impulses, the German pharmacologist Otto Loewi showed that these impulses are achieved only when neurons first release chemicals into the synaptic spaces between cells. He called these messengers chemical transmitters. They are now known as neurotransmitters. By Carlsson's time, six neurotransmitters had been identified. Dopamine, he proved, was one of them. He won a Nobel Prize for it.

Heinz Lehmann had conducted his first trial of Thorazine on psychiatric patients in 1954. Not only did it reduce agitation, the bane of every psychiatric hospital attendant, but it suppressed internal psychotic symptoms. That was not all it did. Although it mercifully rid schizophrenic patients of their auditory hallucinations, it also made them stiff, rigid, slow moving, and tremulous—a condition dubbed *parkinsonism* because of its similarity to the symptoms of Parkinson's disease. If the dosage of Thorazine was reduced or discontinued, the parkinsonism receded but the psychotic symptoms returned. In this zero-sum game, patients faced a difficult choice: suffer with the physical rigidity and the agonizing feeling of being physically trapped, or deal with recurring horrific hallucinations. A few years after Thorazine became the go-to drug in mental institutions, yet another unexpected side effect became apparent: the delayed onset of excessive face, tongue, and limb movements known as tardive dyskinesias. The convergence of the three effects—antipsychosis, parkinsonism, and tardive dyskinesias—gave rise to a revolutionary model of mental disease based on neurochemical imbalances in the brain. This suggested a basis for genuine brain disease without any visible brain damage

As a result, in 1966, the Dutch physician Jacques van Rossum proposed a theory of schizophrenia based on overactive dopamine pathways. An excess of dopamine receptors, he suggested, produced psychosis and hallucinations. This would explain how Thorazine, a dopamine blocker, could suppress these symptoms, and how too much of it could result in the parkinsonism described by Lehmann. The human brain responded to prolonged exposure to the drug with a proliferation of dopamine receptors. This produced oversensitivity to normal amounts of dopamine, and the very opposite of parkinsonism: excessive involuntary movements all over the body.

It seemed Lehmann was right. If insanity is a chemical problem, the patient's environment and upbringing could not be blamed, and psychodynamic theories, notably psychoanalysis, would go out the window. But if chemical imbalances are genetically determined, then degeneration theory would come back into the picture, as would Kraepelin's original assumption about schizophrenia as a genuine disease, differentiated from

177

other psychiatric disturbances. Its driving mechanism, unobservable in his time, would take place on a chemical level. Hallucinations, depression, mania, and paranoia could now be tied to chemical imbalances. Also gone with the neurochemical world view of mental pathology was any emphasis on the *content* of what mentally disturbed individuals actually thought and said.

By the 1960s, with neurosyphilis a rarity and all but forgotten, the neurochemical hypothesis offered a fresh outlook on mental illness and insanity. Psychiatry glided into the age of neuropharmacology, riding the popularity of Prozac, Wellbutrin, and Xanax. The easy attribution of mental illnesses to disorders of chemical systems—dopamine for schizophrenia, norepinephrine or serotonin for depression (depending on which class of drug was ascendant in a given moment)—led to a web of plausible but unsubstantiated theories, and these proved to be at least as compelling to an eager public as psychoanalysis had been just a few years before. The new drugs also offered an alternative version of the psychopathology of everyday life, one couched in authoritative scientific terminology, with relief achievable through the convenience of a pill. But there was still a nagging unanswered question. If insanity is neurochemical, how could a chronic inflammation of the brain brought about by neurosyphilis produce most of the same features of mental illness explained by chemical imbalances?

Over the course of a century, syphilis had filled the insane asylums and Thorazine had emptied them. If penicillin cured the brain, Thorazine cured the mind, or seemed to. But the analogy is not perfect. Penicillin killed the spirochetes in the body, but it did not reverse the neurological damage wrought by either tabes dorsalis or general paresis. Those who received treatment too late would remain either paralyzed or mentally compromised. Thorazine, for its part, did not cure psychosis. It merely addressed the worst symptoms and relieved the suffering mind. But it is not clear which mind Thorazine relieved of suffering—the one residing in each person as a cluster of experiences, or the brain's processing platform where the cluster is created and stored.

The first of these, the distressed mind, is like a surrealistic painting, while the second, the brain, is like a painter's palette. In the painting, the patient's life experiences collide with innate characteristics we call personality. Qualities of anxiety, passivity, obsessiveness, risk-taking, aggressiveness, narcissism, even pessimism congregate in a disordered background. These traits color the stream of thoughts and behaviors. As for the painter's palette, the brain's sensory processing platform, Thorazine and other neuroleptic drugs modulate the application of paint to canvas. They do not change the content of the painted images, but merely steady the brush. Hallucinations diminish in frequency, and though bizarre thoughts may persist to varying degrees, the medication allows the patient to recognize them as unreal. Thorazine alters something in the brain, but not the stream of internal thought and experience directly. That is, it does not impact the mind as much as it blocks the effect of brain disease on the mind. It calms almost any psychosis, no matter what the underlying cause. Of course, beyond any theoretical considerations, it frees the patient from the crippling effects of mania and paranoid delusions, and allows him or her to function as a social being.

Still, it is not a perfect drug. As the former head of the National Institute of Mental Health once cautioned:

> It appears that what we currently call "schizophrenia" may comprise disorders with quite different trajectories. . . . We need to realize that reducing the so-called "positive symptoms" (hallucinations and delusions) may be necessary, but is rarely sufficient for a return to normal functioning. Neither first- nor second-generation antipsychotic medications do much to help with the so-called "negative symptoms" (lack of feeling, lack of motivation) or the problems with attention and judgment that may be major barriers to leading a productive, healthy life.

Consequently, Thorazine and related drugs are more successful in reducing the positive symptoms of schizophrenia (hallucinations and delusions), but less effective with the negative ones of apathy, flattening of emotion, illogical thought patterns, reduced speech, depression, and poor organizational performance. Evidently, the systems affected by Thorazine do not tell the whole story of schizophrenia. There is a part of a disordered brain it does not reach.

In a precursor of Isaac Asimov's *Fantastic Voyage*, French psychiatrist Jacques-Joseph Moreau de Tours wondered what it would be like to enter the mind (rather than the brain) of an insane person through the ingestion of hashish. He thought it might even have therapeutic value. Though he fell short of delivering a breakthrough, others would pick up where Moreau left off, but it took another century to happen.

LSD, or lysergic acid diethylamide, was first synthesized in 1938, and then tested by the man who synthesized it, Swiss chemist Albert Hofmann. He reported feeling "affected by a remarkable restlessness, combined with a slight dizziness. . . . I perceived an uninterrupted stream of fantastic pictures, extraordinary shapes with intense, kaleido-scopic play of colors." There seemed to be no aftereffects, and as with Moreau's hashish experience, he remained conscious and aware of his sensations the whole time. Hofmann had opened, to use Aldous Hux-ley's phrase, "the doors of perception."

It is difficult now to imagine a time when tightly controlled and highly illegal substances were part of the warp and weft of mainstream medicine. Cocaine, for instance, besides being touted as a wonder drug by Sigmund Freud, served as the active ingredient of Coca-Cola until 1903. A bottle of the stuff had contained about a tenth of the amount of cocaine in an ordinary "line." The soft drink 7 Up (invented in 1929, just before the worldwide stock market crash) conveniently contained a healthy dose of lithium citrate, the same form of lithium used in mental hospitals starting in the 1970s to treat mood disorders, bipolar illness, and mania. As 7 Up Lithiated Lemon Soda, it was marketed both as a soft drink and as a patent medicine. LSD only became a Schedule I controlled substance in the United States in 1968. Prior to then, it not only served as a driving force in the counterculture but was widely tested as an experimental psychiatric treatment, usually with disastrous results.

With the outbreak of the Korean War, communist agencies in China, North Korea, and the Soviet Union began to cooperate in the testing and development of mind-control techniques, including hypnosis, mind-altering drugs, and other methods of brainwashing. The U.S. government, in order to keep pace, decided to experiment with LSD, mostly in secret. In 1953, Allen Dulles, the director of the CIA, sanctioned a series of top-secret research projects in pursuit of the same objective: the testing of psychotropic drugs as part of a larger effort to develop enhanced interrogation techniques. Anyone who has read the 1959 novel *The Manchurian Candidate* or has seen the 1962 film of that name starring Frank Sinatra will find the real-life counterpart of the brainwashing scenes in the interrogations of U.S. prisoners of war in the Korean conflict, and in the emulation of these techniques by the CIA over the ensuing decade. The experimentation was carried out, usually with funding from front organizations, at over forty U.S. colleges and universities, as well as at hospitals and prisons.

In 1957, Ken Kesey, the son of a Colorado dairy farmer, received his bachelor's degree in speech and communication from the University of Oregon, where he had also starred on the school's wrestling team. Hoping to become a writer, but lacking the undergraduate background to pursue a master's degree in English, he enrolled at the noncredit creative writing workshop at Stanford University run by the novelist Wallace Stegner. At first regarded by Stegner as a "fairly talented illiterate," Kesey began to show some promise under the tutelage of such teachers as Malcolm Cowley and Frank O'Connor. To help pay the bills, he took a job working the night shift as an orderly in the psychiatric unit of the local veterans hospital in Menlo Park, where he heard about an opportunity to make some fast cash. He was given few details. All he knew was that a few Stanford scientists wanted to test some drugs, and as Kesey put it, "they didn't have the guts to do it themselves." The drugs included mescaline, psilocybin, and LSD.

The full extent of Project MKUltra, as the CIA dubbed it, will never be known. When finally exposed in the 1970s, then CIA director Richard Helms ordered all of the files destroyed. But some files survived, and these formed the basis of a Senate investigation launched by the

Rockefeller Commission. As usually happens in covert experimental programs run with little oversight, many lives were damaged or destroyed, the credibility of institutions was irreparably damaged, and little or nothing of any value was found. We do know that aside from Ken Kesey, the Grateful Dead lyricist Robert Hunter participated. We also know that the gangster James "Whitey" Bulger, while in an Atlanta prison for armed robbery, volunteered for the study with the assurance that he would be helping to come up with a cure for schizophrenia. Over a period of eighteen months, he and other prisoners were given psychotropic drugs, driving him, as he later admitted, to the "depths of insanity."

The catch with LSD, its considerable downside, is the relatively high likelihood of a bad trip, meaning a psychotic episode. The CIA discovered this when it secretly laced its own employees' cups of coffee with the stuff, and one of them jumped out a window to his death. Instead of reducing psychotic symptoms, the drug could produce panic attacks, paranoia, severe depression, and anxiety. The risk of such a reaction is higher in those predisposed to those symptoms—in other words, in schizophrenics. LSD produces a unique psychosis, a temporary form of insanity characterized by visual hallucinations and distortions with no consistency. People tripping together can have widely different experiences, one hallucinating paisley, another Lilliputian, and yet another cubist. It became fleetingly popular to use these experiences as a form of insight therapy, but the idea collapsed when the hallucinations, though vivid and recallable, could not be connected to the person's past experiences. The brain again provided a substrate for the internal mental environment, but had almost nothing to offer by way of insight into word-for-word content. "This is your *brain* on drugs," as the public service messages used to warn. But it is most certainly not your *mind*.

Ken Kesey and Robert Hunter were lucky. Their experiences, especially with LSD, engaged their creative sides. For Kesey, it fueled his conversations with the inmates of the psychiatric ward where he worked. Those tripped-out conversations led to his first published novel, *One Flew Over the Cuckoo's Nest*, which came out in 1962, just a year after Thomas Szasz's book. Kirk Douglas immediately optioned both the stage and the film rights, and starred with Gene Wilder in a Broadway version. Ultimately, Douglas's son, Michael Douglas, produced the film version starring Jack Nicholson and directed by Miloš Forman. It won five Academy Awards. Nicholson's character, Randle P. McMurphy, became the poster child for the abuses of asylum psychiatry, and although many psychiatrists loved the film, it fomented a deep public distrust of the profession.

One Flew Over the Cuckoo's Nest exposed the brutal reality of electroshock therapy and frontal lobotomy in a way that had eluded the mainstream media and whistle-blowers. It was one thing to hear about it, to wonder what might be happening in those gothic asylums dotting the landscape, and quite another to see it happen to Jack Nicholson. It was as though Elwood P. Dowd, played by James Stewart in the 1950 film *Harvey*, had been updated to reflect the counterculture generation, and the innocuous injection of "formula 977," with the promise to make Elwood "normal," had been turbocharged into a highly coercive, invasive, and violent act. The recent fallout from the McCarthy hearings added to a pervasive fear of conspiracies, not just from outside of the institutional structure, but from within. Although he knew nothing of MKUltra or of the CIA's involvement, Kesey was prescient enough to equip one of his lead characters, the Native American narrator, Chief Bromden, with a conspiracy theory of his own. The entire country, Bromden says, is controlled by a central enterprise called "the Combine." The psychiatrists take this sober thought as a sure sign of his schizophrenia.

Ultimately, MKUltra had much in common with the research apparatus set up by Jean-Martin Charcot at the Salpêtrière Hospital. Neither involved informed consent. Both took advantage of subjects who had little choice and no power. Everyone was under observation, and insufficient caution was exercised. In both cases, the goal was to try to control behavior under the guise of trying to understand it, but neither objective was met, and the reputations of the principal actors were damaged in the aftermath. In the wake of MKUltra, the big winner turned out to be the pharmaceutical industry.

With the success of Thorazine, pharmaceutical companies, recognizing a potential gold mine, produced a succession of breakthrough drugs for the treatment of depression, anxiety, mania, and psychosis. These included such well-known brand names as Prozac, Wellbutrin, and Miltown. As a result, psychiatry made an abrupt shift from the talk therapy of psychodynamics to the pill dispensing of psychopharmacology. Psychoanalysts, already in decline, saw their place in academic medicine all but eclipsed when, in 1980, the editors of *DSM-3* excised the unconscious from psychiatric nosology. Homosexuality was no longer a mental illness. Nor was Tourette syndrome. With Freud expunged from the canon, psychiatrists became specialists in dosages, effects, and side effects. They decided to treat mental disorders as *syndromes*, meaning "disturbances of cognition, emotion, or behavior that reflect underlying dysfunctions." Dysfunctions would be identified through "statistical reasoning" rather than through "causal structure." In this way psychiatry became psychopathologically agnostic. "Treat 'em and street 'em" emerged as the operant maxim.

In adequate doses, Thorazine has the inconvenient side effect of making people into zombies—staring, remaining almost motionless, lacking in impulse. Some patients report feeling empty, devoid of thought or the desire to act. Meprobamate (brand name Miltown), a tranquilizing drug developed at about the same time as Thorazine and the forerunner of the class of medications allied with Valium (including Klonopin, Xanax, and Ativan), also calms people, reduces anxiety, and induces sleep. Unfortunately, it does not help schizophrenics. In fact, like LSD, it often makes their hallucinations worse, more vivid and out of control. Thorazine's effects on hallucinations are more specific than those of sedative antianxiety drugs. It seems to influence a particular system in the brain, but not thoughts themselves, and by changing brain chemistry, it reduces the level of paranoid ideas common to schizophrenics. The brain provides the substrate for these ideas, and Thorazine modulates their intensity.

Thomas Szasz disputed the notion that a mind can get sick. In the broadest definition of *sick*, internal thinking can be deranged, and the way in which someone experiences or perceives external events can be disordered. This is almost the definition of mental illness. Yet it is not bidirectional. There is no evidence to support the idea that "the brain changes itself," or that environmental circumstances alter the structure of the cortical regions that produce thoughts. This is the modern equivalent of mind-cure: a popular notion touted in a few bestselling books, but lacking scientific evidence. As general paresis showed, the substrate of a sick brain can pervert the way in which thinking is organized and experienced. Does Thorazine calm the mind or does it calm the brain? Does LSD unhinge the mind or does it disrupt the functioning of the brain? If the content of thoughts could be reduced to the firing of specific synapses or to an excess or deficiency of a neurotransmitter in a particular part of the brain, then both drugs would indeed act directly on the mind via the brain, and Szasz would be satisfied. But if the phenomenon of mind merely *emerges* from the brain without a direct correspondence between thoughts and specific neuronal interactions, then Thorazine and LSD must act directly on the brain and only indirectly on the mind. This seems more likely.

The consistency with which the generic aspects of mental illnesses manifest themselves—auditory hallucinations, paranoia, delusions—suggests a uniformity of the brain functions underlying them. Consider extreme obsessiveness. Normal individuals can slide in and out of periods of excessively focused activity and thought. This is one facet of personality, developed to a greater or lesser degree in any individual. People whose lives are disordered by obsessiveness share the same overall trait, but have little in common with each other when it comes to the target thought or action. Many people feel compelled to repeatedly check their stoves or light switches, and do so in a way that is seemingly beyond their control. If there is no obvious object to focus on, the obsessive mind chooses another target. In other words, obsessiveness is a category of mind disorder with an overall similarity across affected individuals, but it does not determine the particulars of any individual's obsession. The idiom is the same, but the content is different. The form remains consistent, but the content of these experiences is personal. The "unreason" (Michel Foucault's term for the existential aspects of schizophrenia) stays the same across affected individuals, but the content depends on the available material. In many cases of psychosis, some themes do recur: dread of parasites (delusional parasitosis), persecution by authority, suspicion of infidelity (Othello syndrome), and religious grandiosity (messiah complexes). But these reflect general experience or possible evolutionary fears, and do not result from hardwiring in the brain. Irrelevance of content also applies to different types of tics in Tourette syndrome. The existence of the tics does indicate a brain problem, but the type of tic cannot be attached to a specific idea or thought. It has no meaning, despite what the psychoanalysts might say.

Thorazine, then, is the final link in a chain of neurochemical discoveries born in the attempt to cure malaria, then syphilis, and finally schizophrenia. Of the three, schizophrenia remains the most poorly defined and understood, and in the current era of psychopharm, it is unmoored from its historical precedents. It might be caused by a dynamic lesion, but then what circumstances could produce such a lesion? Is it hereditary? These are the questions that finally brought neurology and psychiatry back together.

CHAPTER 16

THE FEVERED DREAM OF
A SCIENTIFIC PSYCHOLOGY

In the spring of 1895, while returning to Vienna by train from a visit
to his friend Wilhelm Fliess in Berlin, Sigmund Freud began to sketch
out a speculative fantasia on the neuronal basis of the conscious and
unconscious workings of the human mind. Neurons, discovered some
five years earlier, along with synapses, axons, and the whole neuronal
theory, had swept through the clinics of neuroanatomists across Europe, with the finely rendered drawings of Camillo Golgi and Santiago
Ramón y Cajal establishing a new and exciting paradigm for the mind
as a product of electrical connections dancing around in the brain. By
year's end, Freud had filled three notebooks with speculations on how
it all worked, how a system of cellular interactions could produce passion, fear, inhibition, and anguish. As the two men hashed out the details by correspondence, Fliess enthusiastically, Freud more hesitantly
as the collaboration wore on, a book took shape.

Fliess was an unlikely partner. A well-heeled ear, nose, and throat
man, he ran in the same medical circles as Freud, and had originated a
baseless but persistent theory of sexuality connecting the penis and the
nose. His most enduring contribution may be his suggestion, backed
more by feeling than by facts, that men have twenty-three-day cycles
and women have twenty-eight-day cycles, and these regulate their personal health and mental lives. The differential calculus of Fliess's cycles,

prefiguring what we now call biorhythms, attracted many adherents, Freud among them. Fliess was very supportive of Freud's early work, and although a contemporary, in fact two years younger, he played the role of mentor at a time when Freud was insecure and uncertain of his future.

Freud aspired to be an idea man of Fliess's caliber, but he got off to a rocky start. In 1884, he published a short paper extolling the virtues of cocaine as a wonder drug. He experimented with it by taking it nasally and far too regularly. Finding it invigorating, he began to prescribe it to patients as a means of kicking a morphine addiction. Too late, he recognized his mistake—cocaine, it turned out, amplified rather than diminished an addict's cravings. His good friend Ernst von Fleishl-Marxow died of a cocaine psychosis in 1891, on a prescription written by Freud; he had become hooked on cocaine in addition to morphine. It took Freud another five years to fully give up the habit himself.

Fliess's influence only made Freud's dalliance with cocaine worse. In his paper titled "The Relations Between the Nose and the Female Sex Organs from the Biological Aspect," Fliess proposed an intimate connection between the nose and genitals, claiming he could cure all manner of nervous illness by operating on or applying cocaine to specific spots inside the nasal cavities. Freud allowed Fliess to operate on his own nose several times for the purpose of curing him of migraine, with predictably gruesome and counterproductive results. Fliess's obsession went so far as to use nasal surgery and cocaine to treat back pain, chest tightness, digestive disturbances, insomnia, and anxious dreams. Extending his nasal-genital connection to women, he would later perform useless and damaging nasal surgeries for gynecological conditions from dysmenorrhea to miscarriages.

Freud's three notebooks full of primordial notions on psychodynamics, along with Fliess's bizarre sexual theories, coalesced into something Freud called "Psychology for Neurologists." When it was finally published, half a century later, long after Freud had given up on it, someone slapped on a catchier title: *The Project for a Scientific Psychology*. It would not be a bestseller.

In the original manuscript, Freud describes three types of neurons: permeable neurons, impermeable neurons (facilitating memory), and perceptual neurons. Admitting that he has invented these distinctions rather than discovered them, he describes how the content of consciousness is supplied by release and transference of qualities and quantities of these basic building blocks. Pleasure, pain, wishfulness, attraction, repression, the ego, and attention: he explains all in terms of speculative processes based on a peculiar biology of the brain. The prose is dry and difficult to follow, and reads more like science fiction than like science.

Several problems became apparent to Freud before he tried to get the work published. It was unconvincing, unreadable, tentative, and full of qualified statements ("we are thus driven to assume . . . ," "in the absence of evidence . . . ," "I venture to assume that . . ."). The *Project* is not completely without interest, but has only one really readable passage dealing with the sexual origin of neurosis. It is the lone case history he chose to include.

When Emma was twelve, some boys in a shop laughed at her, or so she thought. Since then she has been unable to go into a shop alone. Freud unearths the fact that at the age of eight, Emma was groped by a leering shopkeeper, and the memory of the incident has gone repressed for years. Her sexual attraction to one of the boys awakened a latent comprehension of what the shopkeeper had in mind. "Every adolescent carries memory traces which can only be understood after his own sexual feelings have appeared," Freud wrote. "Every adolescent, accordingly, must carry within him the germ of hysteria." The story ends there.

Freud ran his neuronal theory by some colleagues, but quickly realized that for his ideas to succeed he would have to bypass an academic audience and go directly to ordinary people who buy books. Fortunately, he had something else in the works, his collaboration with Josef Breuer—*Studies on Hysteria*—and he wisely set the *Project* aside. It was not published during his lifetime.

Studies on Hysteria (1895) contains the case histories of Anna O. and four others. It combines the therapeutic method of catharsis aided by hypnotic techniques, in all five cases working back into the subject's unconscious memories to locate the original trauma, then attaching to it the latent sexual realization of its meaning. This entailed the fabrication of details in case histories to fit his overall theory, but the book achieved one of Freud's goals: it made for compelling reading, far more so than the turgid *Project*. He followed this up with *The Interpretation of Dreams*, in which he introduced the notion of the unconscious. In the year of its publication, Freud still lacked confidence in his vision. He wrote to Fliess to ask: "Do you suppose that some day a marble tablet will be placed on the house, inscribed with these words: 'In this house on July 24, 1895, the secret of dreams was revealed to Dr. Sigm. Freud'? At the moment I see little prospect of it." He eventually got his plaque, not so much for the interpretation of dreams as for psychopathologizing everyday life.

Is a scientific psychology possible? More to the point, can the theory of psychoanalysis be placed on a scientific foundation? This has been the Achilles' heel of Freudian analysis from the moment Freud set aside his *Project*. Can the mind and the brain be connected by a causal chain? The philosopher Joseph Levine called the difference between physical events in the brain and the nature of conscious experience the "explanatory gap." Although the neurosciences have tried to close this gap, the psychoanalytic establishment has largely given up trying. Psychoanalysts instead settled for a therapeutic method based on the elicitation of freely associated streams of thought interpreted through a system of metaphors (complexes and issues rooted in totems and myths), without the need for scientific backing, simply because, in their estimation, it works all the same. Given the sheer variety of psychoneurotic experience and the paucity of brain-based explanations for it, they have a point.

A young man is unable to function. Tremors, headaches, body pains, and a persistent cough plague his days. The doctors cannot pinpoint a source. At times he feels unable to get out of a chair.

Another man under the influence of hashish hears sounds as colors. "An overturned glass, a cracking chair, a whispered word, sounded and resounded in me like claps of thunder. My own voice seemed so loud to me that I dared not speak for fear of knocking down the walls or exploding like a bomb. More than five hundred clocks chime the hour in their glass, copper, or silver voices. . . . Never had I been so overwhelmed by radiant bliss."

Guy de Maupassant, roaming the grounds of the Passy asylum, declares himself the younger son of the Virgin Mary. He plants twigs in the garden plots of the clinic, telling everyone how they will sprout into little Maupassants. He howls like a dog and licks the walls of his cell. According to Dr. Auguste Marie:

> In his moments of delirium, he fancied his thoughts had escaped from his head, and searched anxiously for them, asking everybody: "You haven't seen my thoughts anywhere, have you?" Then suddenly he fancied he saw them, he had found them again and seemed radiant with happiness. There they were all around him and he saw them in the form of butterflies, infinitely varied and colored according to their subjects: "Black thought for sadness, pink thought for merriment, golden butterflies for glory." And then suddenly he would cry out: "Oh what a fine shade of red: it is the butterfly of sanguinary adulteries." He seemed to follow the butterflies in their flight, and made gestures as though trying to catch them as they flitted near.

What qualitative difference distinguishes these three cases, one a transient hysteria, one a transient high, the last a terminal syphilitic delirium? Does the content have any meaning? Or is it fair game to attach any meaning to it?

At any point during its progression, a disease involves both a state and a trait. The state is the patient's moment-to-moment experience, his symptoms. The trait is the underlying disease or syndrome producing the symptoms. If someone comes to the emergency room complaining of the symptom of shortness of breath (the state), the cause will be found to be something like water backing up into the lungs from congestive heart failure (the trait). The state of a delirious patient may involve hallucinations, paranoia, delusions, or disorganized and illogical thinking. Each of these must have a correlate in brain function at some level. The corresponding trait could be any number of things that affect the brain, from a psychoactive drug like PCP to schizophrenia.

The explanatory gap for Maupassant was simple. His state was manic psychosis. His trait was general paresis of the insane—a syphilitic brain inflammation causing cells to die off in his frontal and temporal lobes. As for the other two cases, the first case might be one of hysteria or possibly one of drug withdrawal. The second is the poet Théophile Gautier under the influence of potent hashish, as recorded by Jacques Moreau de Tours in 1850. It is poetic and exhilarating, and the state is schizophrenic-like, but the trait most likely corresponds to a transient disruption of signals between nerve cells. It is impossible to know to what extent Moreau's experiment bridged the explanatory gap, but we can say something about what was going on in Gautier's brain. Auditory hallucinations produce brain states that are indistinguishable from those of normal brains reacting to real voices. Not surprisingly, activity in the auditory cortexes of schizophrenics supports their reported experience of hearing voices. The same may be true of visual hallucinations.

Researchers trying to create a comprehensive scientific explanation for human behavior today are keying in on ensembles of brain regions activated during complex acts and experiences. These are described as neural networks, and collectively referred to as the connectome. There are two types of connectome, one mapping nerve fiber bundles that bridge different areas of the brain—the anatomical connectome—and the other based on regions that are simultaneously charged up during a thought or an experience—the functional connectome. These bundles of activity and connectivity, detected through MRI scans and analyzed using big data methods, afford a new way of exploring some of the most complicated human experiences and behaviors. For schizophrenics who hear voices, neuropathologists long ago abandoned the possibility of a visible brain lesion as the cause. If we no longer think of brain disorders as the result of single lesions and instead compare the activity of large brain networks in psychotic patients and brains of normal people, it may be possible to find the regions that are necessary (but perhaps not sufficient) for distressing symptoms such as hallucinations to emerge.

One of my colleagues has taken the idea a step further by exploring correlations in network patterns among large numbers of patients with traits such as obsessive-compulsive disorder or sociopathy, and has uncovered regions not previously known to be involved in any psychiatric illnesses. Network analysis can also pinpoint targets for treatment. It might even nail down what is different about the brains of people with schizophrenia or Tourette syndrome. This is uncannily similar to Charcot's idea of a dynamic lesion. But mapping potential trouble spots in the brain has a long way to go before it unravels the traits behind mental illness. According to a durable theory of Charcot's era, it may not even be possible.

At the outset of his career, Freud had the noble goal of trying to account for the gap by attempting to explain mental states in terms of cerebral biology. Rudolf Virchow and the great pathologists of the era were applying scientific principles to diseases of every organ; the goal of understanding the mind as a biological entity seemed within reach. Freud's abandonment of the *Project* is a testament to his good sense and his growing misgivings about Fliess, but he may have abandoned it in favor of a competing concept of mind and brain he found even more compelling. He called it *dependent concomitance*. The idea originated with the philosopher-mathematician Gottfried Wilhelm Leibniz, and was introduced into medicine by the English neurologist John Hughlings Jackson. It has served ever since as a tenuous dividing line between psychiatry and neurology, between brain and mind.

John Hughlings Jackson is mostly remembered today by the Jacksonian seizure, named for him by Charcot. It is both a wondrous and frightening thing to observe, and the description of it resulted from the observation of scores of patients, the first of whom was Hughling Jackson's own wife, combined with astute deduction. In the 1860s, before Charcot had taken up the study of hystero-epilepsy, Hughlings Jackson was deeply immersed in trying to identify the source of epileptic convulsions. Just as Charcot had effectively "decoded" ALS and Parkinsonian tremors, Hughlings Jackson began to see a pattern in classic convulsive seizures. They typically began with a twitch in a small part of the body, perhaps the side of the mouth. In a few seconds, the entire side of the face would become involved. The spasms would then concatenate down the shoulder to the elbow to the wrist and fingers, setting off a rhythmic dance of simultaneous convulsions in the affected body parts. If the seizure did not stop there, it would progress down the torso and hip to the leg and finally to the foot. Hughlings Jackson surmised that by this time, so much of one side of the brain was having a massive rhythmic electrical discharge that the patient might fall to the ground unconscious. His brilliance lay in recognizing that the sequence, no matter where it started and in which direction it spread, must reflect the intimate structure of the motor cortex on the side of the brain opposite the side of the convulsions. Older textbooks of neurology devoted many pages to refined descriptions of various patterns of these seizures. This was an example of classic clinical neurology—close observation of signs leading to precise and ultimately verifiable mappings of motor functions onto the surface of the cerebral cortex.

In 1878, Hughlings Jackson helped to found *Brain*, the first journal to link experimental and clinical neurology. As one of the leading neurologists of the era, he delivered a series of lectures in 1884 in which he laid down a heuristic called concomitance—the inspiration for Freud's dependent concomitance. The *heuristic* value of a scientific idea lies in its utility rather than in its elegance or fundamental logic. If it works, it's good. On multiple-choice tests, a common heuristic is to rule out incorrect answers rather than ruling in the correct ones. Another heuristic is Occam's razor, the timeless principle that between two competing hypotheses, the simpler one is generally the better. Hughlings Jackson's heuristic of concomitance applies Occam's razor to competing theories of mind and brain. He began with the assumption that the human nervous system is an "exclusively sensorimotor machine." The workings of the brain and the state of the mind at any given moment are linked for only two of the brain's functions: producing motion and registering sensation. Thoughts, on the other hand, cannot be traced back to a brain state. In other words, brain and mind are correlated, but not causally linked. The oversimplified example often given is of two clocks set to the same time: they have no direct connection to each other but will ring the hour simultaneously. In the case of brain and mind, there is a connection, but mental phenomena emerge from the brain in an unpredictable way. Two people at opposite ends of the earth can have the same thought at the same moment, and though their mental processes may be the same—they have the same idea—the brain process in each case is unique. The mind is then said to be an emergent property of the brain. It is not an automaton.

Emergence itself is another tricky concept. An emergent entity cannot be broken down into a cause-effect chain of processes. Life itself, for example, is an emergent property of chemistry. A hurricane is an emergent phenomenon of air and water currents. The human body is a machine, but the mind, although its flights coincide with the functioning of the machine, cannot be explained even by a microscopic consideration of the interactions of neurons within that machine. In other words, the brain is not a Rube Goldberg device in which sensory experience goes in one end and stimulates a pinball firing of neurons, and thoughts come out the other end. Yet it is still a device, and its structure and functioning can be observed in various ways that fall short of explaining where thoughts come from. One popular way of observing the brain at work is the functional brain scan: PET or fMRI. The images are striking and are almost always misinterpreted as portraying the mind. But they are decipherable only as depictions of brain processes at work, not as representations of actual thoughts.

When Freud weighed the competing prospects of locating the neuronal systems housing the unconscious or simply layering a philosophy of mind onto abnormal behaviors, he chose the latter. In one of his earliest monographs, entitled "On Aphasia," he gave his full support to Hughlings Jackson's theory.

> It is probable that the chain of physiological events in the nervous system does not stand in a causal connection with the psychical events. The physiological events do not cease as soon as the psychical ones begin; on the contrary, the physiological chain continues. What happens is simply that, after a certain point of time, each (or some) of its links has a psychical phenomenon corresponding to it. Accordingly, the psychical is a process parallel to the physiological—"a dependent concomitant."

The very idea of a "Project for a Scientific Psychology" is preempted by this assumption. Writing in *Brain* a century after its founding by Hughlings Jackson, neurologists George K. York and David A. Steinberg note that:

> The Doctrine of Concomitance has had two practical consequences for front-line physicians. First, it has allowed diagnosticians to focus on sensorimotor signs and symptoms, excluding the mental. The resulting neurological diagnosis has the virtue of reasonable consistency. Like Hughlings Jackson, most physicians are only too aware of the effect of the mind on health, but these symptoms are excluded from physical diagnosis. Secondly, the Doctrine of Concomitance further separated the disciplines of neurology and psychiatry conceptually and institutionally. Before Hughlings Jackson, alienists had cared for the mentally ill, often in large institutions. The Doctrine of Concomitance meant that neurologists could attend to sensorimotor symptoms while psychiatrists attended to the mental, a separation that extended to the laboratory.

Nevertheless, a cause-and-effect relationship between neurons firing and the act of thinking remains the darling of popular psychology and an essential goal of modern neuroscience. This is, simply put, an attempt to resurrect Freud's *Project*. It has perpetuated a culture of reductionist biologic explanations for every sort of behavior, mostly based on reading more meaning into functional brain imaging than the actual data can bear. What Hughlings Jackson could not have anticipated was the problem posed by neurosyphilis—a brain disease producing both sensorimotor and psychological symptoms. It would require a combined effort from neurology and psychiatry to solve.

Freud's star has been retrograding since the 1970s as revelations of his personal failings, as well as the failure of psychoanalysis to outperform placebos, have come to light. Over the same period, the invention of CT, MRI, and functional brain imaging has turned clinical neurology into an almost mechanized practice, with brain scans replacing the refined clinical skills once required to analyze brain function. The models of localization that formed the bedrock of clinical neurology offered a basis from which psychiatry could start to examine the causes of insanity, but the proliferation of psychotropic drugs has similarly mechanized the practice of psychiatry. Mood stabilizers, antidepressants, and antipsychotic drugs were great practical advances, but they changed the culture and outlook in both specialties. As a result, neurology and psychiatry have settled into a kind of algorithmic minuet, dispensing diagnoses and drugs while each one dances around the central question of the nature of mental illness.

In 1950, Freud's *Project for a Scientific Psychology* first saw the light of day when the original German version was published. An English translation followed a few years later. For a time, it energized Freudian thinkers with the possibility of establishing their scientific bona fides once and for all. But like a mirage, the goal kept receding into the distance. Even so, there remain stolid holdouts for psychodynamic theory within mainstream neuroscience. The eminent scientist and Nobel Prize winner Eric Kandel, a psychoanalyst by training, has written extensively on the prospect of closing the explanatory gap between Freud's theory of the unconscious and observable neuroanatomical and neurophysiological changes in brain cells. In a 1999 article entitled "Biology and the Future of Psychoanalysis," he wrote: "It is intriguing to think that insofar as psychoanalysis is successful in bringing about persistent changes in attitudes, habits, and conscious and unconscious behavior, it does so by producing alterations in gene expression that produce structural changes in the brain. We face the interesting possibility that as brain imaging techniques improve, these techniques might be useful not only for diagnosing various neurotic illnesses but also for monitoring the progress of psychotherapy." In the two decades since he wrote this, neither of these things has come to pass. While investigation of networks and connectomes has flourished, psychiatric research using imaging has focused primarily on schizophrenia and autism, and psychoanalysts have remained obstinately opposed to the collection and analysis of their own data.

Kandel's assertion that changes in mental states result in changes in brain structure has been partly confirmed. He carefully avoids asserting causation, but some anatomical connections between mind and brain have been made. London taxicab drivers, for example, who once had to memorize every street name and the most direct routes through a massive and tangled city, demonstrated a unique growth of brain matter volume in the hippocampus, a region central to memory. But this is a generic brain function; overtraining memory has nothing to do with actual thoughts. The same is true for violinists. Kandel notes how brain images of string players show structural uniqueness in the motor regions controlling the second to fifth fingers of the left hand. But the structural change relates to a purely motor skill. It would be a huge leap to get from there to identifying a brain pattern for neurosis.

It is also true that after prolonged exposure to narcotics or alcohol, a brain's synaptic sensitivities do change. Addiction effectively facilitates the triggering of certain pathways: the receptors for certain neurotransmitters multiply and make a pathway more likely to fire, though it is unlikely that new pathways are created. Besides, addiction is a diagnosis made through observation of behavior. It consists of a cluster of sociopathic behaviors involving lying, self-deception, and betrayal. Addicts are declared to be addicts through their behavior and not through the mapping of their neural pathways. It is not clear whether the behaviors or the changed wiring come first, or if faulty and susceptible wiring is inherited. Current thinking about addiction places emphasis on a genetic component. Addiction tends to run in families, and some brains seem to be more vulnerable than others are. Is this an example of a dynamic lesion, or is it conditioned from birth?

Functional imaging, biochemistry, and network analysis may ultimately reveal unique patterns for depression, schizophrenia, obsessive-compulsive disease, and perhaps even structural personality disorders such as sociopathy, or less delineated clinical states such as addiction and alcoholism. These patterns may expose the biological causes of aberrant brain function, while not necessarily advancing our understanding of the underlying psychology. We may ultimately be obliged to think of mental illness as the product of abnormal brain networks, without being able to associate types of thought with types of networks. Freud's great insight was to leapfrog all of this brain science and conclude that a self-referential, internally consistent psychology was required to explain hysteria, and later, neurosis. Once he had shelved his *Project*, Freud saw no further use in trying to match neuroses to brain function. The mental life of each individual case is its own thing, he realized, subject to fluid rules and interrelationships. The brain is another thing.

In general paresis of the insane, damage to specific parts of the brain causes mental disorders similar to those arising spontaneously from conventional mental illness. Thus the name: the great imitator. But the analogy to mental illness is limited. A system that purports to explain the individual's experience of depression, for example, is no longer connected to the neural correlates of the actual problem as experienced by that patient. An explanation of why someone has become depressed may be helpful, reassuring, cathartic, calming, and most likely of practical use to the patient. Defenders of psychoanalysis argue that reflection and realization change the brain. But they cannot provide any convincing evidence for this. Certainly psychoanalysis and talk therapy generally can change someone's internal narrative, and this can alter patterns of activity in a brain scan, but not the brain itself.

The disconnect between mind and brain also works in reverse. A deranged mind has motifs of derangement, including paranoia, delusions, and hallucinations, but the content of insanity, debility, compulsion, or crippling anxiety is personal, and not likely to be illuminated by brain science. No amount of parsing of the contents of mental illness can explain much about the corresponding brain illness. Any system, psychoanalysis included, may have something to say about the human psyche, but when it claims to plumb the depths of the brain, it is doomed. Visible or invisible, the same principles apply in psychiatry as they do in neurology; disturbances in parts of the brain produce mental changes, but only in form, not in content.

Neurology is now in a position to explain how general paresis produces the sequence of mental and physical deterioration experienced by

Guy de Maupassant. Neurosyphilis, it turns out, is not even a metaphoric imitator. It has no volition, no plan, and no design for survival. It is what it is. Darwinian evolution is not driven by cunning. Instead it involves a natural process of weeding out genetic mutations least suited to an environment, allowing better-suited ones to propagate. Within the human body, the lining and adjacent outer surface of the brain affords a very hospitable environment for spirochetes to flourish. When they do, the inflammation they produce damages three regions: the anterior parts of the frontal lobes, the undersurfaces of the frontal lobes, and the anterior tips of the temporal lobes. This has been known since the disease was first described by Antoine Bayle. Many theories have been offered for this distribution. Perhaps the circulation of new spinal fluid, constantly being produced and reabsorbed, is least efficient in these regions, and the inflammation is not washed away. Over a few years, the inflammation erodes the underlying cortex. The neurosyphilitic then displays the behaviors expected from damage to these three lobes of the brain. The manic, delusional dementia is from damage to the anterior temporal lobes. Softening of the very anterior parts of the frontal and prefrontal lobes impairs the ability to check experience and thinking against reality, allowing delusions generated by damage to the other two areas to be absurdly grandiose. A similar form of damage to frontal and temporal lobes, with an entirely different cause, presents in much the same way. Called frontotemporal dementia, it has only recently been classified and studied.

Psychoanalysis was a clever way of working with the content of mind, but as with all other such systems, attempts to make it into brain science are severely limited. Thinking is a creative act we repeat throughout each day. It is not captured in any meaningful way by recording electrical activity or by admiring real-time images from a stimulated brain. For neuroscience, attaching meaning and metaphor to mental disease is a continuation of its original sin. Psychiatry and neurology, for their part, split when Charcot included hysteria, neurosis, and neurasthenia under "nervous disease" and assigned them to neurology. Insanity, anchored in neurosyphilis and brain disease in general, was left to psychiatry. This reversed the appropriate division of labor between the two specialties. Neurosis is now a psychiatric concern; brain disease belongs with the neurologists.

When psychoanalysis took over academic psychiatry during the middle half of the twentieth century, it prioritized its particular and peculiar theories of mind over the study of the brain, and emphasized life experience over biology. With its demise, neurology and psychiatry have reunited in a grudging and unacknowledged agreement with Thomas Szasz. Behavior deemed to fall outside of socially accepted norms, without an underlying disease state, should not be pathologized. But in defiance of Szasz, the current consensus allows some pathological states, notably schizophrenia, bipolar illness, and Tourette syndrome, to qualify as true disorders without a confirmed etiology. The standard of care assumes that these afflictions, including insanity, are biological and thus medically correctable. Charcot, maligned by history, appears to have gotten it right. His idea of a "dynamic lesion," as applied to hysteria and other aberrant mental experiences, has an internal frame of reference in the workings of the mind. It is a product of the brain but not explainable by brain science. At least not yet.

CHAPTER 17

THE LESSONS OF NEUROSYPHILIS

I DO have one interesting case of neurosyphilis." Hannah was referring to Martin, the "man from Honduras," as she had been calling him. "When I first saw him, all his tests were positive—syphilis and HIV. He came to us because he had had a bunch of strokes, which left him with a hemiparesis on the left side. His cognitive abilities were terrible."

At first blush, it came as a complete surprise to find a case like this. Hannah had just returned from a two-year fellowship at Johns Hopkins in Baltimore, where there was plenty of syphilis, but neurosyphilis? A nineteenth-century disease, a disease of mad poets, novelists, painters, and musicians? Here in Boston? Unlike tuberculosis, which has been kept in check through stringent reporting measures, syphilis has been scrubbed from the medical most-wanted list. It is thought to pose no threat to the public weal, which is true—at least for anyone with access to a doctor and a pharmacy and an ability to visit them. But that leaves out broad swaths of the population, through which the disease is borne via its favorite vector, sex.

Spirochetes have colonized the human race. They still move from host to host, greatly aided by human foibles unlikely to ever disappear. One theory blames the rise on apps like Tinder and Grindr, along with head-in-the-sand attitudes. But those factors are merely accelerants. Syphilis has turned out to be the cockroach of the bacterial world, destined to survive the antibiotic holocaust, its complete eradication just wishful thinking. From the encouragingly low number of new infections of the 1960s, it has made a steady comeback, spiking with the AIDS epidemic in the 1980s, then growing exponentially ever since. A front-page article in *The New York Times* from August of 2017 highlights the dual challenges of finding its victims and then convincing them to undergo treatment; mistrust runs high. In Oregon, syphilis rates increased tenfold between 2007 and 2014. The state has created a website, syphaware.org, with the tagline: "Oregon is known for many things: natural beauty, coffee, beer and pinot noir. Did you know that Oregon is also known for syphilis?" In Bakersfield, California, there have been double digit percent increases in rates of infection over the last few years, leading to a rise in congenital syphilis in infants.

The current rate of syphilis in the United States is about 7.5 cases per 100,000 citizens. This translates into about 225,000 people with active infections, and the number is climbing back to levels above those of the early 1950s. This would have appalled Mahoney and Parran. After the introduction of penicillin, it was thought that incidental exposure to antibiotics for innocuous infections like sore throats would wipe out the disease, but in the United States, in men aged twenty-five to twenty-nine, the rate is now 41.8 per 100,000, with a higher incidence among men who have sex with men. For women in the same age cohort, the rate is 4.5 per 100,000. If left undetected and untreated, perhaps as many as 15 percent of these cases will progress into dementia over the next ten to twenty years. A few will show up in neurology practices and be mistaken for Alzheimer's disease or strokes.

The essential problem is the same one faced by Parran in the 1920s— the deprioritization of a manageable public health threat. There is no vaccine for syphilis but there is a simple and inexpensive cure, and if the disease were spread passively, like tuberculosis, rather than sexually, testing those at risk of exposure would be straightforward. But when it comes to sex, as Freud told us, nothing is straightforward. Add to this a disturbing new disease profile involving a mild, almost unnoticeable first stage followed by a quick progression to neurosyphilis in compromised immune systems, and the situation promises to get worse.

The disease could be contained, but the collective willpower to do it does not exist and probably never will.

Martin was living in Jamaica Plain, a district of Boston near the hospital. One day he left the house telling his aunt he was going out to get some milk. He didn't come back. "We eventually found Martin when his HIV doctor saw his name on a missing persons list," Hannah said. "He turned up in Lincoln Medical Center in the Bronx. They called me and said, 'We have your patient here.' It became a big deal because we didn't tell them he had HIV—we couldn't tell them because of HIPAA protocols. I had to talk to the social worker, but we couldn't give out any information. All I could say was that his family wanted to know where he was and that he was okay."

Martin had been a carpenter and handyman, and his skill set, despite his partial paralysis, remains more or less intact. He can assemble a bookcase, but if you asked him to design one, he wouldn't know where to begin. Neurosyphilis has robbed him of organizational skills. It has also taken away his judgment and common sense. For better or worse, it has left his initiative and determination intact.

"He later told us that when he had gone out for the milk he decided on the spot that he had to go back to El Salvador, where his wife was. He got it into his head that he was going to walk there from Boston. So he started walking and just kept walking. He got picked up somewhere on the highway and made it as far as New York, where he realized he needed to take his medications. He hadn't brought any with him. So he stopped at a hospital in order to get a dose of his medicine. He was dirty and he wasn't making any sense, but he managed to give them the number of this hospital, and that's how they contacted us. They extradited him. His aunt talked him into coming back to Boston by making a deal with him. If he took his medications, she would take him to El Salvador."

Medicine has acknowledged the distinction between observable organic illness and symptom-defined illness in the terms *disease, disorder,* and *syndrome*. Diseases have well-understood chains of causation called etiologies. We know the etiology of Martin's problem because we can detect the presence of spirochetes in his brain, we know how they got there and what kind of damage they have wreaked. Schizophrenia and bipolar illness are disorders that have not yet risen to the status of diseases, although it is assumed to be only a matter of time. A syndrome, on the other hand, is a collection of symptoms and signs with no commitment as to cause. Tourette syndrome was recently upgraded to a disorder because its response to drugs ties it to specific brain functions. Drug addiction, alcoholism, and obsessive-compulsiveness have been upgraded from disorders to brain-based diseases despite the lack of supporting evidence. The possibility that they have an exclusively mental basis seems to have been abandoned. Chronic fatigue remains a syndrome; whether it will someday be upgraded or discarded is not known. Some disorders—multiple personality, for example—have virtually disappeared, as allegedly has hysteria. Over the course of two centuries it has been variously thought of as a syndrome, a disorder, a disease, and a sham. Done in by its historical connotations, in current classification schemes it has been renamed into oblivion. In other words, it no longer officially exists.

Yet the modern equivalent of Charcot's *grande hystérie* is everywhere, its prevalence far outpacing syphilis or AIDS, and because it is a product of the mind, it will never go away. Estimates put the proportion of neurological outpatients ultimately diagnosed with medically unexplained or psychogenic neurological symptoms at about one out of every five. The symptoms vary among cultures and epochs, often shaped by social factors. The World Health Organization's *International Classification of Diseases* (*ICD*), an exhaustive listing of every possible affliction, takes an agnostic stance on historical terminology. Telegrapher's cramp, for example, still has a billable code. So does nervous prostration and psychogenic writer's block. The number of classifications branching off from *hysteria* includes neurasthenia, nervous collapse, nervous instability, psychasthenic neurosis, hysterical psychosis, dissociative disorder, conversion neurosis, and operational fatigue. The listings grouped under "conversion disorder," Freud's loaded term for the psychosexual origins of hysteria, have expanded with almost every revision of the *DSM*. Psychogenic disorders currently classified under "Psychiatry" in the *ICD* will soon be cross-listed under "Neurology" so that neurologists will not have to resort to euphemistic misclassifications in order to bill their hysterical patients. In this perverse way, driven by billing codes, neurology and psychiatry have been unified in a grudging servitude to an oppressive administrative dictum.

They have also found common ground in an explosion of so-called shadow syndromes, conditions exhibiting mild or single symptoms of mental dysfunction not serious enough to qualify as true illnesses. Shadow syndromes do not reflect doctors' efforts to classify disease so much as the noble goal of relieving suffering. Examples abound in my practice. A woman unable to quell her temper with her kids; a young adult unable to keep on task at a new job; a middle-aged man who is unusually pessimistic—each one is assigned to a box with the labels "anger dyscontrol disorder," "adult ADHD," and "dysthymic depression," respectively. A child who is not achieving by second grade or does not fully look adults in the eye is similarly suspect. Every deviation from an idealized societal norm must now be a syndrome—not pathologized, strictly speaking, but validated.

In 1774, Franz Anton Mesmer did much the same thing. He cleverly medicalized the psychic complaints of his clients by blaming almost everything on the nerves. "The exaggerated irritability of the nerves produced by the aberration of harmony within the human body," he wrote, "is what we designate as nervous disease." Thus did he conveniently ignore the fact that some people are anxious by nature, not because of disease. Others become overwhelmed by the circumstances of their lives and become depressed, but also are not diseased. Yet Mesmer knew they could still benefit from his help, and he promised to "cure nervous disorder directly and other disorders indirectly" through the natural medium of animal magnetism. To his credit, he succeeded with most of his clients.

A century later, Charcot dispensed with magnetism but retained the concept of nervous disease and applied it to a vivid form of hysteria. Thomas Szasz was right to complain about the proliferation of disease categories based entirely on symptoms and not on pathology, but he was wrong to paint everything with one brush. Charcot was indeed guilty of inventing grand hysteria, but his now-discredited theory grew out of an honest attempt to distinguish real from imitation seizures and paralyses. With the meager tools at his disposal, he decided there had to be something in between—"psychic disturbances that are just as real as those arising from an organic lesion"—and he labeled these *névroses*. Specifically, he assumed that the brain experience, or the brain state, was the same in neurological diseases and the psychiatric illnesses that mimicked them. As we now know from brain scans, he was partly right.

There is an area of the midbrain that, once stimulated, can produce a state of profound depression. No one is quite sure of its precise location or whether it is the same from person to person, but its existence would seem to make depression a brain trait rather than a mind state. Yet even if the midbrain can produce a state of extreme depression with a single touch, that does not explain depression. That is, the vast majority of depressed people do not have a brain disease, even though their experience of depression is genuine. It is likely that if someone is depressed as a result of bipolar illness, the parts of their brain that are active (or inactive) are the same ones active or inactive in any depressed person. The broad outlines of depression can be detected in the scan in either instance. This means there is a biology of depression, and its existence can theoretically be confirmed on a brain scan. But how you get to that state makes all the difference. If depression is the result of a constitutional and inherited disorder, we consider the brain to be compromised, and we look for answers and treatments there rather than in the patient's past experience.

In the same way, a sense of anxiety and the experience of an overactive amygdala nucleus deep in the brain always coincide, no matter how a person gets there. If a brain disorder such as epilepsy stimulates the amygdala, it produces an aura of extreme anxiety and fear. The same thing happens to most people following an exceptionally frightening experience such as being physically attacked, the difference being that the non-epileptic can roll back these experiences and calm those areas of the brain through talk therapy. The temptation to treat such experientially triggered states with medications is overwhelming, and we physicians often resort to a quick fix by prescribing drugs intended for patients with brain disorders. These rarely solve the deeper problem. On the other hand, if someone's nervous system is compromised with epilepsy, bipolar depression, Huntington's disease, or general paresis, talk therapy may mute the problem for a while, but is unlikely to fix it.

The human brain does three things very well—it produces movement, registers sensation, and generates thoughts. Consequently, a disease of the brain can lead to a disorder of movement, a loss of sensation, or a problem with thinking. But unlike the liver or the kidneys, the brain has one other special attribute. By constantly monitoring the internal experience of consciousness, it can and does create its own reality. In idle moments, it has a habit of surveying what it has created and is easily convinced it is not well.

Mesmer and Freud recognized that in order to talk someone out of a psychological state (a neurosis) it helps to have a method. Both men employed hypnotism supplemented with some shamanistic trappings—a robe, a tub, and a magic wand; a Viennese accent, a couch, and a cigar. Cognitive behavioral therapy (CBT), the system that has edged out psychoanalysis over the last three decades, is the most recent recursion of the genre: mesmerism without animal magnetism, psychoanalysis without the unconscious. It does not dispense entirely with trappings. The patient, now called a client, still has to go to an empathic, authoritative practitioner who has a body of experience and a system that validates it as an effective therapy. And most important, the client has to listen and respond. Medication requires no such involvement.

For the most part, CBT works as well as or in many cases better than antidepressants because it gives the patient coping strategies rather than explanations; it attempts to change the internal conversation but it does not attempt to alter the brain. Nor does the brain alter itself, despite the common conceit that talk therapy can affect the brain in some material way, that the brain heals itself. Changes in brain scans following psychotherapeutic successes may appear to support this, but only superficially. The stream of thoughts—good, bad, or in between—cannot be reduced to brain activity. The working mind is different from the working brain. Scans might provide a snapshot of brain events occurring simultaneously with mind events; they cannot explain how those events are connected, or establish the direction of causality. If the patient feels better and the brain scan looks better, it is impossible to know which came first because the scan has to be interpreted within the context of the patient's story, and this is where the reach of medicine often exceeds its grasp.

A century ago, institutional psychiatry treated most forms of mental illness as disease—if not of the brain, then of the body. Standard treatments included restraints, cold baths, electroshock, insulin coma, and ultimately, lobotomy. Freudian analysts resisted this trend by insisting on a solely mental etiology even of true diseases like cancer, asthma, and ulcers, attributing them to the psychosomatic conversion of repressed trauma. Today, most lay therapists, taking their cue from Freud himself (rather than his followers), limit their practices to problems of the mind, leaving bodily disease to physicians. Psychiatry, for its part, has abandoned Freud and allied itself with modern neuroscience, holding out for a day when statistical analyses will produce a Rosetta stone for decoding brain scans. That day is nowhere in sight.

Diseases, as Susan Sontag has pointed out, have always been saddled with meaning, imbued with agency, accused of having motives, and treated as persecutors, avengers, and adversaries. Sontag would have none of it. "Nothing is more punitive," she wrote, "than to give a disease a meaning—that meaning being invariably a moralistic one." Real diseases have no meaning; only cause, progression, treatment, and outcome. For centuries syphilis was thought of as a scourge of God. In time it was shown to signify nothing more than the proliferation of a colony of microorganisms and the body's response to their presence. With the discovery of a cure, the stigma attached to it diminished, but did not disappear. Yet any moralistic judgment layered into it cannot subvert its scientific explanation.

Mental illness is different. Unlike cancer or AIDS or neurosyphilis, it is intrinsically metaphorical. It has no scientific explanation. Freud got this much right. If someone is caught up in a mind state *sans* brain problem, the therapist will say, "Tell me what it is like for you," and the patient will reply, "It is like this." Psychotherapy operates on the principle that all experience is subjective, and that metaphors can be used to great effect in treating problems of the mind. But they can also be unreliable. Patients experiencing life problems may insist that "it's my nerves" or "it's in my blood" or "I'm just wired differently," but these phrases have no practical meaning, and serve mainly to shift attention away from the real issue. It is easier to blame the body than one's own mind. People who have survived a cerebral hemorrhage are usually happy to talk about it, even if it resulted in cognitive impairment. They have no need for a therapist because the bleed happened *to* them and was beyond their control. It is much easier to say "I had a stroke" or "I had a heart attack" than "I'm depressed" or "I tried to commit suicide." Those who feel depressed, anxious, or suicidal may even pursue a drug regimen for a brain condition they do not have. Similarly, drug and alcohol addiction are routinely rationalized as brain diseases and medically treated as such, partly to alleviate the social stigma, but also because of a problem with terminology. Mental illness, nervous disorder, psychosis, neurosis, dependence, dysphoria, insanity, brain disease: these are loaded terms, they say different things, yet they have come to be used too casually, almost interchangeably, even though what they attempt to describe can properly be assigned to only one of two categories—mind or brain.

The fact that a psychological state can induce the same pattern of brain activity as a truly diseased state with similar symptoms does not prove the existence of mind/brain states lying between brain disease and mental illness, between psychiatry and neurology. There may be many kinds of psychological problems, just as there are many diseases of the brain, but the two do not intersect. Grief after the loss of a loved one closely resembles depression, but is not a brain disease. Hysteria is also not a brain disease but rather the mirror of it—the mirror of neurosyphilis. It is a profound mind problem that makes the sufferer act as if he or she were diseased. Neurosyphilis is the opposite: a brain disease that can produce a simulacrum of mental illness. Yet our everyday vocabulary, even in informal conversations among physicians, has not caught up with this fact. The terms we use offhandedly have the effect of legitimizing all kinds of in-between states such as neurasthenia, nervous exhaustion, chronic fatigue, and nervous breakdown. These terms may no longer be officially recognized by the profession, but they continue to influence the way we think about mental illness, and neurosyphilis was largely to blame.

Guy de Maupassant's physical and mental deterioration was regarded by Charcot and others through a triple lens: one part biological, one part psychological, and one part social. Degeneration theory explained both the biological and psychological components. The social component, Parisian nightlife, provided Maupassant with motive and opportunity. Current psychiatric models still seek to formally explain mental illness as a product of three factors. This is called the biopsychosocial model of clinical care. The way someone metabolizes alcohol, for example, combined with his or her psychic pain and exacerbated by various social influences can result in addiction. None of the three factors alone can explain it. But today, unlike in Charcot's time, the biological component has coopted the triad. The allure of brain scans and the power of genetics have made it a de facto explanation for many disabling conditions, thereby overwhelming the psychological and social contributions needed to make the model an effective basis for treatment and recovery.

The false promise of neurosyphilis was that all mental illness would turn out to be attributable to the brain; that all forms of anguish, anxiety, torpor, paranoia, dread, depression, and addiction would be located in identifiable neurons and networks. This has not happened. Despite the grandiose claims of modern neuroscience, a one-to-one correspondence between mental events and physical ones may never be firmly established. Current neuroscientific research may seem to be converging toward a final answer, but only asymptotically. We have yet to answer the fundamental questions that Charcot, Freud, and Kraepelin struggled with: What is hysteria? What is madness? What causes someone to become "alienated from reason"? There may be nothing in between brain disease and mental illness, but there are very many things we are still unable to definitively assign to one camp or the other. What we tend to forget is that the brain is just a platform for the mind, not its blueprint. A brain trait, to the extent we can observe and measure it, cannot account for every discordant thought, nor does discord necessarily imply disease.

For now, psychiatrists and neurologists faced with patients who have symptoms but no signs to show for them still have to explain to the suffering individual what is causing his or her problem. We in the profession should begin by acknowledging that the final common pathway for people with true brain disease, with neurosyphilis as the exemplar, and those with life-altering disruptive experiences tends to look the same, but are very different. History has shown us as much. In neurosyphilis, the brain truly loses its mind. In hysteria (we are still waiting for a better term), the mind simply loses its way.

NOTES

INTRODUCTION

9   **"he who knows syphilis"**: A common paraphrasing of a comment by William Osler in an address to the New York Academy of Medicine in 1897.

CHAPTER 1. A CLINICAL LESSON

14   **Louis de Meurville's dismissive remark**: Mary Hunter, *Face of Medicine*, p. 167.

15   **"No one anywhere in the civilized world"**: Richard Webster, *Why Freud Was Wrong: Sin, Science, and Psychoanalysis*, p. 54.

16   **Elaine Showalter calls hysteria**: Elaine Showalter, *Hystories*, p. 15.

18   **"grand asylum of human misery"**: Georges Gillain, *J.-M. Charcot, 1825–1893: His Life—His Work*, trans. Pearce Bailey, p. 35.

18   **"museum of living pathology"**: Jonathan W. Marshall, *Performing Neurology*, p. 53.

19   **Marie Wittman**: Blanche's life story is detailed in Asti Hustvedt, *Medical Muses*, pp. 35ff.

20   **"Are you amorous?"**: Guy de Maupassant, "Une Femme," *Gil Blas*, August 16, 1882.

20   **"[Charcot] produces on me"**: Guy de Maupassant, "Magnetism."

21   **"I've the pox!"**: Marlo Johnston, *Guy de Maupassant*, p. 195 [letter to Pinchon].

21   **"I am obsessed by women"**: Ibid., p. 713.

21   **"Many symptoms to which I"**: Ibid., p. 195.

22   **"I can hardly see out of"**: Ibid., p. 306 [letter to Flaubert].

22   **"an abominable hypochondria"**: Ibid., p. 894 [letter to Dr. Bouchard].

22   **"I'm losing my mind"**: Ibid., p. 972 [letter to Dr. Robin].

23   **"On the last occasion"**: Robert Harborough Sherard, *Twenty Years in Paris* (London: Hutchinson, 1905), pp. 56–57.

23   **"Look, François, at what I've done"**: Johnston, *Guy de Maupassant*, p. 1,042.

23   **"He accused François"**: Michael Lerner, *Maupassant* (New York: George Braziller, 1975), p. 273.

CHAPTER 2. WHAT IS A DISEASE?

25   **"walking his post"**: The account of the Chomentowski case relies on Jeffrey Oliver, "The Myth of Thomas Szasz," *The New Atlantis*, summer 2006, pp. 68–84.

25 **"The people now have the original Davy Crockett"**: Jeffrey Oliver, "The Myth of Thomas Szasz," *The New Atlantis* (Summer 2006): p. 71.

26 **"Psychiatry is conventionally defined"**: Thomas S. Szasz, *The Myth of Mental Illness*, p. 1.

26 **"People say these are illnesses that doctors can cure"**: Oliver, "The Myth of Thomas Szasz," p. 79.

27 **"This is a colossal and costly mistake"**: Szasz, "The Myth of Mental Illness," p. 38.

27 **"Being called a psychiatric patient"**: Oliver, "The Myth of Thomas Szasz," p. 79.

29 **an abnormal gene on chromosome 4**: James F. Gusella et al., "A Polymorphic DNA Marker Genetically Linked to Huntington's Disease," *Nature* 306 (November 17, 1983): 234–38.

30 **Catherine Dekeuwer has defined**: "Defining Genetic Disease," in Philippe Huneman et al. eds., *Classification, Disease and Evidence* (Springer, 2015), 147–64, p. 155.

30 **Kraepelin "provided the single most significant insight"**: Edward Shorter, *A History of Psychiatry*, p. 100.

31 **"I ensured that a Zählkarte"**: Andrew Moskowitz and Gerhard Heim, "Eugen Bleuler's *Dementia Praecox or the Group of Schizophrenias* (1911): A Centenary Appreciation and Reconsideration," *Schizophrenia Bulletin* 37.3 (May 2011): 471–79, p. 472.

31 **he used them selectively**: M. Weber and E. Engstrom, "Kraepelin's 'Diagnostic Cards': the Confluence of Clinical Research and Preconceived Categories," *History of Psychiatry* 8 (1997): 375–85, p. 383.

32 **"I call dementia praecox 'schizophrenia'"**: Moskowitz and Heim, "Eugen Bleuler's *Dementia Praecox*," p. 473.

32 **"lent their authority"**: Thomas Szasz, *The Myth of Mental Illness*, p. 24.

32 **"Paresis was *proved* to be"**: Ibid., p. 12.

32–33 **"Charcot made it easier"**: Ibid., p. 24.

33 **the population of American psychiatrists**: Leon Eisenberg and Laurence B. Guttmacher, "Were We All Asleep at the Switch? A Personal Reminiscence of Psychiatry from 1940 to 2010," *Acta Psychiatrica Scandinavica* 122 (2010): 89–102.

33 **"The enterprise of inventing mental diseases"**: Ibid., p. 13.

CHAPTER 3. PYGMALION AND GALATEA

35 **"a singularly impressionable nature"**: George du Maurier, *Trilby* (Oxford: Oxford University Press, 1995), p. 50.

36 **Maria Theresia von Paradis informed**: Described in F. A. Mesmer, *Dissertation on the Discovery of Animal Magnetism* (Paris: 1779), pp. 45ff. See also Thomas Szasz, *The Myth of Psychotherapy*, pp. 54 ff.

37 **"Mesmer stands in the same sort of relation to Freud and Jung"**: Szasz, *Myth of Psychotherapy*, p. 43.

38 **a certain Fräulein Oesterline**: Mesmer, *Dissertation*, p. 33.

38 **"I am now less happy"**: Stefan Zweig, *Mental Healers: Franz Anton Mesmer, Mary Baker Eddy, Sigmund Freud* (New York: Frederick Ungar, [1932], 1962), p. 11.

40 **A scientific panel convened by King Louis XVI**: *Rapport des commissaires chargés par le Roi de l'examen du magnétisme animal* (Paris: L'Imprimerie Royale, 1784).

40   **A second royal commission**: Alexandre Betrand, *Du magnétisme animal en France* (Paris: J. B. Baillière, 1826).

41   **verges on the ecstatic**: Paul Buchanan, *The American Women's Rights Movement: A Chronology of Events and of Opportunities from 1600 to 2008* (Boston: Branden Books, 2009), pp. 80–81.

42   **He initially called it neurypnology**: James Braid, *Neurypnology; or the Rationale of Nervous Sleep, Considered in Relation with Animal Magnetism* (London: J. Churchill, 1843), pp. 12–13.

42   **"Living in this way"**: Georges Gillain, *J.-M. Charcot, 1825–1893: His Life—His Work*, trans. Pearce Bailey, p. 135.

43   **hysterical women had "attacks"**: Georges Didi-Huberman, *Invention of Hysteria*, p. 76.

43   **"ephemeral, changeable"**: Ibid., p. 77.

CHAPTER 4. THE INVENTION OF HYSTERIA

45   **"More than once his closest pupils"**: Georges Gillain, *J.-M.Charcot, 1825–1893: His Life—His Work*, p. 53.

46   **"Everything in his lectures"**: Ibid., p. 55.

47   **"There is something mystical"**: Félix Platel, *Les Hommes de Mon Temps* (Paris: Bureau de Figaro, c. 1878).

47   **he isolated an extreme form**: See Paul Richer, "Étude Descriptive de la Grande Attaque Hystérique," thesis of 1879.

48   **Charcot introduced hypnosis in 1878**: J. Bogousslavsky, O. Walusinski, and D. Veyrunes, "Crime, Hysteria, and Belle Époque Hypnotism: The Path Traced by Jean-Martin Charcot and Georges Gilles de la Tourette," *European Neurology* 62.4 (2009): 193–99, p. 195.

49   *artificial* **hysteria . . . unfolded**: Diana P. Faber, "Jean-Martin Charcot and the Epilepsy/Hysteria Relationship," *Journal of the History of the Neurosciences* 6.3 (1997): 275–90, p. 283.

50   **In 1882, Charcot presented this theory**: J-M Charcot, "On the Various Nervous States Determined by Hypnotization in Hysterics."

50   **Why did Charcot medicalize hysteria**: Jan Goldstein, "The Hysteria Diagnosis and the Politics of Anti-Clericalism in Late Nineteenth-Century France," p. 234.

51   **Binet and Charles Féré**: Alfred Binet and Charles Féré, *Animal Magnetism* (New York: D. Appleton, 1888).

51   **"When it came time to take off her corset"**: Asti Hustvedt, *Medical Muses*, p. 80.

52   **among the "stars of hysteria"**: Jane Avril, *Mes Mémoires* (Paris: Phébus, 2005).

52   **He renamed the condition** *pithiatisme*: Joseph Babinski, "Hystérie et Pithiatisme," *Éxposé des Travaux Scientifiques* (Paris: Masson, 1913).

52   **called the Babinski sign**: Joseph Babinski, "Sur le Réflexe Cutané Plantaire dans Certaines Affections Organiques du Système Nerveux Central," *Comptes Rendus des Séances de la Société de Biologie* 3 (1896), p. 207.

53   **"for the most part, a mental illness"**: C. G. Goetz, "Charcot, Hysteria, and Simulated Disorders," *Handbook of Clinical Neurology* 139 (2016): 11–23, p. 17.

53   **"Never has an actor or painter"**: Jules Claretie, *Le Temps*, July 11, 1884.

54   **"If we were put to sleep"**: Alphonse-Marie Baudouin, "Quelques Souvenirs de la Salpêtrière," *La Presse Médicale* 21 (1925): 517–20.

54   **The French government bought**: Mary Hunter, *The Face of Medicine*, p. 189.

54 **psychiatry and neurology as cooperative specialties**: Charcot, "Introduction," *Archives de Neurologie*, July 1880, p. 2.

CHAPTER 5. THE PAPUAN IDOL

57 **"a fragment of poetry"**: Julien Bogousslavsky, *Following Charcot*, p. 75.

57 **the scandalous nature of these trials**: J. Bogousslavsky, O. Walusinski, and D. Veyrunes, "Crime, Hysteria, and Belle Époque Hypnotism," *European Neurology* 62.4 (2009): 193–99, p. 197.

58 **Argyll Robertson pupil**: Douglas M.C.L. Argyll Robertson, "Four Cases of Spinal Miosis: With Remarks on the Action of Light on the Pupil," *Edinburgh Medical Journal* 15 (1869): 487–93.

58 **Macdonald Critchley provided detailed accounts of the disease**: Macdonald Critchley, *The Divine Banquet of the Brain*, pp. 203–205.

59 **Armour . . . Long conversation . . . Not once:** Daudet, *In the Land of Pain*, pp. 14, 23, 24.

62 **"What a bizarre story!"**: Quoted in Olivier Walusinski and Gregory Duncan, "Living His Writings: The Example of Neurologist Georges G. de la Tourette," *Movement Disorders* 25 (2010): 2,290–2,295.

62 **"I was unable to shake off"**: Asti Hustvedt, *Medical Muses*, p. 136.

63 **"Tourette was ugly"**: Walusinski and Duncan, "Living His Writings."

CHAPTER 6. HEARTS OF DARKNESS

65 **"The wilderness . . . had taken him"**: Joseph Conrad, *Heart of Darkness*, chapter 3.

65 **You should have heard him say, "My ivory"**: Ibid., p. 49.

68 **This vignette . . . comes from a lengthy Latin poem**: Girolamo Fracastoro, *La Syphilis: Le Mal Français*, trans. Alfred Fournier (Paris: Adrien Delahaye, 1869).

68 **"On their flippant way through Italy"**: Cited by John Frith in "Syphilis—Its Early History and Treatment Until Penicillin and the Debate on Its Origins," *Journal of Military and Veterans' Health* 20.4, p. 50.

69 **"know syphilis, and the whole of medicine"**: William Osler, "Internal Medicine as a Vocation," in *Aequanimitas, with Other Addresses to Medical Students, Nurses, and Practitioners of Medicine* (Philadelphia: R. Blakiston's Son & Co., 1905).

70 **"The entire body is so repulsive"**: Camillo Di Cicco, *History of Syphilis*, p. 10.

71 **"the disease itself was never . . . more rife"**: William Clowes, *A Brief and Necessary Treatise Touching the Cure of the Disease Now Usually Called Lues Veneris*, 1596.

72 **"You cannot catch a double dose of syphilis"**: Deborah Hayden, *Pox*, p. 138.

72 **the 74-gun British warship HMS *Triumph***: M. P. Earles, "A Case of Mass Poisoning with Mercury Vapour on Board H.M.S. *Triumph* at Cadiz, 1810," *Medical History* 8.3 (July 1964): 281–86.

73 **Karen Wetterhahn**: Karen Endicott, "The Trembling Edge of Science," *Dartmouth Alumni Magazine*, April 1998.

75 **"It pains me to speak in a journal"**: Marlo Johnston, *Guy de Maupassant*, p. 1,125.

76 **" 'The king died' "**: E. M. Forster, *Aspects of the Novel* (New York: Harcourt, Brace, 1954), p. 86.

CHAPTER 7. THE SOUL OF A NEW DISEASE

78 **"He does not belong"**: Gilbert Lely, *Vie du Marquis de Sade* (Paris, 1965), p. 640.

79 **"I shall have attained the objective"**: Antoine Bayle, "Recherches sur L'arachnitis Chronique," Thèse No. 247, Paris, 1822.

80 **"the opening of the body"**: E. H. Hare, "The Origin and Spread of Dementia Paralytica," *Journal of Mental Science* 105.440 (July 1959): 594–626, p. 605.

80 **"A subject is mad or delirious"**: Wayne Petherick and Grant Sinnamon, eds., *The Psychology of Criminal and Antisocial Behavior* (Academic Press, 2017), p. 493.

80 **"Its gravity," Bayle noted**: Antoine Bayle, "Traité des Maladies du Cerveau et de Ses Membranes," Paris, 1826.

81 **He estimated that a fifth of all admissions**: Hare, "Origin and Spread," p. 605.

81 **"father of the concept that a specific disease of the brain"**: Moore and Solomon, *Contributions of Haslam, Bayle, and Esmarch and Jessen to the History of Neurosyphilis*, p. 808.

81 **"I am aware that this locution"**: Louis-Florentin Calmeil, *De la Paralysie Considérée chez les Aliénés* (Paris: J. B. Baillère, 1826), p. 9.

82 **"The malady afflicts men of every rank"**: Ibid., p. 375.

83 **"so little is to be found in the special psychiatric literature"**: Moore and Solomon, *Contributions*, p. 831.

84 **"He who is generally paralyzed"**: E. H. Hare, "Origin and Spread," p. 594, fn. 1.

84 **"Psychological diseases are diseases of the brain"**: Wilhelm Griesinger, *Die Pathologie und Therapie der Psychischen Krankheiten* (Stuttgart: Krabbe, 1845).

85 **"he is Emperor Napoléon"**: Moore and Solomon, p. 811.

85 **The Bicêtre asylum**: Laure Murat, *The Man Who Thought He Was Napoleon*, p. 112.

86 **"Syphilis is in a sense the making of psychiatry"**: Southard and Solomon, *Neurosyphilis*, p. 8.

86 **Fracastoro's poem**: Girolamo Fracastoro, *La Syphilis: Le Mal Français*, trans. Alfred Fournier (Paris: Adrien Delahaye, 1869).

87 **He was accused . . . of "seeing syphilis everywhere"**: M. A. Waugh, "Alfred Fournier, 1832–1914: His Influence on Venereology," *British Journal of Venereal Disease* 50.3 (1974): 232–36, p. 235.

87 **syphilis-*related*, or what he called *parasyphilitic***: Alfred Fournier, *Les Affections Parasyphilitiques* (Paris: Rueff et Cie, 1894).

88 **"I made myself a collector"**: J. Darier, "Alfred Fournier, 1832–1914," *Journal of Cutaneous Diseases Including Syphilis* 36 (1918): 482–93, p. 492.

CHAPTER 8. THE UNSETTLED TERRITORIES OF THE MIND

89 **"On the day that the writer"**: Charles Baudelaire, *Intimate Journals,* trans. Christopher Isherwood (2006), p. 85.

89 **"this disgusting and ignoble disease"**: L. P. Rudnick, *Suppressed Memoirs of Mabel Dodge Luhan*, p. 131.

89 **"They didn't think it funny"**: D. H. Lawrence, "Introduction to These Paintings," *Late Essays and Articles* (Cambridge: Cambridge University Press, 2004), p. 188.

90 **"No man can look without a sort of horror"**: Ibid.

90 **"ghastly secret things"**: Rudnick, *Suppressed Memoirs*, p. 131.

92 **"Syphilis in the male parent"**: Freud, *A Case of Hysteria*, footnote to p. 20.

92 **"The appearance of syphilis in our midst"**: Lawrence, "Introduction," p. 189.

93 **"The disease I have as my birthright"**: Henrik Ibsen, "Ghosts," act 3, *Ibsen's Prose Dramas* (New York: Scribner's, 1906), p. 96.

93 **"an open drain; a loathsome sore"**: quoted in G. B. Shaw, *The Quintessence of Ibsenism* (New York: Brentano's, 1913), p. 93.

93 **"They called it Locomotus attacks us"**: Rudyard Kipling, *Soldiers Three and Other Military Tales, Part II* (New York: Charles Scribner's Sons, 1897), p. 335.

96 "It seemed that my body was dissolving": Jacques-Joseph Moreau de Tours, *Hashish and Mental Illness,* p. 11.

97 "In order to know how a madman loses reason": Ibid., p. 17.

97 "There is not a single, elementary manifestation": Ibid., p. 18.

98 "Does psychosis . . . depend upon organic lesions?": Ibid., p. 207.

99 "*One is insane or one isn't*": Benjamin Ball, *Les Frontières de la Folie,* pp. 72–73.

99 "The astuteness of the Moslems": Ibid.

100 "walked about the streets, lonely and full of longing": Freud, *The Psychopathology of Everyday Life, Standard Edition* 6, p. 149.

CHAPTER 9. THE DIFFICULT CASE OF ANNA O.

103 "talking cure": This follows a useful recapitulation and reassessment of the case in Mikkel Borch-Jacobsen, *Remembering Anna O.*

104 "it was not any kind of emotional excitation": Freud, *Autobiographical Study* (New York: W. W. Norton, 1952), pp. 42-43.

104 "extraordinarily underdeveloped": Ibid, p. 40.

104 "the great man showed no interest": Freud, "Autobiography," *Standard Edition* 20, pp. 19–20.

105 "Bertha is once again in the sanatorium": John Forrester, "The True Story of Anna O.," *Social Research* 53.2 (Summer 1986): 327–47, p. 341.

105 "Now the child I have from Dr. Breuer": Letter from Sigmund Freud to Stefan Zweig, June 2, 1932. E. L. Freud, ed., *Letters of Sigmund Freud,* trans. Tania and James Stern (New York: Basic Books, 1960), p. 266.

106 "No one else has affected me": Freud, letter to Martha Bernays, November 24, 1885, *Standard Edition* 3, p. 10.

106-107 "So greatly did Charcot overestimate heredity": Freud, "Charcot," *Standard Edition* 3, p. 23.

107 "our civilization is built up on the suppression of instincts": Freud, "'Civilized' Sexual Morality and Modern Nervous Illness," *Standard Edition* 9, p. 186.

107 "We may therefore regard the sexual factor": Ibid.

107 "They spring from the sexual needs of people": Ibid.

107 "We must therefore view all factors": Ibid.

107 "a quota of affect and a sum of excitation": Freud, "The Neuro-Psychoses of Defense," *Standard Edition* 3, pp. 60–61.

CHAPTER 10. THE DEVIL AND ADRIAN LEVERKÜHN

112 "A poet is a light and winged and sacred thing": Plato, *Ion,* trans. by W. R. M. Lamb, Loeb Classical Library (Cambridge: Harvard University Press, 1971), 534B–C.

112 "infirmity alone makes us take notice": Marcel Proust, *Sodom and Gomorrah (In Search of Lost Time,* vol. 4).

112 "Great minds that are healthy": Guy de Maupassant, "The Englishman of Étretat" [1882].

112 "What was it that drove Nietzsche": Thomas Mann, "Nietzsche's Philosophy in the Light of Contemporary Events," Address to the Library of Congress, April 29, 1947, p. 71.

114 "I was endeavoring to convert an artificial base": Simon Garfield, *Mauve,* p. 36.

115 **Experimentation with coal tar derivatives**: See Garfield, *Mauve*, pp. 154 ff. for more on the applications of aniline compounds.

116 **"Herewith the discussion is closed"**: Paul de Kruif, *Men Against Death* (New York: Harcourt, Brace, 1932), p. 225.

118 **The Wassermann blood test for syphilis**: A detailed contemporary account of the test was provided by Wassermann's assistant Felix Plaut in *The Wassermann Sero-Diagnosis of Syphilis in Its Application to Psychiatry*, trans. Smith Ely Jelliffe and Louis Casamajor (New York: Journal of Nervous and Mental Disease Publishing, 1911).

120 **"Afflicted creature that I am"**: All quotations from *Doctor Faustus* come from the translation of John E. Woods (New York: Knopf, 1997).

123 **Salvarsan was of no use**: Cynthia J. Tsay, "Julius Wagner-Jauregg and the Legacy of Malarial Therapy for the Treatment of General Paresis of the Insane," *Yale Journal of Biology and Medicine* 86.2 (June 2013): 245–54, p. 249.

124 **Julius Wagner-Jauregg . . . was awarded a Nobel Prize in 1927**: Wagner-Jauregg became a eugenicist and argued for the forced sterilization of the insane. His reputation recently came in for a stark reassessment when the Vienna City Council decided to look into the lives of two hundred Austrians commemorated in the city's central cemetery. Wagner-Jauregg's name had been plastered on streets, schools, and hospitals around the city as one of its favorite sons. When the council dug up his application to join the Nazi Party in 1939, they faced an awkward decision. Fortunately for all concerned, acute embarrassment was avoided when it was discovered that his application was denied on account of his Jewish first wife. He died in 1940, before he got a chance to reapply. The council let the matter drop. Ibid., pp. 251–52.

CHAPTER 11. SEX AND THE NEW WOMAN

126 **"I had never heard this word before"**: Rudnick, *Suppressed Memoirs*, p. 198.

127 **"Take long vigorous walks . . . and eat plenty of beefsteaks"**: Rudnick, *Intimate Memories*, p. 109.

127 **"Edwin had flowed out"**: Ibid., p. 112.

128 **"The trouble with Freudians"**: Bernard Sachs, *The Normal Child* (P. B. Hoeber, 1926), p. 89.

128 **According to Mabel, "he thought it would be advisable"**: Rudnick, *Intimate Memories*, p. 121.

128 **"a man of prodigious intellect"**: Lois Palken Rudnick, *Mabel Dodge Luhan: New Woman, New Worlds* (Albuquerque: University of New Mexico Press, 1985), p. 131.

130 **"Is there really that much syphilis"**: Rudnick, *Intimate Memories*, p. 199.

131 **Maurice "skulked down the street"**: Rudnick, *Suppressed Memoirs*, p. 132.

131 **"He did not seem at all embarrassed"**: Ibid., p. 133.

132 **An estimated 20,000 stillbirths in England**: David Nabarro, "Some Aspects of Congenital Syphilis," *British Journal of Venereal Diseases* 25.3 (September 1949): 133–46.

133 **"I certainly didn't plan to revolutionize all medicine"**: Kendall F. Haven, *Marvels of Science: 50 Fascinating 5-Minute Reads* (Littleton, CO: Libraries Unlimited, 1994), p. 182.

134 **A year later, he published the results of his experiments with penicillin**: Alexander Fleming, "On the Antibacterial Action of Cultures of a Penicillium," *British Journal of Experimental Pathology* 10.3 (1929): 226–36.

135 **It increased the yield of penicillin tenfold**: Gwyn Macfarlane, *Alexander Fleming: The Man and the Myth* (Cambridge: Harvard University Press, 1984).

CHAPTER 12. WINNING THE BATTLE AND LOSING THE WAR

136 **he could not utter the words**: Courtesy of Social Welfare History Archives, University of Minnesota Libraries, Box 070, Folder 04, p. 2; Folder 05, p. 10; and Folder 06, p. 5.

137 **"To break down this taboo in the U.S."**: *Time*, October 26, 1936, p. 61.

137 **"One of the principal obstacles"**: American Medical Association statement published through various state medical society journals.

138 **adoption in the 1970s of the term**: Charles E. Campbell and R. Jeffrey Herten, "VD to STD: Redefining Venereal Disease," *American Journal of Nursing* 81.9 (September 1981): 1,629–35. Campbell and Herten did not introduce the term STD, but declared VD "out of date."

138 **"The young uncle had numerous mucous patches"**: Alfred Fournier, *The Treatment and Prophylaxis of Syphilis*, p. 411.

140 **War Advertising Council . . . withdrew its support**: *Time*, October 16, 1944, p. 56.

143 **Mahoney launched his landmark study**: John F. Mahoney, R. C. Arnold, and A. D. Harris, "Penicillin Treatment of Early Syphilis: A Preliminary Report," *American Journal of Public Health* 33 (December 1943): 1,387–91.

143 **"probably the most significant paper"**: John Parascandola, *Sex, Sin, and Science*, p. 129.

143 **"New Magic Bullet"**: *Time*, October 25, 1943, p. 38.

143 **penicillin should be used to first treat soldiers**: Henry K. Beecher, "Scarce Resources and Medical Advancement," *Daedalus* 98.2 (Spring 1969): 275–313, pp. 280–81.

144 **The CDC declared the United States polio-free in 1994**: https://www.cdc.gov /mmwr/preview/mmwrhtml/00032760.htm.

145 **"Bad blood"**: The phrase used as a euphemism for syphilis. See James H. Jones, *Bad Blood: The Scandalous Story of the Tuskegee Experiment*.

145 **"the natural history of syphilis in the Negro race"**: William Bender, "Did a U.S. Surgeon General Come Up with the Idea of the Notorious Tuskegee Syphilis Experiment?" *Philadelphia Inquirer*, July 20, 2017.

145 **Guatemala syphilis experiment**: Exposed by Susan M. Reverby in "'Normal Exposure' and Inoculation Syphilis: A PHS 'Tuskegee' Doctor in Guatemala, 1946–48," *Journal of Policy History*, Special Issue on Human Subjects, January 2011.

146 **a formal apology by President Barack Obama**: *Washington Post*, October 1, 2010.

146 **the number of cases of syphilis was halved**: CDC Division of STD Prevention, https://www.cdc.gov/std/stats/syphilis-stats-all-years.htm.

146 **A variant of "herd immunity"**: N. C. Grassly, C. Fraser, and G. P. Garnett, "Host Immunity and Synchronized Epidemics of Syphilis Across the United States," *Nature* 433 (January 27, 2005): 417–21.

147 **Every man, woman, and child in the United States**: "End of Syphilis by Mass Use of Penicillin Seen," *Chicago Daily Tribune*, February 7, 1946, p. 14.

147 **The last to have the requirement**: Mississippi State Department of Health, https://msdh.ms.gov/msdhsite/_static/31,0,175.html.

CHAPTER 13. THE PSYCHIC INTERPRETATION OF DISEASE

148 **"a barbarous system of coercion"**: *The Westminster and Foreign Quarterly Review*, October 1847–January 1848 edition.

149 **the therapies enthusiastically proposed at that time**: John Romano, "American Psychiatry: Past, Present, and Future," in G. Kriegman, R. D. Gardner, and D. W. Abse, eds., *American Psychiatry, Past, Present, and Future* (Charlottesville: University of Virginia Press, 1975), p. 34.

150 **"much of our century's most influential psychiatric writing"**: C. E. Rosenberg, "The Crisis in Psychiatric Legitimacy," in Kriegman, Gardner, and Abse, eds., *American Psychiatry, Past, Present, and Future*, p. 142.

150 **They require a libido**: Freud, *Beyond the Pleasure Principle* (1920), p. 50.

150 **"The cells of the malignant neoplasms"**: Ibid.

151 **"No one of course would dream"**: Sándor Ferenczi, "Psycho-analysis and the Mental Disorders of General Paralysis of the Insane" [1922].

151 **"Dr. Jelliffe told me his fascinating theories"**: Lois Palken Rudnick, *Intimate Memories*, vol. 3, "Movers and Shakers," p. 109.

152 **"a moralist in the guise of a scientist"**: Thomas Szasz, *The Myth of Mental Illness*, p. 153.

152 **"The process of mental illness"**: Lawrence Kubie, "The Myths of Thomas Szasz," *Bulletin of the Menninger Clinic* 38.6: 497–502, p. 499.

153 **"Preconscious coded signaling"**: Lawrence Kubie, "Psychoanalysis and the Scientific Method," *Journal of Nervous and Mental Diseases* 131 (1960): 495–512, p. 510.

153 **"I maintain," writes Kubie, "that whenever"**: Lawrence Kubie, "The Myths of Thomas Szasz," p. 500.

153 **"The mathematicians . . . who offer these"**: Thomas Szasz, *The Meaning of Mind: Language, Morality, and Neuroscience* (Westport, CT: Praeger, 1996), p. 76.

154 **By the 1950s, there were half a million patients**: Deanna Pan, "Timeline: Deinstitutionalization and Its Consequences," *Mother Jones*, April 29, 2013.

CHAPTER 14. A BEAUTIFUL NAME FOR A HORRIBLE DISEASE

156 **She was a twenty-four-year-old Italian American**: The description of this case relies on Arthur K. Shapiro and Elaine Shapiro, "Treatment of Gilles de la Tourette's Syndrome with Haloperidol," *British Journal of Psychiatry* 114.508 (March 1968): 345–50.

158 **They usually first appear in childhood**: James F. Leckman et al., "Course of Tic Severity in Tourette Syndrome: The First Two Decades," *Pediatrics* 102 (July 1998): 14–19.

158 **By the age of eighteen**: Ibid.

159 **about 10 percent of Touretters exhibit coprolalia**: R. D. Freeman et al., "Coprophenomena in Tourette Syndrome," *Developmental Medicine and Child Neurology* 51.3 (March 2009): 218–27.

159 **Japanese ticcers do not curse as profusely**: Y. Nomura, M. Kita, and M. Segawa, "Social Adaptation of Tourette Syndrome Families in Japan," *Advances in Neurology* 58 (1992): 323–32.

159 **the disorder is tentatively called**: Ashutosh Kumar, William Trescher, and Debra Byler, "Tourette Syndrome and Comorbid Neuropsychiatric Conditions," *Current Developmental Disorders Reports* 3.2: 217–21.

160 **"it feels just right"**: "'Just Right' Perceptions Associated with Compulsive Behavior in Tourette's Syndrome," J. F. Leckman et al., *American Journal of Psychiatry* 151.5 (May 1994): 675–80.

160 **As Georges Gilles de la Tourette scanned**: *Le Constitutionnel,* July 10, 1884, "Necrologie."

160 **Tourette himself made the news that summer**: see *Le Temps,* July 11, 1884.

161 **A two-page summary of her case by a Dr. Itard**: J-M. Itard, "Mémoire sur Quelques Fonctions Involontaires des Appareils de la Locomotion, de la Préhension, et de la Voix," *Archives Générales de Médecine* 8 (1825): 385–407.

161 **Victor of Aveyron**: Jean Marc Gaspard Itard, *The Wild Boy of Aveyron (L'enfant Sauvage): First Developments of the Young Savage,* trans. George and Muriel Humphrey (New York: Appleton-Century-Crofts, 1962).

162 **her stock phrases were**: Howard I. Kushner, "Medical Fictions: The Case of the Cursing Marquise and the (Re)Construction of Gilles de la Tourette's Syndrome," *Bulletin of the History of Medicine* 69.2 (Summer 1995): 224–54, p. 225.

162 **Who was Mme de D . . . ?**: Probably Mme. Emilie Ernestine Prondre de Guermantes, contesse Picot de Dampierre (b. 1820, d. July 8, 1884).

162 *écarts de langage*: These were attributed to Eulalie Picot de Dampierre (Eulalie de Thoulazon, b. 1803, d. February 26, 1889).

163 **American neurologist George Beard**: George Beard, "Experiments with the 'Jumpers' or 'Jumping Frenchmen' of Maine," *Journal of Nervous and Mental Disease* 7 (1880): 487–90.

164 **"As for the essential nature of the affliction"**: Gilles de la Tourette, "Étude sur une Affection Nerveuse," p. 200.

164 **"I always felt an urgent need to imitate"**: Henry Meige and E. Feindel, *Les Tics et Leur Traitement* (Paris: Masson, 1902), p. 183.

165 **"The initial motivation becomes lost"**: Ibid., p. 10.

165 **"should be reserved solely for those cases"**: Ibid., p. 180.

165 **"a ticcer has a neuropath for a father"**: Ibid., p. 180.

166 **"[He] never ceased to carry out certain stereotyped actions"**: Sándor Ferenczi, "Psycho-analytical Observations on Tic," *International Journal of Psycho-Analysis* 2 (1921), p. 3.

166 **exposure and response prevention techniques**: Victor Meyer, "Modification of Expectations in Cases with Obsessional Rituals," *Behaviour Research and Therapy* 4.1–2 (1966): 273–80.

167 **Shapiro's patient was "a naïve and immature woman"**: Shapiro and Shapiro, "Treatment of Gilles de la Tourette's Syndrome with Haloperidol," *British Journal of Psychiatry* 114 (1968), p. 346.

167 **"Acquaintances looked oddly at her"**: Ibid., p. 347.

168 **"Improvement might have been due"**: Ibid., p. 349.

168 **Shapiro ultimately amassed records**: Arthur K. Shapiro et al., *Gilles de la Tourette Syndrome.*

170 **a strong argument to be made**: Joseph Jankovic, "Tourette Syndrome," *New England Journal of Medicine* 345.16 (October 18, 2001): 1,184–90.

170 **according to physiologist Derek Denny-Brown**: Ropper, Samuels, and Klein, *Principles of Neurology,* 10th ed., p. 67.

171 **a controversial entity called PANDAS**: S. E. Swedo et al., "Pediatric Autoimmune Neuropsychiatric Disorders Associated with Streptococcal Infection:

Clinical Description of the First 50 Cases," *American Journal of Psychiatry* 155.2 (February 1998): 264–71.

172   **Haldol . . . is not unique**: Ropper, Samuels, and Klein, *Principles of Neurology*, 10th ed., pp. 110–11.

CHAPTER 15. MEDICINAL LOBOTOMY: THE INVENTION OF THORAZINE

173   **"I asked an army psychiatrist"**: H. Laborit, P. Huguenard, and R. Alluaume, "Un Nouveau Stabilisateur Végétatif (le 4560 RP)," *La Presse Médicale* 60 (February 13, 1952), p. 206. The drug was called 4560 RP.

174   **The first drug treatment of a case of psychosis**: J. Hamon, J. Paraire, and J. Velluz, "Remarques sur l'Action du 4560 RP sur l'Agitation Maniaque," *Annales Médico-Psychologiques* 110 (1952): 331–35, p. 331.

174   **"By May 1953, the atmosphere in the disturbed wards"**: Stephen A. Maisto, Mark Galizio, Gerald J. Connors, *Drug Use and Abuse*, 8th ed. (Boston: Cengage, 2018), p. 328.

174   **an article in the *Annals of Clinical Psychiatry***: F. López-Muñoz et al., "History of the Discovery and Clinical Introduction of Chlorpromazine," *Annals of Clinical Psychiatry* 17.3 (2005): 113–35.

175   **"Psychiatry needed a big contribution"**: Heinz Lehmann, interviewed by William Bunney Jr., December 12, 1994.

176   **a British researcher discovered**: K. A. Montagu, "Catechol Compounds in Rat Tissues and in Brains of Different Animals," *Nature* 180 (August 3, 1957): 244–45.

176   **Arvid Carlsson found a way**: A. Carlsson, "Thirty Years of Dopamine Research," *Advances in Neurology* 60 (1993): 1–10.

176   **Hornykiewicz . . . developed and tested a drug**: Oleh Hornykiewicz, "A Brief History of Levodopa," *Journal of Neurology* 257, Suppl 2 (November 2010): S249–52.

176   **He called these messengers chemical transmitters**: Otto Loewi, Nobel Lecture, "The Chemical Transmission of Nerve Action," December 12, 1936.

177   **Jacques van Rossum proposed a theory of schizophrenia**: J. M. van Rossum, "The Significance of Dopamine-Receptor Blockade for the Mechanism of Action of Neuroleptic Drugs," *Archives Internationales de Pharmacodynamie et de Therapie* 160.2 (1966): 492–94.

179   **"'schizophrenia' may comprise disorders"**: Thomas Insel, "Antipsychotics: Taking the Long View," NIMH blog post, August 28, 2013.

180   **"affected by a remarkable restlessness"**: Albert Hofmann, *LSD: My Problem Child*, trans. Jonathan Ott (New York: McGraw-Hill, 1980), p. 15.

181   **"fairly talented illiterate"**: Philip L. Fradkin, *Wallace Stegner and the American West* (New York: Knopf, 2008), p. 131.

181   **"they didn't have the guts to do it themselves"**: Ken Kesey, 1998 interview with *Stanford* magazine.

182   **James "Whitey" Bulger . . . volunteered for the study**: Michael Havis, "Notorious Gangster in Shock Confession: I Was in Secret CIA Mind Experiments," *Daily Star*, May 16, 2017.

184   **"disturbances of cognition, emotion, or behavior"**: "The *DSM* Conception of Mental Illness and Its Critics," *Stanford Encyclopedia of Psychiatry*, section 2.2.

185   **"unreason"**: In *Madness and Civilization* (1964), Michel Foucault contrasts rationality and reason with unreason and madness. He attributes the latter not to illness but to social and historical conditions.

186 **Some themes do recur [in psychosis]**: Angelo Picardi et al., "Delusional Themes Across Affective and Non-Affective Psychoses," *Frontiers in Psychiatry* 9 (2018), p. 132.

CHAPTER 16. THE FEVERED DREAM OF A SCIENTIFIC PSYCHOLOGY

187 **Men have twenty-three-day cycles**: William Sims Bainbridge, *Dynamic Secularization: Information Technology and the Tension Between Religion and Science* (New York: Springer, 2017), p. 115.

188 **A short paper extolling the virtues of cocaine**: S. Freud, "On Coca," in *The Cocaine Papers* (Vienna and Zurich: Dunquin Press, 1963).

188 **Fliess's obsession**: Peter Perkins, "Fliess, Freud, and the Nose," *Journal of the Royal Society of Medicine* 100.9 (September 2007), p. 398.

189 **the lone case history**: Freud, "Project for a Scientific Psychology," *Standard Edition* 1, p. 353.

190 **"Do you suppose that some day"**: Freud, letter to Wilhelm Fliess, June 12, 1900.

190 **the "explanatory gap"**: See Joseph Levine, "Materialism and Qualia: The Explanatory Gap," *Pacific Philosophical Quarterly* 64 (1983): 354–61.

190 **"An overturned glass"**: Moreau de Tours, *Du Hachisch et de l'Aliénation Mentale* (Paris: Fortin, Masson, 1845), pp. 71–72.

191 **"In his moments of delirium, he fancied"**: Macdonald Critchley, *The Divine Banquet of the Brain and Other Essays* (New York: Raven Press, 1979), p. 213.

194 **"exclusively sensorimotor machine"**: John Hughlings Jackson, "Notes on the Physiology and Pathology of the Nervous System," *Medical Times Gazette* 2 (1861), p. 526.

195 **"It is probable that the chain"**: Freud, "On Aphasia: A Critical Study," *Standard Edition* 14, p. 207. NB: The phrase *dependent concomitant* is from Hughlings Jackson, "On Affectations of Speech from Diseases of the Brain," *Brain* 1 (1878–79), pp. 304–30; 2 (1879–1880), pp. 203–22, 323–56. These citations make up his Croonian Lectures.

196 **"The Doctrine of Concomitance"**: George K. York III and David A. Steinberg, "Hughlings Jackson's Neurological Ideas," *Brain* 134.10 (October 2011): 3,106–113, p. 3,110.

197 **"insofar as psychoanalysis is successful"**: Eric Kandel, "Biology and the Future of Psychoanalysis," *American Journal of Psychiatry* 156.4 (April 1999): 505–24, p. 519.

CHAPTER 17. THE LESSONS OF NEUROSYPHILIS

203 **A front-page article in *The New York Times***: Jan Hoffman, "Hunting a Killer: Sex, Drugs, and the Return of Syphilis," *New York Times*, August 24, 2017.

203 **In Bakersfield**: Anna Gorman, "Record STD Rates Drive Syphilis in Newborns," *Kaiser Health News*, March 1, 2017, https://www.cnn.com/2017/03/01/health/syphilis-newborns-partner/index.html.

203 **The current rate of syphilis in the United States**: CDC Sexually Transmitted Diseases Surveillance.

204 **Martin.** This patient's details have been de-identified.

206 **"The exaggerated irritability of the nerves"**: F. A. Mesmer, *Maxims on Animal Magnetism*, trans. Jerome Eden (Mount Vernon, NY: Eden Press, 1958), p. 50.

207 **"psychic disturbances that are just as real"**: Asti Hustvedt, *Medical Muses*, p. 310.

209 **"Nothing is more punitive"**: Susan Sontag, *Illness as Metaphor*, p. 58.

SELECTED BIBLIOGRAPHY

Alexander, Franz G., and Sheldon T. Selesnick. *The History of Psychiatry: An Evaluation of Psychiatric Thought and Practice from Prehistoric Times to the Present.* New York: Harper & Row, 1966.

Ball, Benjamin. *La Morphinomanie: Les Frontières de la Folie.* Paris: Asselin et Houzeau, 1885.

Bernheim, Hippolyte. *Suggestive Therapeutics*, trans. Christian A. Herter. New York: G. P. Putnam's Sons, [1889] 1998.

Bleuler, Eugen. *Dementia Praecox or the Group of Schizophrenias*, trans. Joseph Zinkin. New York: International Universities Press, 1950.

Bogousslavsky, Julien, ed. *Following Charcot: A Forgotten History of Neurology and Psychiatry.* Basel: Karger, 2011.

Borch-Jacobsen, Mikkel. *Remembering Anna O.: A Century of Mystification*, trans. Kirby Olson. New York: Routledge, 1996.

Charcot, Jean-Martin. *Charcot the Clinician: The Tuesday Lessons*, trans. Christopher G. Goetz. New York: Raven Press, 1987.

———. *L'Hystérie: Texts Choisis et Présentés par E. Trillat.* Toulouse: Edouard Privat, 1971.

Conrad, Joseph. *Heart of Darkness and Other Tales.* Oxford: Oxford University Press, 2008.

Critchley, Macdonald. *The Divine Banquet of the Brain and Other Essays.* New York: Raven Press, 1979.

Daudet, Alphonse. *In the Land of Pain*, trans. Julian Barnes. New York: Knopf, 2002.

Di Cicco, Camillo. *History of Syphilis: A Night with Venus, a Lifetime with Mercury.* Camillo O. Di Cicco: 2007.

Didi-Huberman, Georges. *Invention of Hysteria: Charcot and the Photographic Iconography of the Salpêtrière*, trans. Alisa Hartz. Cambridge, MA: MIT Press, 2003.

Eisenberg, Leon. "Mindlessness and Brainlessness in Psychiatry," *British Journal of Psychiatry* 148.5 (May 1986): 497–508.

Eisenberg, Leon, and Laurence B. Guttmacher. "Were We All Asleep at the Switch? A Personal Reminiscence of Psychiatry from 1940 to 2010," *Acta Psychiatrica Scandinavica* 122.2 (August 2010): 89–102.

Ellenberger, Henri F. *The Discovery of the Unconscious.* New York: Basic Books, 1970.

Faber, Diana P. "Jean-Martin Charcot and the Epilepsy/Hysteria Relationship," *Journal of the History of the Neurosciences* 6.3 (December 1997): 275–90.

Ferenczi, Sándor. *Further Contributions to the Theory and Technique of Psycho-analysis*, trans. Jane Isabel Suttie et al. London: Karnac Books, 2002.

Fournier, Alfred. *La Syphilis du Cerveau*. Paris: Masson, 1879.

———. *The Treatment and Prophylaxis of Syphilis*, trans. C. F. Marshall. New York: Rebman Company, 1907.

Freud, Sigmund. "The Aetiology of Hysteria." *The Standard Edition of the Complete Psychological Works of Sigmund Freud*. 24 vols., trans. James Strachey. London: Hogarth Press, 1953–74, 3: 187–222.

———. "Charcot." *Standard Edition*, 3: 11–23.

———. *Dora: An Analysis of a Case of Hysteria*, ed. Philip Rieff. New York: Collier Books, 1963.

———. *On Aphasia: A Critical Study*, trans. E. Stengel. New York: International Universities Press, 1953.

———. *Project for a Scientific Psychology. Standard Edition*, 1: 281–391

———. *The Psychopathology of Everyday Life*, ed. James Strachey. New York: W. W. Norton, 1960.

———. *Three Essays on the Theory of Sexuality. Standard Edition*, 7: 123–243.

Freud, Sigmund, and Josef Breuer. *Studies on Hysteria*, ed. James Strachey. New York: Basic Books, 2000.

Garfield, Simon. *Mauve: How One Man Invented a Color That Changed the World*. New York: W. W. Norton, 2000.

Gillain, Georges. *J.-M. Charcot, 1825–1893: His Life—His Work*, ed. and trans. Pearce Bailey. New York: Paul B. Hoeber, 1959.

Gilles de la Tourette, Georges, "Étude sur une Affection Nerveuse Caracterisée par de l'Incoordination Motrice Accompagnée d'Echolalie et de Coprolalie (Jumping, Latah, Myriachit)," *Archives de Neuologie*. Paris: Bureau de Progrés Médical, 1885.

Gilman, Sander. *Disease and Representation: Images of Illness from Madness to AIDS*. Ithaca: Cornell University Press, 1988.

Gilman, Sander, et al. *Hysteria Beyond Freud*. Berkeley: University of California Press, 1993.

Goldstein, Jan. "The Hysteria Diagnosis and the Politics of Anti-Clericalism in Late Nineteenth-Century France," *Journal of Modern History* 54.2 (June 1982): 209–39.

Goldwater, Leonard J. *Mercury: A History of Quicksilver*. Baltimore: York Press, 1972.

Hale, Nathan G. Jr. *The Rise and Crisis of Psychoanalysis in the United States: Freud and the Americans, 1917–1985*. New York: Oxford University Press, 1995.

Hayden, Deborah. *Pox: Genius, Madness, and the Mysteries of Syphilis*. New York: Basic Books, 2003.

Haymaker, Webb, and Francis Schiller. *The Founders of Neurology: One Hundred and Forty-Six Biographical Sketches by Eighty-Nine Authors*. Second edition. Springfield, IL: Charles C Thomas, 1970.

Hunter, Mary. *The Face of Medicine: Visualizing Medical Masculinities in Late Nineteenth-Century Paris*. Manchester: Manchester University Press, 2016.

Hurn, Juliet D. *The History of General Paralysis of the Insane in Britain, 1830 to 1950*. Doctoral dissertation, University of London, 1998. Retrieved from http://discovery.ucl.ac.uk/1349281/1/339949.pdf.

Hustvedt, Asti. *Medical Muses: Hysteria in Nineteenth-Century Paris*. New York: W. W. Norton, 2011.

Johnston, Marlo. *Guy de Maupassant*. Paris: Fayard, 2012.

Jones, James H. *Bad Blood: The Scandalous Story of the Tuskegee Experiment—When Government Doctors Played God and Science Went Mad.* New York: Free Press, 1981.

Kandel, Eric R. *The Age of Insight: The Quest to Understand the Unconscious in Art, Mind, and Brain, from Vienna 1900 to the Present.* New York: Random House, 2012.

———. *In Search of Memory: The Emergence of a New Science of Mind.* New York: W. W. Norton, 2006.

King, Lester S. *Medical Thinking: A Historical Preface.* Princeton: Princeton University Press, 1982.

Kraepelin, Emil. *General Paresis*, trans. J. W. Moore. New York: Nervous and Mental Disease Publishing Company, 1913.

Laureno, Robert. *Raymond Adams: A Life of Mind and Muscle.* Oxford: Oxford University Press, 2009.

Malcolm, Janet. *Psychoanalysis: The Impossible Profession.* New York: Knopf, 1981.

Makari, George. *Revolution in Mind: The Creation of Psychoanalysis.* New York: HarperCollins, 2008.

Mann, Thomas. *Doctor Faustus: The Life of the German Composer Adrian Leverkühn as Told by a Friend*, trans. John E. Woods. New York: Knopf, 1997.

Marshall, Jonathan W. *Performing Neurology: The Dramaturgy of Dr. Jean-Martin Charcot.* New York: Palgrave Macmillan, 2016.

Martino, David, and James F. Leckman. *Tourette Syndrome.* New York: Oxford University Press, 2013.

Masson, Jeffrey Moussaieff, ed. *The Complete Letters of Sigmund Freud to Wilhelm Fliess, 1887–1904.* Cambridge: Belknap Press of Harvard University Press, 1985.

Mayer, Andreas. *Sites of the Unconscious: Hypnosis and the Emergence of the Psychoanalytic Setting.* Chicago: University of Chicago Press, 2013.

McNally, Kieran. *A Critical History of Schizophrenia.* New York: Palgrave Macmillan, 2016.

Merritt, H. Houston, Raymond D. Adams, and Harry C. Solomon. *Neurosyphilis.* New York: Oxford University Press, 1946.

Moore, Merrill, and Harold C. Solomon. *Contributions of Haslam, Bayle, and Esmarch and Jessen to the History of Neurosyphilis: Haslam's* Observations on insanity, *Bayle's* Recherches sur l'Arachnitis Chronique, *and Esmarch and Jessen's* Syphilis und Geistesstörung. Chicago: American Medical Association, 1934.

Moreau, Jacques-Joseph. *Hashish and Mental Illness*, trans. Gordon J. Barnett. New York: Raven Press, 1973.

Mroczkowski, Tomasz F. *History, Sex and Syphilis.* Booklocker.com, 2016.

Murat, Laure. *The Man Who Thought He Was Napoleon*, trans. Deke Dusinberre. Chicago: University of Chicago Press, 2014.

Nonne, Max. *Syphilis und Nervensystem: Ein Handbuch in Zwanzig Vorlesungen für Praktische Ärzte, Neurologen und Syphilidologen.* Berlin: S. Karger, 1921.

Parascandola, John. *Sex, Sin, and Science: A History of Syphilis in America.* Westport, CT: Praeger, 2008.

Paris, Joel. *Prescriptions for the Mind: A Critical View of Contemporary Psychiatry.* New York: Oxford University Press, 2008.

Philippon, Jacques, and Jacques Poirier. *Joseph Babinski.* Oxford: Oxford University Press, 2008.

Richer, Paul. *Études Cliniques sur l'Hystéro-Épilepsie ou Grande Hystérie.* Paris: Adrien Delahaye, 1881.

Ropper, Allan H., Martin A. Samuels, and Joshua P. Klein. *Principles of Neurology*, 10th ed. New York: McGraw-Hill, 2014.

Rosenberg, C. E. "The Crisis in Psychiatric Legitimacy," in G. Kriegman et al., eds, *American Psychiatry, Past, Present, and Future*. Charlottesville: University of Virginia Press, 1975.

Rudnick, Lois Palken, ed. *Intimate Memories: The Autobiography of Mabel Dodge Luhan*. Albuquerque: University of New Mexico Press, 1999.

———. *The Suppressed Memoirs of Mabel Dodge Luhan: Sex, Syphilis, and Psychoanalysis in the Making of Modern American Culture*. Albuquerque: University of New Mexico Press, 2012.

Shapiro, Arthur K., et al. *Gilles de la Tourette Syndrome*, 2nd ed. New York: Raven Press, 1978.

Shorter, Edward. *A History of Psychiatry: From the Era of the Asylum to the Age of Prozac*. New York: Wiley, 1997.

Showalter, Elaine. *Hystories: Hysterical Epidemics and Modern Media*. New York: Columbia University Press, 1997.

Skal, David J. *Something in the Blood: The Untold Story of Bram Stoker, the Man Who Wrote Dracula*. New York: Liveright Publishing, 2016.

Solomon, Harold C., and Maida H. Solomon. *Syphilis of the Innocent: A Study of the Social Aspects of Syphilis on the Family and Community*. Washington: United States Interdepartmental Social Hygiene Board, 1922.

Sontag, Susan. *Illness as Metaphor*. New York: Farrar, Straus and Giroux, 1978.

Southard, Elmer E., and Harry C. Solomon. *Neurosyphilis: Modern Systematic Diagnosis and Treatment, Presented in One-Hundred and Thirty-Seven Case Histories*. Boston: W. M. Leonard, 1917.

Szasz, Thomas S. *The Myth of Mental Illness: Foundations of a Theory of Personal Conduct*. New York: Harper, 1974.

———. *The Myth of Psychotherapy*. Syracuse: Syracuse University Press, 1988.

Thomas, Evan W. *Syphilis: Its Course and Management*. New York: Macmillan, 1949.

Tone, Andrea. *The Age of Anxiety: A History of America's Turbulent Affair with Tranquilizers*. New York: Basic Books, 2009.

U.S. Department of Health, Education, and Welfare. Public Health Service. *Syphilis: A Synopsis*. Washington, DC: U.S. Government Printing Office Publication 1660, 1967.

Veith, Ilza. *Hysteria: The History of a Disease*. Chicago: University of Chicago Press, 1965.

Webster, Richard. *Why Freud Was Wrong: Sin, Science, and Psychoanalysis*. New York: Basic Books, 1995.

INDEX

Page numbers set in *italic* indicate paintings.

A NOTE ABOUT THE AUTHORS

Dr Allan H. Ropper is Professor of Neurology at Harvard Medical School and Raymond D. Adams Master Clinician of the Department of Neurology at Brigham and Women's Hospital. He is also a deputy editor of the *New England Journal of Medicine* and a fellow of the American Academy of Neurology, Royal College of Physicians, and the American College of Physicians. Dr Ropper is an author of the most widely consulted textbook of neurology, *Principles of Neurology*, currently in its eleventh edition, and co-author with B.D. Burrell of *Reaching Down the Rabbit Hole*.

B.D. Burrell is a member of the mathematics faculty at the University of Massachusetts Amherst. A teacher and writer, he is the author is several books, including *Postcards from the Brain Museum*, *The Words We Live By*, and, jointly with Dr Allan H. Ropper, *Reaching Down the Rabbit Hole*.